Round
Ireland *with*
a fridge

Round Ireland *with a fridge*

TONY HAWKS

St. Martin's Press ⚓ New York

THOMAS DUNNE BOOKS.
An imprint of St. Martin's Press.

ROUND IRELAND WITH A FRIDGE. Copyright © 1998 by Tony Hawks.
All rights reserved. Printed in the United States of America.
No part of this book may be used or reproduced in any manner
whatsoever without written permission except in the case of
brief quotations embodied in critical articles or reviews.
For information, address St. Martin's Press,
175 Fifth Avenue, New York, N.Y. 10010.

Photography by Shane McCarthy and Tony Hawks

ISBN 0-312-24236-0

First published in Great Britain by Ebury Press,
an imprint of Random House UK Limited

First U.S. Edition: March 2000

10 9 8 7 6 5 4 3 2 1

To Sylvia

Author's Note

All the events described in this book actually took place, and all the characters depicted really exist. I have used real names except on one or two occasions when, out of respect for a person's privacy, they have been re-christened. I should like to express my heartfelt thanks to all of those who have helped me in the lead up to publication of this book, not least the characters about whom I have written. I hope I have done you justice.

Prologue

I'm not, by nature, a betting man. However, the pages that follow in this book do not bear testimony to that. In fact they exist wholly as the result of a bet.

I'm not, by nature, a drinking man. However, the making of the bet which led to this book does not bear testimony to that. Because I made it when I was pissed.

Everything you read from this moment forth is a tribute to what can be achieved as a result of a shabby night of booze.

1
If Only

In 1989 I went to Ireland for the first time. I don't know why it had taken so long. Some parts of the world you make a conscious effort to visit and others have to wait until fate delivers you there.

When the moment arrived for me to set foot on the Emerald Isle, it was as a result of a badly written song. An Irish friend from London, Seamus, had urged me to compose a piece for him and his mate Tim to sing at an International Song Competition which was held each year in his home town. Qualification for the final, he explained, was a formality provided I agreed to do a twenty-minute stand-up comedy set for the audience whilst the judges were out. Seamus wanted to perform a humorous song, and had asked me to come up with something that would 'set it apart' from the other mundane entries. In the event, what would set it apart would be a quite significant drop in standard.

The song I had written was called 'I Wanna Have Tea With Batman'. Now I consider myself to be a good songwriter (in spite of my only commercial success being a one-off hit record called 'Stutter Rap' by Morris Minor And The Majors), but this song was . . . how can I put it? . . . yes, that's it – poor. To their credit, Seamus and Tim conjured up a performance to match it.

In an extraordinary gesture which was at best surreal and at worst embarrassing, they dressed as Batman and Robin. At least that's what they had aimed to do, but a limited costume budget had left them in borrowed tights, miscellaneous lycra and academic robes doubling as capes. They resembled a couple of children entered for a fancy dress competition by uninterested parents. Seamus seemed unconcerned, his theory of comedy being that if you had an 'outrageous' outfit, that was enough; and then he announced his master stroke that one of them would carry a teapot and the other a kettle.

One had to admire his courage, for he was performing in front of his home town and everyone he had grown up with was there. Friends, family, teachers, shopkeepers, barmen, drunks and priests were all rooting for him. If one was going to let oneself down very badly – and Seamus was most definitely going to do that – it would be difficult to imagine an assembled throng with which it would have more resonance.

Seamus and Tim took centre stage. The audience responded with an audible inhalation of breath. For them, there was little to suggest that the two characters before them were supposed to be Batman and Robin, and they were clearly taken aback by this magnificent fusion of colour, tights and kitchen appliances.

I watched from the back, experiencing for the first time a curious blend of wonderment and discomfort, and could see in the faces of both performers that their self belief in the costume selection was ebbing away with each elongated second. Thankfully, from the congregation, astonishment subsided into applause. The conductor caught the eye of our superheroes and they nodded to establish they were ready. The band struck up. The musical introduction finished but neither Tim nor Seamus began singing. They looked accusingly at each other. Paralysed with nerves one of them had missed their cue. Somebody near me allowed their head to drop into their hands. Seamus, man of the moment, stepped forward and signalled to the conductor to stop the band. Astonishingly the maestro ignored him. He was pretending he couldn't see Shea's frantic signals. For God's sake, how bad could his eyesight be? Was it possible not to notice the flapping arms of a multi-coloured caped crusader brandishing a teapot in anger?

That conductor was more focused than most of us could ever hope to be. He had a long evening to get through and he was going to get through it in the shortest available time. Going back and starting again for those who had screwed up wasn't on the agenda, even if it was 'Good old Seamus' from down the way. And so, with all the obduracy of a first world war general, his head stayed firmly down and the band played on.

Time went into stasis. I simply have no way of knowing how long it was before Seamus abandoned his frenzied gesticulations, punched Tim, and they both began singing. Indeed, I can't recall how badly they performed the rest of the song. Who cares? The audience applauded, they won 'Most Entertaining Act', and so began my fascination with Ireland.

Aside from the song contest débâcle, there had been another incident which had made this first trip to Ireland stand out in my mind. On arrival at Dublin Airport, I had been met by Seamus's lifelong friend Kieran and driven to Cavan. As we headed north and discussed Batman and Robin's prospects (Kieran was peculiarly guarded on the subject, but later I understood why when I learned that he had watched their rehearsals), I noticed a figure by the side of the road, hitch-hiking. I looked closer, as one does with hitch-hikers, to make that split-second assessment of their appearance to judge their suitability for travel companionship. This was odd. Very odd. He had something alongside him and he was leaning on it. It was a fridge. This man was hitch-hiking with a fridge.

'Kieran, was that man hitch-hiking with a fridge?'

'Oh yeah.'

There was nothing in Kieran's tone of voice to suggest the slightest hint of surprise. I had clearly arrived in a country where qualification for 'eccentric' involved a great deal more than that to which I had become used.

Years passed. (I've always wanted to write that.) The Song Competition had become an anecdote which was given an airing at dinner parties approximately once every two years, and a reference to the fridge hitch-hiker always accompanied it as something of a postscript. For some reason, the image of this man and his large white appendage was indelibly stamped on my memory. I could still see him there by the roadside, something in his face demonstrating a supreme confidence that the presence of his refrigerator would in no way impair his chances of a ride. Sometimes I wondered whether I had imagined him, but no, Kieran had witnessed the miracle too.

Had it not been for Kieran, I could have allowed my imagination to develop 'Fridge Man' into some kind of spiritual revelation; an apparition, an angel who had appeared to me as a symbol of optimism in a bleak, cynical world. I could be the apostle who spread the message that we could all transport our burdens with the ease of 'Fridge Man', if only we trusted in our fellow man to stop and help us on our way. I could hand out leaflets at railway stations and arrange meetings, steadily recruiting followers into a utopia where, when you opened your door to the world, a little light came on and illuminated your groceries.

Alternatively, I could pull myself together.

And that is exactly what I did. The fridge incident was forgotten, banished to the recesses of my mind where matters of infinitesimal consequence belonged. It took alcohol in excess to throw it back up again.

The occasion was a dinner of party with some friends down in

Brighton. A vast quantity of wine had been consumed and the atmos-phere was, shall we say, lively. Round about midnight those present set-tled on a short discussion on the merits of the new fridge which Kevin had bought, and then, by a series of turns, our raddled attention was given to a trip he was planning to Ireland. The juxtaposition of the two triggered a triumphal re-emergence of my fridge hitch-hiking story, which I relayed to the guests via a long-winded collection of badly slurred words. Kevin's response was unambiguous.

'Bollocks.'

'It's not bollocks,' I countered. I had hoped this would see him off, but there was more.

'Yes, it is. Nobody could ever get a lift with a fridge.'

'They could in Ireland, it's a magical place.'

'Magical! So's my arse!'

I let the subject drop. Experience had taught me that someone men-tioning how magical their arse was tended not to precede stimulating and considered debate.

When I woke in the morning, in a physical condition which served as a reminder as to what had taken place the night before, I found a note by my bed:

'I hereby bet Tony Hawks the sum of One Hundred Pounds that he cannot hitch-hike round the circumference of Ireland, with a fridge, within one calendar month.'

And there was Kevin's signature, and below it, an illegible squiggle which I took to be mine.

And so, the bet was made.

Now, it's no good me pretending that the gauntlet had been thrown down and that my honour was at stake if I didn't pick it up and rise to the challenge set down before me. I had been drunk and so had Kevin, and if people were held to things said when sloshed, then we'd all be tragic heroes, ensnared in miserable lives enforced upon us by our own reck-less words. I'd still be with Alison Wilcox who I'd told I would 'love for-ever' in the midst of a lager-sodden teenage one-night stand. I find it difficult to imagine us still together now – mortgage, kids and Ford Mondeo, given that the only thing we really had in common was a fail-ure to remember each other's names in the morning.

In fact when I did get round to calling Kevin, he had only a very sketchy recollection of the whole sorry saga. The last thing he was going to do was to hold me to something he could barely remember having taken place. So why, a month later did I find myself seriously considering taking the bet on? There was no need, no need at all, and yet there I was looking at a map of Ireland and trying to work out the mileage involved in making its coastal circuit. Alas, I had been struck down with what psychoanalysts refer to as G.T.D.S.B.S. syndrome*.

Naturally, the adopted logic of those suffering from G.T.D.S.B.S. syndrome is flawed and can be easily exposed. I cite a short conversation I had with a mountaineer (mountaineers are probably the most common casualties of this phenomenon) as an example of how easily this may be achieved: 'Why, in the bitter conditions of an Alpine winter, are you tackling the dangerous and challenging northeastern face of the fearsome Mattherhorn?' 'Because it's there.'

'But so are your slippers and the TV remote.' Q.E.D., I think.

Why subject yourself to untold pain and deprivation when popping to the shops and back followed by a bit of a sit down, is an option? Why *explore* when you can *tidy*? Why *sail singlehandedly* when you can *read singlehandedly*, *trek* when you can *taxi*, *abseil* when you can *take the stairs*, *stand* when you can *sit*, or *listen to Neil Sedaka's Greatest Hits* when you can *take your own life*?

And it's no good pretending that G.T.D.S.B.S. syndrome is rare, because we all know someone who has been touched by it. Someone at work, or their brother, or someone in the aerobics class, has run a marathon. Twenty-six miles. Twenty-six pointless miles. And do we know anyone who has enjoyed it? Of course we don't. They might pretend they enjoyed it, but they're lying. Life is full of mysteries, doubts and unfathomables but if we can be certain of one thing in this world then it is this:

Running twenty-six miles is *no fun*.

I think it was probably an American who came up with the adage 'if it ain't hurting, it ain't working'. It would be nice to think that shortly after he uttered those words someone smacked him in the mouth by way of demonstrating how well it was working for him.

---

*G.T.D.S.B.S. syndrome = GOING TO DO SOMETHING A BIT SILLY syndrome. *(Source – Freud,* Dreams and the Unconscious, *published 1896.)*

And yet I was just as deluded as the marathon runner, maybe even more so. All logic defied what I found myself contemplating. I would sit up late at night weighing up the pros and cons. All right, the cons won hands down, but there were times when I managed to make the whole thing seem glamorous. An adventure, the unknown, the chance to do something no one had done before. Wow! – something no one had done before. That's something most of us can only dream of.

If you're not sure of the lengths to which people are prepared to go in order to set themselves apart from their fellow Man, then have a browse through *The Guinness Book Of Records* next time you find yourself with a couple of free minutes in the reference library. That's exactly what I found myself doing one morning – checking the entries under Refrigerators and Hitch-hiking, just to confirm that the whole Ireland/fridge venture hadn't already been successfully undertaken by a seventeen-year-old biology student from Sheffield. Research brought relief when I discovered that nobody had done it, but honestly, you wouldn't believe some of the things they *had* done.

Akira Matsushima of Japan unicycled a distance of 5,244 km from Newport Oregon, to Washington DC, from 10 July to 22 August 1992.

Quite impressive given that most people would be chuffed just to make it across a room. But the efforts of Akira must have pissed off another aspiring unicyclist, Ashrita Furman of the US, who wanted to establish a unicycling record of his own, but felt unable to eclipse the feat of the one-wheeled Jap. So, what to do? Of course – it's obvious, isn't it? Start practising unicyclying *backwards*.

Ashrita Furman of the US unicycled 85.5 km *backwards* at Forest Park, Queens, US, on 16 September 1994.

Well, I just hope his parents are proud of him. What an invaluable skill their son has acquired. Further study of this most bizarre of textbooks revealed that Ashrita was one of many who adhered to the school of thought that if you couldn't break a world record *forwards*, then your best bet was to have a go at doing it *backwards*.

Timothy 'Bud' Badyna ran the fastest *backwards* marathon – 3 hours 53 minutes and 17 seconds at Toledo, Ohio, on 24 April 1994.

I checked to see whether Timothy 'Bud' Badyna had also managed an entry under 'Biggest Wanker', but I was disappointed to find that he hadn't. Congratulations though to the Conservative MP, Edward Leigh.

Before I returned the book to its shelf, I scoured the pages for an entry under 'Most failed attempts to get into the *Guinness Book Of Records*', hoping to see a list of efforts like:

Most amounts of cheese eaten in a force 8 wind.

Most number of years spent attempting to startle a postman every morning.

Shiniest ears.

Biggest piece of wood coloured in, in crayon.

Widest dog.

Tallest fish.

Smallest pair of swimming trunks.

But alas, I found nothing. One day, I hope, the publishers will see the wisdom of introducing such a category.

So, given the efforts of Ashrita Furman, Timothy 'Bud' Badyna and friends, I was able to conclude that my plans were rational enough, as for the most part I would be moving in the direction known as 'forwards'. Happy in the knowledge that I hadn't lost my mind (in fact I was so happy that I was doing a little jig and singing at the top of my voice in the High Street), I was able to give consideration to another factor in the decision making process. That of regret.

I was reminded of something Nigel Walker had said: 'There are two words I don't want to find myself uttering as an old man, and they are "If only . . ."' If only. We all have our own 'if onlys'. If only I'd studied harder, if only I'd stuck with those piano lessons, if only I'd spoken to that girl at the bus stop, if only I hadn't spoken to that girl at the bus stop, if only I'd remembered Alison Wilcox's name in the morning.

Nigel Walker is a former Olympic hurdler who gave it all up and became a Welsh International rugby player. I had the privilege of meeting him at a corporate function I was hosting, where he was giving a talk about his life with particular reference on the 'need to adapt'. There could have been few people better qualified to talk on the subject. His talk was punctuated with video clips of his sporting achievements, and one particular sporting failure. The 1984 Olympic 110m hurdle semi-final and the culmination of four years of dedicated, exhaustive and sometimes punishing training. As Nigel showed the clip of the race, we all watched in horror as he caught his leading foot on the seventh hurdle and went crashing to the ground. In that moment, everyone present felt Nigel's disappointment as if it was their own – that sudden destruction of a dream held for so long, aspirations of glory brutally subverted by pain, both mental and physical.

Nigel stopped the video clip and smiled. (It must have been a few years before he was able to pull that trick.) 'So, what next?' he said, with characteristic Welsh understatement. He went on to explain that although he had considered a career change at this low moment, it wasn't until he failed to qualify for the 1992 Olympics that he felt he ought to make the change to rugby. Friends and colleagues advised him otherwise, but he was determined, not least because he didn't want to find himself saying at a much later date '*If only* I'd had a serious go at playing rugby'.

The clips that followed were all the more important. They were a compilation of Nigel's magnificent international tries for Wales, and they left the corporate audience uplifted in a way that I had never seen before. But never mind, the managing director's speech, 'Corporate re-structuring in the domestic marketplace', soon put paid to that.

However, before the managing director proudly strode behind the lectern and embarked on his speech which would deaden the senses of a now uplifted audience, I was required to join Nigel on stage to conduct a short interview. There was one question I simply couldn't resist asking him.

'Nigel, was there any point when you thought to yourself, as you were lying prostrate on the Olympic track alongside an upturned hurdle with two badly grazed knees, "If only I'd jumped a bit higher . . .?"'

2

A Prince And A Coconut

Of course, the question I had asked Nigel had been a tad cruel, but the laugh which followed easily justified its inclusion. (In my book anyway.) Nigel had been able to laugh along with the rest, enough healing time having elapsed since his horrors of 1984. And although I had made a joke about it, the fact was that I believed that Nigel was offering a first-rate perspective on life. I liked the idea of doing all you could to reduce the chances of you, as an old person, saying 'if only'.

The deeper point behind my question, if I can pretend there was one, was to illustrate that 'if onlys' are inevitable, an inescapable part of life. If only that plane hadn't crashed, if only that volcano hadn't erupted, if only I hadn't stepped in that dogshit. The trick is to be masters of our own destiny in so far as we have control, and take the rest on the chin with a wry smile. But we must go for it. Only a fool would squander the rich opportunities which life affords us. And so it was that I found myself in an electrical superstore looking at fridges.

And my, there are some magnificent models on the market.

Darren was most attentive. I knew his name was Darren because he had a badge on saying 'Darren', with 'I'm here to help' written underneath. He must have been in his late teens, early twenties, and was sweating nervously. He wore a tie awkwardly and with an obvious reluctance. The company 'uniform' of blue sweater and matching slacks hardly communicated a message of corporate success when Darren was its model. For him, 'style' was little more than a word between 'stutter' and 'stymie' in the dictionary. Everything about him suggested that he was in the job not because he was ahead of the rest of the pack when it came to selling electronic goods, but because the reward for doing it was a magnificently insubstantial hourly rate.

We surveyed the fridges. A mass of white filled an entire corner of the superstore. Who says choice is a good thing? This amount of choice wasn't going to make my life any easier and you could be sure it made Darren's an absolute nightmare.

'What exactly is it you're looking for?' he said at insufficient volume.

Difficult one that. What *are* you looking for in a fridge? You can't answer with the obvious – 'Well, I'm after something which will keep things cold.' What other considerations are there? It's not like buying a car, is it? I can't express a preference for an automatic, or demand power steering or even spend time deliberating over what colour. All their fridges were white. White, pristine white. So, denied the comfortable ease of 'Well, Darren, I'm looking for one in a light blue', I found myself offering up, 'What's the lightest model you sell?'

Darren went pale. Nothing in his superficial training had begun to prepare him for this.

'Lightest?'

'Yes, lightest.'

'Why? Are you going to be moving it about much?'

'You could say that, yes.'

I didn't make a purchase that day. It wasn't Darren's fault; in fact his spectacular ignorance of 'all things fridges' endeared him to me greatly. I don't want a load of technical jargon – what I'm looking for is exactly the kind of exchange I was able to have with Darren.

TONY: 'Ah, this one is another fifty quid, it must be better.'

DARREN: 'I suppose so.'

Darren understood that the customer is always right. For him this was founded on the supposition that he was almost always wrong. But I made no purchase because I didn't wish to become embroiled in the secondary selling which these poor salesmen are required to engage in. Having already got you to commit to a purchase by telling you how efficient and reliable the product is, they then embark on getting you to sign up for an insurance policy by pointing out how inefficient and unreliable the product is. It's a difficult stunt for the salesman to pull off and I didn't wish to see Darren attempt it. I had too much respect for the man.

Besides I had some negotiating to do with Kevin before making any purchase. I wanted to take a small fridge which was about two feet square, because one like this would fit on the back seat of a saloon car and greatly enhance my chances of a ride. OK, the original hitchhiker I had seen all those years before had been heroic enough to undertake the task with a full-size fridge with freezer at the top, but the chances were that he was only going up the road and wasn't attempting a journey of similar magnitude to mine.

*

Negotiations were easier than I expected. As it turned out, Kevin didn't for one moment believe I was actually foolish enough to see this thing through, so had no problem agreeing to my request. In fact he was predictably smug about the whole thing.

'Size isn't important,' he quipped.

I have never adhered to this view. As far as I'm concerned, people who say size isn't important, aren't big enough to admit that they're wrong.

Kevin included one stipulation. After a glance at the map he insisted that my journey should take in Tory Island at the extreme northwestern tip of Ireland, Cape Clear Island in the extreme southwest and Wexford in the southeast. Apart from that I was free to take whichever route I saw fit, provided I was hitch-hiking. With a fridge. I was allowed the luxury of taking a bus for the first few miles out of Dublin, and my argument was accepted that Northern Ireland be excluded since there was a distinct possibility the fridge might be mistaken for a bomb. It's difficult to put a price on a bet worth risking your life for, but £100 falls some way short.

Now, it would be foolish to take on a journey of this nature without rigorous planning but, given the ridiculous nature of the challenge, making any adequate preparations wouldn't have been in the spirit of things. Instead I felt that the best course of action in the weeks prior to my departure was to close off my mind to the reality of what lay ahead. Although I was talking about the trip a good deal and gaining kudos from friends and colleagues who had a nagging admiration for what they saw as a romantic whimsy, when it came down to considering basic logistics I would quickly find something else to think about. I was just like any self-respecting schoolkid – I wasn't going to do my essay until the night before it needed handing in, and then it would be sloppy and rushed, but just competent enough to keep me out of trouble. At least I hoped so.

I had decided that I wanted to make my journey in the month of May, a time which I hoped would see Ireland dryish and warmish but not overrun with tourists. My agent and I had arrived at a suitable departure date. I had been asked to do a six-minute stand-up spot at the Prince's Trust Royal Gala at the Opera House, Manchester. The plan was to perform in front of HRH The Prince of Wales and a two-thousand-strong audience at one of the star-studded theatrical events of the year, and then bugger off to Ireland the next morning and stand by the side of the road with a fridge. As plans go, it had a nice shape to it. The words chalk, sublime, cheese and ridiculous immediately sprang to mind, but not in that order.

With two days to go, instead of focusing my energies on preparing for a performance at the Royal Gala which could greatly further my career, I was taken up with worrying about what would follow the day after. My imagination was working overtime in providing pictures of bleak rain-swept roadsides and uncompassionate drivers. I had begun to do something very close to panic.

What had seemed amusing in the pub had now become a reality. Suddenly I was making calls trying to get a friend of a friend to purchase a fridge for me in Dublin, looking at different kinds of trolleys which might be best suited for its daily transportation and staring at a map of Ireland trying to decide whether to go clockwise or anti-clockwise. But I was scared. I was scared that I was heading towards a deep embarrassment. I'd been embarrassed before – who hasn't? – but I felt I was headed for the kind of big-time embarrassment which leaves a scar on your soul and can disrupt sleep patterns.

When I was about ten years old I used to go and watch Brighton and Hove Albion football club with my father and we would stand on the East Terrace at every home game. I used to stand on a box and thrill at the whole spectacle. I was mesmerized, not just by the football (it was Brighton and Hove Albion after all) but by all the cheering, chanting, ritual display of partisan colours and the rattatatt sound of the rattles. The rattles particularly. I don't think you see or hear them anymore, they seem to have fallen out of fashion, but then it was very popular for fans to swing a wooden rattle whenever the fancy took them.

One Christmas I got given a toy machinegun. When you pulled the trigger it made exactly the sound of a rattle. I decided I would take it to the next home game and fire it off in exactly the same manner as the other 'rattlers'. I can't think why, but my heart was set on it, and my father and I embarked on the twenty-minute walk to the ground and I carried my toy machinegun in my hand. Just before we reached the turnstile two much bigger boys saw the gun and put their hands in the air shouting 'Don't shoot! Don't shoot!' Suddenly all eyes seemed to be on me. There was much laughter. I felt humiliated, frightened and ludicrous all at the same time. The moment passed quickly but there were still a few little jokes being made about the gun by the people in the queue behind us. I was distraught, frantic with worry that when we went into the ground the whole crowd would turn towards me and shout

'Don't shoot! Don't shoot!'

I looked up at my father and he was smiling at some of the jokers. It was all right for him – it hadn't been *his idea* to bring the gun. What an idea. What had I been thinking of?

I asked him to take the machinegun and put it under his coat. He told me not to be silly but then when I asked him again, and he could see the tears welling up in my eyes, he did what a father has to do in these situations – he had to watch a football match whilst holding a toy machinegun.

I was now beginning to feel that I was heading for an embarrassment as deep as that. I would just start to pull the fridge to the roadside to begin my hitching and someone would make a wisecrack and that would be me finished – the whole escapade shot to pieces at the first instance. And I wouldn't have my father to suffer my embarrassment for me this time. That's growing up I suppose – you have to hold your own toy machineguns. Or be like most people and use toy machineguns for playing with at home and fridges for keeping things cold in kitchens.

The night before I was due to leave was a very sleepless one. There are occasions when the night can seize upon problems and worries and magnify them to such an extent that by about 3.30 am they seem completely insurmountable. I genuinely started to fear for my life. What if I got stuck on some remote rural road, miles from anywhere and simply couldn't get a lift and night fell? If the temperature dropped (it had been snowing recently) and I failed to find adequate shelter I could die of exposure.

The next morning I went straight to London's top camping shop to look into the purchase of a tent and sleeping bag. When I got there I immediately dismissed the tent idea, even the smallest ones were too large, and I knew I would die of frustration trying to erect the thing before the threat of exposure had even begun to become a factor. Instead I bought the top-of-the-range sleeping bag. It was small and light and over a hundred quid, but on leaving the shop I felt death to be a more distant proposition than it had been the previous night.

I packed in sombre mood. I'm very rarely jolly when packing anyway because there are few things I dislike more, unpacking being one of them. I was in a hurry because packing is something which you always do at the last minute. Anyone who packs two days before departure should seek counselling. Balanced people are still shoving stuff into their bag as they are leaving the house. That's normal.

I was having an especially bad time because I'd dug out an old ruck-sack for this journey and I had forgotten what displeasing items of lug-gage they are. Their only advantage is that you don't need hands to carry them, but that's not enough; the same can be said of contagious dis-eases. I seemed to have the worst model available on the market – it was like a kind of inverse tardis. Big on the outside, it seemed to hold sod all. The inclusion of two shirts, a jumper, a pair of trousers, shoes and a healthy quota of pants and socks left it overflowing, and a measure of undignified 'shoving down' of things was required before the bloody thing would shut. Or close. Or whatever it is a rucksack does when it isn't open anymore. Then I remembered that I hadn't included water-proofs. So, I had to tug once again at the abundant array of strings and cords which seemed to be all over it in order to get the bloody thing open again, take everything out and go through the whole infuriating process one more time. I hoped that my relationship with the fridge would be more serene. Anyway, I had done it, I had packed everything I needed. I was starting to feel rather pleased with myself when my heart sank, because there in the corner of the room sat the sleeping bag.

Well, I wasn't going without that – it could save my life. I slumped down next to the rucksack and tried to work out what I could sacrifice to make room. Pants? One month without pants hitching round Ireland with a fridge? No, I was doing it with pants or I wasn't doing it at all. I stared at the rucksack and resisted the temptation to get up and give it a good kicking. Then I suddenly realised that all the tags, tassles, cords and ropes which hung from it weren't just there to make the carrier of the bag feel like an accomplished traveller, but that they did, after all, have a function. The designer of the bag had realised that he had created one which held next to nothing and so had made provision for numerous items to be secured on the outside. An hour and a half and a good deal of swearing later, the sleeping bag was successfully tethered to the exterior of my rucksack. I forced my way between its shoulder straps, hauled it around on to my back and stood proudly in front of the mirror. I was pleased with what I saw. I really did look a hardy and experienced traveller. But for the bedroom slippers.

I was ready. I waited for the taxi to arrive and remembered that it was Royal Gala day. I wondered if the other artistes had been preparing for performance in the same way that I had.

I was going to fly straight on to Dublin the following day, so I was wearing the gear I would be in for the next month. I had my suits for the performance and after-show reception in a suit holder which my agent would bring back to London after the show. Carlton Television were providing the taxi to take me to the airport where I would fly up to Manchester. Hardly worth getting the plane for such a short journey, but they had offered it and somehow it seemed more glamorous than the train. I wasn't dressed for glamour – windcheater, scruffy trousers, hiking boots and holding a rucksack. The taxi arrived, except it wasn't a taxi but a stretch limo. The TV company must have got me mixed up with Phil Collins. I expect he was well pissed off with the seven-year-old Datsun Cherry waiting outside his door.

And so my neighbours were treated to the unusual sight of a scruffy hiker having a peak-capped chauffeur holding the door open for him whilst he climbed into the back of a shiny black stretch limo. It may have appeared that I hadn't fully embraced the true spirit of backpacking.

In Manchester another impressive car was waiting to meet me at the airport. I remember thinking that I should enjoy this, the zenith of travel experience, for the nadir was surely to come. I arrived at the theatre to find hordes of photographers and autograph hunters. Were they here for me or was there just a chance they might be more interested in The Spice Girls, Phil Collins or Jennifer Anniston? I emerged from the limo and a wave of confusion engulfed the onlookers and, at a stroke, their excitement was supplanted by bemusement. Was there a band called The Backpackers on the bill? Was there a new member of The Spice Girls called Itinerant Spice? I made my way to the stage door, rucksack over my shoulder, and a strange kind of silence fell over the crowd. It almost felt like resentment. How dare I get out of a car like that and not be someone they were excited about. If a frown made a sound, the noise would have been deafening. As it was you could hear a head drop.

The show went fine. Not great – just fine. I wasn't sure how well I had done but as we lined up for the finale bow, one of the dancers from Kid Creole And The Coconuts gave me the thumbs up. That was enough for me, I was happy to have the approval of a Coconut. That's why we do it. The show's producers, whilst rewarding me with a position in the front row for the curtain call, had put me right at the end of the line which meant that when I was required to turn to my right and bow to the Prince, I was so far across the stage that I was just bowing directly into the wings. There before me, instead of HRH Prince Charles, the Prince of Wales, was a fat member of the stage crew who acknowledged my bow by giving me the wanker sign and pissing himself with laughter. I smiled, largely because I couldn't think of what else to do.

Moments later the curtain had dropped and I was in a line waiting to be greeted by Prince Charles. As he worked his way up towards me I could hear the kind of mind numbingly superficial conversation that he had to engage in. This kind of social intercourse clearly wasn't something that came naturally to him but years of experience had left him accomplished enough in the brief inanity. I felt sorry for him – but for an accident of birth that could have been my gig.

Finally, he arrived at me, having had the relative ease of chatting with performers from Cirque du Soleil who had made life easy for him by coming from all over the world and having performed a spectacular and unusual act involving contortion and acrobatics. It all went rather well – there was even a slight moment of amusement when he asked the Russian girl how she got her body into that position. Then me. The bloke who came on and talked to the audience for six minutes, got a few laughs and then went off again. He shook my hand. I could see from his eyes that the poor guy could think of absolutely nothing to say to me. A moment of complete silence. What is it about me? I haven't got the rucksack on now. I looked into his eyes – he looked right through mine. He wasn't focusing, he was trawling his brain for a suitable question.

'Have you had to travel far to be here?' he eventually managed.

'Not really, London.'

I hadn't given him much to get his teeth into there. He could hardly say,

'Oh, London – that's where my mother lives – she's got a little place in SW1.' Again the flash of panic in his eye. Come on Charles, hang in there – two more questions and you're on to Frank Bruno, he's going to be much easier.

'And were the audience difficult?' This was better, but although meant well, isn't exactly a question a comedian longs to be asked. In an ideal world you would have been so funny and the audience would have lost themselves in laughter to such a degree that a question like that would have been redundant.

'Oh, they were okay.'

I wasn't really helping him very much here but I suppose there was a part of me that didn't want to. What *was* the point of this? My instinct was to say 'Look, let's talk properly or not at all', but there seemed little point in making this thing any more gruelling for him than it already was.

Prince Charles seemed to relax slightly, perhaps in the knowledge that however unsuccessful his next conversational gambit might be, at least it was his last one with me.

'And what are you up to next?'

I waited a moment and then offered in my best deadpan delivery, 'I'm hitch-hiking round Ireland with a fridge, Your Highness.'

His response was a Royal masterstroke. He simply smiled and pretended not to hear. Or understand. Or both. And who can blame him? My answer had invited the kind of follow-up question for which there simply wasn't time. I warmed to him as he smiled again and moved on – after all, why ask when you don't care? Oddly our little exchange had afforded him a rare opportunity to show some honesty. For that, I'm sure he will be eternally grateful.

The flight from Manchester to Dublin is only forty minutes or so. It feels slightly longer when there is a stag party three rows back. I was sat next to a matronly looking middle-aged woman whose tuts and sighs were more irritating than the unpleasant noises emanating from the stag boys. It was only 11.30 am and they were already quite drunk. Nothing like pacing yourself. The woman was reading a very impressive, thick hardback book. I couldn't see what it was called but the chapter she was on was entitled 'Domination and Hegemony'. I concluded that she was either an academic or a sado masochist. I closed my eyes and let the gentle rhythm of the safety instructions lull me to sleep. I was woken soon enough by the stag party who had broken into song. I wanted to stand up, turn round and say 'Please stop, I beg you' but I didn't need to because matronly lady had taken roughly the same approach only with a less supplicatory tone. Needless to say, her words had the reverse effect, causing an increase in volume and the personalisation of a number of songs in her honour. Suddenly I found it all more relaxing. The lyrics were more entertaining now they had found a focus, and the woman's increasing discomfort somehow had a soothing effect upon me.

Ignoring the surrounding turbulence I began to study my map of Ireland. I knew very little about the place and had no real idea of the distances involved, but my brain wasn't up to the taxing task of trying to work them out now. I gave some thought to what I might try and tackle on my first morning. My intention was to get a bus out of Dublin in the direction of Cavan and try and start hitching in roughly the area where I reckoned I had seen the original 'Fridge Man' all those years ago. This, I decided, was somewhere around Navan. I looked out of the window. It was raining. Ireland is good at that. To cheer myself up I started to scan the map for places with silly names. I noticed a Nobber and another place Muff. Muff was on the coast and I was momentarily amused by the idea of going there and attempting to hire some diving gear.

The plane touched down. The Odyssey had begun.

3

This Bus Is Going To Cavan

Shane must be a very good friend of Seamus. I can just imagine his face when he got the call.

'Oh hi Shane, it's Seamus here – could you do a favour for me?'

'Sure.'

He had already made mistake number one by not finding out the nature of the favour first.

'There's this friend of mine Tony and he's going to hitch-hike round Ireland with a fridge.'

'Hmmmmm.'

'Could you buy a small fridge and a trolley for it and pick him up at Dublin airport? He'll give you the money when he gets there.'

'Er–'

'Good, grand . . . I'll ring you Friday with the flight details.'

And there he was at the airport, the man who had been entrusted with the responsibility of purchasing someone's travelling companion for the next month, a role more commonly associated with Bangkok than Dublin. Although we'd never met, we knew each other instantly. He must have been able to recognise the wild apprehension in my eyes and I could see the dismay in his. He greeted me cordially enough and we made our way to the car. That was where the fridge was, he told me, accurately assessing that its whereabouts were my main concern.

I was rather nervous about meeting it. He'd been given detailed instructions and he seemed bright enough, but what if he'd bought the wrong kind of fridge? I suddenly felt it had been a mistake to have abdicated responsibility for this, the most important of all my pieces of baggage. After all I knew so much about fridges having been given the lowdown by an expert like Darren. But it had to be like this because today was a Sunday and not a good day for fridge shopping, and I wanted to make a start first thing in the morning. It was almost like starting a new job – in on Monday morning, bright and early, looking your best and keen to impress.

We climbed the stairs in the surprisingly odourless multi-storey car park. I found Shane to be a reticent man but assumed he was more so today because his thoughts were occupied trying to work out the size of favour he would demand from Seamus in return for having done this one. It was certain to be a biggy, along the lines of 'There's this man I want you to kill . . .' Then I saw the fridge for the first time. Shane had done well. Exactly what I had been looking for, a white cube about two feet square. I patted it affectionately and Shane looked away allowing us a moment of intimacy. Then he produced the trolley and in reverent silence we strapped the fridge to it, respectful witnesses at the birth of a truly symbiotic relationship.

I wheeled the fridge around the car park a bit like a sportsman warming up, and it felt good. Me, the fridge and the trolley were going to get along just fine. We would have been the dream team if it hadn't been for the rucksack. Initiation ceremony out of the way we headed off. Shane had exceeded his initial brief by organising bed and breakfast accommodation for me in an area south of the River Liffey called Donnybrook. He started to relax and we chatted more freely. He revealed himself to be quite amused by my prospective expedition and suggested that I get in touch with a radio show on RTE FM 2 called *The Gerry Ryan Show*. He said that they liked to get behind wacky ventures and mine fitted the bill perfectly. I hadn't thought of doing anything like that but as we progressed slowly through the gridlocked centre of Dublin the idea grew on me.

We reached Donnybrook and I paid Shane the £130 I owed him for the fridge.

'By the way, how much is the bet for?' he asked.

'A hundred pounds,' I replied.

He was confused for a moment, then he rather hurriedly wished me good luck and drove off with a look on his face which suggested that he was relieved that I wasn't in his car anymore.

I was greeted at the B&B by Rory, a young man who looked as if he'd just graduated and was some way from being the middle-aged maternal lady called Rosie who I imagined ran all these kinds of establishments. He had very thick lenses in his glasses and I found the resulting enlargement of his eyes a little disconcerting. He declared that he had no problems on the vacancy front given that he had no other guests staying. Initially he didn't comment as I wheeled the fridge into his hall, but he surveyed it in such a way as to suggest that he wasn't confident that his thick lenses were thick enough. A few seconds passed and he capitulated.

'Is that a fridge?' he said.

This was an enquiry I was to hear a good deal more in the weeks to come.

'Yes,' I replied accurately.

He didn't pursue this line of questioning and I offered nothing further although I could tell that he was curious. I had made a decision before leaving that I would try not to volunteer information about this fridge unless it was asked of me and then I would tell the truth. I was interested to see how many people wouldn't ask, either through politeness or a general lack of interest. Rory fell into the former category.

Shortly after I'd settled into my room and was embarking on some gentle unpacking there was a knock on the door. It was Rory asking me if I would do him a favour. I carelessly said 'no problem' in a manner of which Shane would have been proud. Rory said that he was popping out for a while and would I mind answering the phone if it went, and once again I obliged with another 'no problem'. Forty minutes and three bookings later, I decided that the best course of action was to go out myself.

I was feeling pretty jaded, with recent sleepless nights and the trauma of the flight taking their toll, but I had two things I wanted to do before I turned in for the night. Firstly, since Shane had pointed out that the RTE studios were fortuitously only five minutes walk away, I saw no harm in dropping a note into *The Gerry Ryan Show* giving them details of the journey I was about to embark on and leaving the phone number of Rory's B&B if they wanted to speak to me in the morning. Also I wanted to take a photograph.

On a previous visit to Dublin I'd gone to a nightclub in a basement in Leeson Street called Buck Whaley's. It was an evening of no significance other than for an estate agent's sign which had caught my eye. Two doors down from Buck Whaleys another basement club had closed down but the dormant neon light letters spelling out the word 'DISCOTHEQUE' remained. Outside an estate agent had placed a board saying:

TO LET

COMMERCIAL PROPERTY

SUIT DISCO

I was impressed. After all that's what you pay your money for. Without the particular expertise of that estate agent and for his aptly chosen words 'SUIT DISCO', heaven knows what doomed commercial venture an entrepreneur might have considered for that property, carelessly clearing out the bars and breaking up the dancefloor in order to open up a shoe shop.

I got there to find the photo opportunity was denied to me since the board was no more, someone wisely having followed its sound advice opening it up as a disco. Commission well earned by Messrs Daly, Quilligan and O'Reilly.

I dropped my explanatory letter into RTE, ate a disappointing takeaway, returned to Rory's, took a shower and went to bed. Fortunately I was so tired that it didn't take me long to fall asleep. If it had, I might have started to become anxious about what the next day held in store.

The next morning I was woken by Rory knocking on my door. I *thought*, 'Oh God, I suppose you're going out again and you want me to man the telephones and make my own breakfast?' but *said*, 'Yes?'

Not such a good line but it came a close second.

'Phonecall for you,' said an excited Rory, 'it's *The Gerry Ryan Show*.'

'Oh. Right.'

Having been awake only a matter of seconds I wasn't exactly on top of what all this meant. I opened the door and Rory handed me one of those cordless phones which nearly always get a bad reception however much the manufacturers promise otherwise. I put it to my ear.

'Hello?'

'Hello Tony, it's Siobhan here from *The Gerry Ryan Show*, I'll put you on hold and you'll be through to Gerry in a minute.'

Gerry? I don't know a Gerry. And why can't he talk to me now? Before I could say anything I found myself listening to Chris Rea and the whole thing dawned on me. Oh no, I was going to be on air after this record! What about my hair? I cleared my throat several times in an effort to make it sound less like I'd just woken up. I tried to ignore Chris Rea's lyrics; after all the thought of being on 'the road to hell' was disturbing enough first thing in the morning, but when you were about to embark on a venture like mine it was almost as if the bastard was taking the piss.

Gerry Ryan's voice cut through the fading record.

'Now, I've got Tony Hawks on the line. Good morning Tony – now you're about to make an interesting journey – would you care to tell us about it?'

I can think of easier things to do one minute after you've woken up.

Actually I didn't do a bad job of explaining what I was up to and why, even managing to be faintly amusing from time to time.

'I've no idea if I'll stay this jolly,' I said to Gerry at one stage, 'it's only because I haven't started yet that I sound this happy.'

'Well, I think maybe if the weather is good for you, you'll probably get a very good response, and indeed knowing the way the national psyche of the people in this country works, you'll probably be made extremely welcome – and it will be a great thing for the peace process.'

'Well, I hope to be passing through Northern Ireland later today, so if I can do anything to smooth things over up there I'd be more than happy – maybe we should all get round the fridge. People have tried getting round tables and it doesn't really work out, the whole body language thing behind a table is all wrong – so let's all get round the fridge.'

'I think you may have hit on something there, Tony – that could be our motto for the peace process – "Let's get round the fridge".'

We must have chatted for six or seven minutes, which surprised me because I was so used to English radio where they want a few quick soundbytes from you before they whack on another record. We even took a call from a pub landlord offering to throw a 'fridge party' when I got to Cork. I thanked him and promised to take him up on the offer, but wondered if he had any idea as to what a fridge party might involve. It didn't seem to matter.

In Gerry Ryan I could tell I was dealing with a very accomplished broadcaster who had mastered the art of calmly coping with four things happening at once whilst talking at the same time. He also seemed to be genuinely intrigued by the absurdity of my undertaking and wound up the interview by saying, 'This is exactly the kind of thing that we like to keep an eye on – we will put the full weight of RTE behind you, will you call us tomorrow?'

'Absolutely, Gerry, I'd be delighted.'

'Good morning.'

'Good morning.'

I sounded happy and indeed I was. But only because I hadn't woken up properly, both in the physical and metaphorical sense, to the reality of what lay ahead of me. Furthermore I hadn't looked out of the window so I was blissfully unaware that it was sheeting down with rain.

Through the phone's earpiece I heard Gerry's summing up, 'Good luck to Tony . . . well, you have to say it's a completely purposeless idea, but a damn fine one.'

I hoped that the rest of Ireland would feel the same.

On my way to the B&B's dining room I was intercepted by a beaming Rory.

'So that's what the fridge is for, you madman.'

He led me into the kitchen and sat me down at a table where I could watch him prepare breakfast. Presumably this was an honour bestowed upon guests who had just been on national radio. In the next few minutes Rory really opened up to me, telling me about his studies, travels and his business partnership with his father, all at the expense of my bacon. He didn't mind. He simply tossed the burnt rashers away and extravagantly produced some fresh ones. All at the expense of my eggs. He wasn't very good at this breakfast business and it might have been easier for me if I hadn't been coerced into watching. It didn't bother him though, he was too busy telling me about the Five-year Economic Plan he and his Dad had worked out.

I don't know what had caused the conversational floodgates to open but I suppose there must be something about *knowing* why someone is travelling with a fridge that sets your mind at ease, however irrational the reason may be. Overnight Rory may have felt that he had a dangerous psychopath as his only guest but now he knew the truth. I was a good-humoured eccentric for whom care with breakfast wasn't a priority. In fact he lavished a service of complete neglect upon me; he disappeared off to answer the phone three times and his prolonged absence necessitated my self-promotion to breakfast chef. Not a problem, for I was a better cook than him and I was pleased he was getting more bookings. Last night's level of occupancy wasn't in accordance with the Five-year Plan.

Rory returned from his last phonecall just as I was completing my first meal of the day.

'Good breakfast?' he enquired, making no apology for his lack of involvement in its creation.

'Lovely. Thanks.'

Twenty minutes later I was in a taxi taking me to the bus station, Rory having charged me half price for the room.

'Ah, if you're staying in guest houses for a month you'll need to save money,' he had said. A nice gesture – or was he trying to tempt me back there to work full time?

The taxi driver had helped me in with the fridge but had failed to see anything in it worthy of conversation. He had his own agenda and he wanted to chat about traffic congestion in the city, unnecessary round-abouts and the mindless introduction of one-way systems. Taxi drivers are the same throughout the world – great levellers. Never mind that Nelson Mandela, President Clinton or Michelle Pfeiffer has jumped into the cab, they'll get no specialist treatment, none whatsoever. The driver will bore them just as shitless as you and me.

At the bus station I was to discover that pulling a fridge on a trolley wasn't easy amongst large numbers of people who were in a hurry. Cornering was harder than I had imagined and going down stairs was a particularly hazardous business. I knew that in the course of the next few weeks I wouldn't want to find myself in a hurry too often. Self-consciously I made my way to the ticket office taking care not to injure small children with my cumbersome load. I was aware now of the heavy rain outside and was approximately at the mid-point of a mood swing from jolly to despairing.

I bought a ticket to Navan where I was to start hitching. I would be happy if I could make it as far as Cavan by nightfall and then take on the potentially difficult journey to Donegal the following morning. As far as I could make out from the map, the roads leading to Donegal dipped in and out of Northern Ireland, and I was anxious not to find myself hitching in that part of the world. Apart from the fact that I'd been told that drivers very rarely stop for hitchers there, I was conscious of the interest a small white container might hold for the security forces. Of all the romantic and heroic ways to leave this world, being part of a controlled explosion with a large kitchen appliance rated very poorly. Folk songs and poems were unlikely to be written, and not just because 'fridge' is a very difficult word to find a rhyme for.

The bus driver, a balding middle-aged avuncular figure, helped me load the fridge into the vast luggage compartment at the rear of the bus. There were no other bags in there and I was concerned that it would slide from side to side every time we went round a corner.

'Isn't it going to slide from side to side every time we go round a corner?' I asked the driver.

'Ah no, it'll be just fine,' he assured me authoritatively.

There were no views to be enjoyed on the fifty-minute busride because the heavy rain meant that the windows had steamed up. I don't understand the physics behind why that happens but I do know that it does little to improve your state of mind. My personal mood swingometer had now left 'jolly' way behind and was nudging 'despair' with a fleeting stop at 'mild wretchedness'.

We ploughed on through the rain towards Navan, five of us dotted around the bus, either reading or, like me, indulging in painful self examination. There were no conversations to distract me from my immediate fate, the only sounds were the hum of the engine and that of the fridge sliding from side to side every time we went round a corner.

Finally we arrived in what I took to be Navan. We went up a hill and on my right I could just make out a sign saying 'NOBBER MOTORS'. Excellent – this cheered me up – a secondhand car dealer's called Nobber Motors. Where the salesmen *really* screw you.

I could fathom two other things from peering through the smudge I'd created in the window's condensation; it was now raining harder than ever, and the town centre of Navan was no place to start hitching because everyone here was either shopping or going to the bank. Thinking there may be a suitable stretch of open road north of the town, I decided to consult the driver.

'Excuse me, but is there a bus stop north of Navan?'

'Where are you headed?'

'Er . . . Cavan.'

'Well, this bus goes to Cavan.'

'Yes . . . er . . . yes . . . but the thing is . . . I want to get out at a spot which might be suitable–'

'You're going to Cavan you say?'

'Yes, but–'

'Well, this bus is going to Cavan.'

'I know that, but–'

'Where are you trying to get to?'

'Er . . . Cavan.'

'Well, this bus is going to Cavan.'

I sat back down again, in absolutely no doubt as to where this bus was going. It was going to Cavan. From my point of view the exchange with the driver had been an abject failure. All I had succeeded in doing was confirming beyond any doubt whatsoever something that I already knew, and I now had a problem with regard to getting off the bus, the driver seemingly now having taken it upon himself to make sure that he delivered me to Cavan. Any attempt by me to try and get him to stop and let me out on the open road would result in his insistence that it wasn't Cavan, and that his bus was going to Cavan.

Now I could have insisted he stop and let me off; it was after all my inviolable right as a passenger, and what was more, I had already travelled further than the validity of my ticket permitted. But I was suffering from the English disease of not wanting to make a scene. Like most English people I fall into the category of those who will suffer a third-rate meal at a restaurant with sloppy service, and then, when faced with the waiter's question 'Is everything okay, sir?' will simply say 'Yes, fine thanks'. Better that way than making a scene. The last thing you want to do is make a scene.

Somehow I had to find a way of not going to Cavan on this bus. *Without* making a scene. I decided to try and sneak off at the next stop, hoping that there would be a reasonable amount of cover created by passengers getting on and off. It was a long shot but it might just work. Fifteen minutes later we stopped on the outskirts of a small town and a few of the people who had joined us in Navan got up and started to make their way off the bus. It was now or never. I quickly jumped to my feet and slipped between an old man, and a woman carrying a baby. It was touch and go whether the driver would see me out of the corner of his eye but I skilfully used my rucksack to obscure my face. I was good. I was very good, and I found myself descending the steps of the bus with freedom in sight. Such was my feeling of elation when I hit the ground and started to move off that I was untroubled by the driving rain which greeted me. Suddenly I stopped in my tracks. The fridge! I'd forgotten the fridge!

I turned round to see the bus doors closing. I scrambled back to the bus and just managed to slam my fist again in the closed door before the bus pulled away. The driver looked down and recognised me. He opened the doors and said, 'This isn't Cavan yet.'

We were back to square one.

'I know. It's just that–'

'Jump back on, this bus is going to–'

'Cavan, yes I know, it's just that I thought I might spend some time here first.'

'In Kells?'

He looked a little surprised, a desire to spend some time in Kells not being a preference often expressed. Looking around me, all I could see was a pub, a shop and the reason for the driver's surprise. Then I became conscious of the rain. Hard driving rain. I remembered my comfortable lifestyle at home and it occurred to me that I needed to be somewhere where there was a pub, a shop *and* a head doctor's.

I responded to the driver's bewilderment, 'Yes, I like the look of Kells. Very much.' I might have been overdoing it. 'I need you to open up the back for me to get my stuff out.'

The driver obliged, but with a lack of enthusiasm bordering on disapproval. He didn't buy this whole 'wanting to spend some time in Kells' yarn and as far as he was concerned I'd let him down badly by not staying on his bus as far as Cavan. He helped me out with the fridge, treating it as if it was a perfectly ordinary piece of baggage, and said 'Goodbye now' with a hollowness which reflected his deep disappointment in me.

Oh well, sometimes you've got to tread on a few toes in this world.

4

Rain, Mud And A Jack Russell

This was it. My reason for being here, the apogee of a dream held dear for so long and the inception of an unlikely and unpredictable voyage of discovery. I had arrived at the point of no return. I had my rucksack, I had my fridge and I had my desire. Nothing was going to stop me now.

Except the rain.

Look, I know it sounds feeble, but it really was raining too hard. To my mind there seemed little point in starting off the whole thing absolutely wet through and miserable. Okay – all right – *and* I needed to acquire some courage of the Dutch variety.

When I wheeled the fridge into the pub, the head of the little old man at the bar span round immediately.

'Is that a fridge?' he said.

'Yes,' I replied, growing quite skilled at this response.

There was a silence as the old man surveyed my baggage pensively.

'Sweet mother of Jesus, I've never seen a man come in here with a rucksack and a feckin' fridge before,' he said. And then smiled, 'Have you got a bomb in it?'

I explained about my bet and he shook his head in amazement, but then conceded, 'It's a very neat little fridge – everyone should have one.'

I agreed and then raised the question of whether there was any possibility that someone might appear behind the bar to serve me a drink.

'Ring the bell and he'll be with you in a moment. He's busy doing stocktaking – counting bottles or something.'

I rang the bell and in the ten minutes it took before it provided any kind of result I learned most of what there was to know about the old man's life. His name was Willy, he lived in Kells, had spent the years between 1952 and 1962 in London, had fought for the British in the second world war in North Africa, was now spending his army pension money on one of his favourite hobbies – whiskey, and his blood group was 'Rh Negative'. I didn't even know what my own blood group was, but already I knew Willy's. He'd just come back from Navan where he'd been giving blood and he was rather proud of the fact that there weren't very many 'Rh Negatives' in Ireland. Lucky him, he had the privilege of being born special; some of us had to lug fridges around to achieve that status.

The landlord eventually emerged from the bowels of his own pub, unflustered and unapologetic, and I ordered a drink.

'He's got his own ice,' said Willy to the landlord, who didn't get the joke because he hadn't yet seen the fridge at the foot of his bar. Still Willy laughed, and I smiled supportively.

'Do you do food?' I asked the confused landlord. He shook his head and mumbled, 'No.'

'Oh.'

'Next year.'

'What?'

'Next year. We start doing food next year.'

I really was getting quite hungry and I figured that next year wasn't going to be soon enough so I nipped over the road to the shop to buy a sandwich.

When I returned the pub was considerably busier and there was much excitement and raised voices. The atmosphere was transformed, the only constant being that for the landlord, the counting of bottles was still taking priority over the selling of them. Two middle-aged couples had come in and Willy was undergoing a rigorous cross examination. As politely as I could, I struggled between them to rescue my pint and sat down to listen in until I had enough information to ascertain exactly what was going on. The newcomers were two sisters, originally from Kells but now living in Canada, and their Canadian husbands. The sisters had left Kells in 1959 and hadn't been back since. Each disclosure of a Kells character that Willy and the two sisters knew was welcomed with a cacophonous enthusiasm which was visibly starting to piss off the husbands. They were already more concerned than their wives at the lack of any tangible barman. An almighty clamour greeted the discovery that the sisters' mother used to do Willy's mother's hair many many years ago. Other discoveries of a similar magnitude followed until the atmosphere was suddenly punctured by a raised and irascible Canadian voice, 'How does anyone get a drink around here?'

Willy gently explained the protocol, the bell was rung and the reminiscing continued, but at a slightly more acceptable volume. It also entered a new domain.

'Do you remember a little woman, auburn hair – a wonderful dancer
. . . Rosie . . . lived beside the church?'

'Yes, of course we do.'

'She's dead.'

'Oh dear. Mind, she must have been a fair old age.'

'That she was.'

'What about her sisters?'

'Dead.'

'And the brother?'

'Dead.'

The next twenty minutes saw the establishment of who was alive and
who was dead from the 1959 population of Kells. The only high point was
the appearance of the landlord which soothed the nerves of the
Canadian contingent and saw my pint glass replenished.

Then the ladies were furnished with two important new facts. That
Willy was an 'Rh positive' and that I was travelling with a fridge. The
sisters thought the latter was hilarious and it even caused some amusement in the long suffering Canadian camp.

'You're carting a ruddy fridge with you – for what?'

I told them about the bet.

'Who the hell is going to give you a ride?'

I told them it would fit in a four-door saloon car.

'Well, I hope you've got good walking shoes and a good ruddy mac.'

More laughter. All of this wasn't instilling me with confidence. The
banter was all good natured but it was undermining my already fragile
state of mind.

I looked at the fridge and saw a toy machinegun.

I hadn't hitched anywhere for about fifteen years. I was hoping the
thumb hadn't lost the old magic. I'd hitched alone in America, my
obliviousness to the danger somehow making me immune to it. On one
triumphant day, I'd made it from Niagara Falls to New York City in a
quicker time than it took the Greyhound bus. I had met a lot of nice
people and experienced much kindness. One guy, seeing that I was
hungry, insisted on buying me a huge lunch and when I thanked him for
his kindness, he simply said, 'Pass it on.' I liked this selfless concept –
repay *me* by rewarding *someone else entirely* with a generous dollop of
goodwill.

The only slightly dodgy experience was in France when I was picked up by an elderly man whose second question to me was what did I think of nude bathing? Having originally said I was headed for Lyons, I immediately revised my destination and insisted he let me off in Chalon-sur-Saône. As I got out of the car he said something in French which I didn't understand but I assume meant something equivalent to, 'But this bus is going to Cavan.'

I hauled my load slowly to a suitable spot by the roadside, noticing with some concern that cars were coming by at alarmingly irregular intervals. In a physical and emotional state close to numbness, I arranged myself by the roadside and tried to force myself to feel optimistic. Although the rain had eased off, it was still spitting and the clouds on the horizon suggested that it wouldn't be long before the waterproofs would have to come out. I surveyed the surroundings with which I hoped I wouldn't become too familiar and saw that I had chosen a bleak unwelcoming stretch of road on which to begin my journey. It wasn't ugly and it certainly wasn't attractive; it was just a dull stretch of Irish road. Electricity pylons, a couple of fields and the back view of a sign pointing the other way which, with any luck, read 'NO SCOFFING AT THE HITCHER'. I put the fridge a little way in front of me and leant the rucksack against it trying to create an impression of normality – that a fridge and a rucksack *should* be seen together, and I stuck my thumb out.

A Ford Fiesta sped past. Then a Vauxhall Cavalier. A Renault next, and then a red car whose make I couldn't fathom. That was four cars and none of them had shown any sign of stopping. What was going wrong? Had they not seen that my thumb was out? Were they not intrigued by the sight of this fridge? A Citroen, a large truck, a Ford Escort and a BMW later I sat on the fridge for a moment and gathered my thoughts. Eight vehicles had been past and I had been there ten minutes. I realised that this was less than one car a minute. I checked the second hand of my watch, and waited a minute. Oh dear. Nothing. Things were going from bad to worse. Even less than one car a minute. I tried to escape from this statistical mire by giving myself a pep talk in which I resolved to think positively for a quarter of an hour or so. I got up off the fridge and attempted to stand in such a way as to present myself as a strong, positive man with an air of vulnerability about him, thinking that this might give me the best 'across the board' appeal to oncoming drivers.

This gave me cramp. So I sat back down on the fridge and wondered how I could have been so naive as to have expected a steady flow of traffic on a main road. Maybe I should have got a piece of card with my destination written on it. Maybe I should have got a card and written 'ANYWHERE' on it. Maybe I should have recognised the difference between a funny idea and the practicality of attempting to act it out. Cars passed with an infrequency which left me having fantasies about traffic congestion. The numbness which I had felt when I began had long since disappeared and instead I now found my emotions lurching from one extreme to the other. Each time I could see a car or truck on the horizon I would become filled with expectation, 'This is it! This is the one!' As it drew nearer I would allow my hopes to rise to such an extent that when it sped by I felt bitterly rejected. Twenty minutes and seventeen bitter rejections later, I was beginning to feel a little low. Three or four weeks of this kind of torment would leave me in need of expensive counselling. My thoughts turned to the bet. I could handle losing a hundred pounds, and the knock to the pride would be considerably less than a daily dose of what I was having to suffer now. Contemplating giving up after less than an hour was not the start I had envisaged. No doubt about it, I was on the ropes. Actually I was on the canvas with the count having reached about six.

Occasionally a couple would go by and I could see what looked like the beginning of a conversation starting between them.

'Was that a fridge?'

'What?'

'That guy back there – hitching – did he have a fridge with him?'

'You're tired, darling. Stop in a minute and I'll take over driving.'

I thought, don't talk about it, stop and pick the poor bugger up! Self-centred bastards, you had room in your car. Never again was I going to leave a hitch-hiker by the side of the road.

I started considering the possibility of hiding the fridge and only revealing its existence when the driver had already stopped and had committed to the lift. I concluded that this wasn't cheating but should be a measure only resorted to after about two hours or if it started to rain heavily. Neither proposition seemed too distant a prospect. I stood up. I tried smiling at cars. This didn't work and probably made me look certifiable. To ease the boredom, I tried to look nonplussed, just to see if it was possible. That must be a mark of a great actor – someone who can look nonplussed at the drop of a hat.

Just when I had least expected it, in fact when I was having a go at looking bewildered, a scruffy red Fiesta van pulled over just in front of me. I couldn't believe it was stopping for me and ran forward to check. A dishevelled looking old man and his Jack Russell dog surveyed me through the open window.

'I'm only going as far as Carrerreraragh,' he mumbled. Not the dog, the man.

At least that was what I thought he'd said, his accent was strong and he obviously felt that talking was best done with the mouth barely open.

'How far is Carr . . . err . . . eraragh?'

'You mean Carrecloughnarreraragh?'

'Yes, Car–, yes, there, how far is that?'

'Carrereraoughnanrrara? It's about three miles.'

Oh God. Three miles is no use to anyone. From my previous experience of hitch-hiking I had discovered that it was sometimes better to turn down a lift than accept one which can land you in the middle of nowhere. I didn't like the sound of Carrerrererreragh, or its ability to sound different every time it was said. I tried to ascertain if Carreranoughnara would be any good for hitching.

'Is there anywhere round there I might–'

'Throw them in, throw them in.' He was pointing to my luggage.

'What's the road like there in Carra–'

'Throw them in, throw them in.' It might as well have been the dog talking for all the progress being made.

'I'm sorry, it's just that sometimes it's best to–'

'Look, jes' throw the feckin' things in the feckin' back, will ya?'

This did the trick. I responded immediately and against all my better judgement I was loading my gear into his tatty van in order to advance a further three miles up the road. Still, as I'd heard somewhere before, a journey of a thousand miles starts with one step.

Both he and the dog watched with interest as I lifted the fridge into the back.

'What have you got there?'

'It's a fridge.'

'Oh. You wouldn't want to be travellin' with a fridge for too long.'

Wouldn't you? No I suppose you wouldn't. I got into the front seat and the dog jumped on to my lap using me as a means of improving its view out of the front window.

'Where are you headed?' I asked.

'The cattle auction up the road here.'

'Are you going to buy a cow?'

'No, I'm just going to kill time.'

I suddenly felt a long way from home. I was in a place where people went to cattle auctions to kill time. Then I noticed something which had been obvious all along but had escaped my attention such had been my preoccupation with trying to decipher what he was saying. The old man was covered in mud. There's some rubbish that biologists or physicists give you about humans being 90% water, but this guy was at least 25% mud. It looked like he'd been rolling in it. Presumably to kill time. The strange thing was, his dog wasn't very muddy at all. How could that have happened? Dogs pride themselves on getting muddy and to be less muddy than your owner must be deeply shameful. I reckoned that's why the dog was so keen to look out of the window – keeping a check on the whereabouts of other dogs so it could avoid them and maintain some kind of respect in the area.

We arrived all too quickly in Carrerrerarse, the six minutes spent in the company of this mud-covered man and his dog having afforded me a brief respite from the notion that I had made a foolish error in my life. This hitching with a fridge business *was* possible. The man had stopped and he had picked up both me and my fridge. It was just bad luck that he was only going a few miles. And it was just bad luck that Carrerrerranoughnabollocks was one of the worst places for hitching in the Northern Hemisphere.

As the old man pulled into the side of the road, he was greeted by three other elderly farmer types who were also covered in mud. They weren't as muddy as him, obviously, but certainly muddy enough to be on the committee of the muddy gang. I got out, collected my gear and said goodbye, conscious of the fact that I was outside a cattle auction in the heart of rural Ireland, with a rucksack, a fridge and an insufficient coating of mud to be welcome in these parts.

All around me were the scenes of traffic congestion I had been dreaming of only minutes earlier. Trucks, wagons, carts, Range Rovers and tatty red Fiesta vans were arriving for the cattle auction and they were of absolutely no help to me. In fact they were an enormous hindrance, making it something of a problem finding a place to stand where through traffic might see me. I lifted the fridge on to its trolley, hoisted the rucksack on to my back and started to walk up the road. Needless to say it was muddy. I looked round to wave goodbye, but the old man had gone and instead I saw his Jack Russell eyeing me disparagingly through the van's windscreen. Instinctively it seemed to know the way I had chosen to travel lacked wisdom. I gave it the finger and continued on my way.

As I walked I could hear the monotone machinegun-fire delivery of the cattle auctioneer over the distant PA. I hoped for his sake that his entire audience wasn't made up of those who were killing time. I walked on. A farmer was staring at me. 'What's his problem?' I thought. I had forgotten that he had just seen an unmuddy man pulling a fridge behind him give the finger to a Jack Russell dog.

Presently I arrived at the hitching location which I considered to be the least unsuitable to those available to me. I was still alongside parked cars but I felt it was worth a try. Just as I had finished arranging myself as attractively as I could, it started to rain. Hard.

I had two alternatives. I could either commence an undignified struggle with my rucksack in an attempt to extricate my waterproofs, or I could go and seek shelter. The problem with the second option was that the only shelter available was the building in which the cattle auction was taking place and I was frightened that a combination of despondency and delirium would see me making a successful bid for a cow. Hitching round Ireland with a fridge *and* a cow really would be pushing it.

With considerable trepidation I took on the rucksack. I had just opened it up and was subjecting the clothes at its apex to the full consequences of the weather conditions when, thank God, a car stopped for me. A blue Datsun estate car, a Sunny, or a Cherry, or one of those – no, I know what it was – the Datsun Saviour. I scurried to the passenger door and opened it.

'How far are you going?' I said.

The driver looked at me with consternation. 'I'm just parking here,' he replied.

Oh. I moved away enabling him to complete his manoeuvre without further interference. Ahead of him another car had stopped and was parking. I really was in a most unsuitable spot. I headed back to my roadside encumbrances. The car ahead tooted its horn. It was obviously having some difficulty parking. Forlornly I went back to rummaging for waterproofs. Then the car ahead did something very strange. Quite suddenly it went into reverse and stopped alongside me. The driver leant over, wound down the passenger window and said, 'I heard you on the radio this morning. I thought you'd be gone by now.'

After a false start, the journey had truly begun.

5

Who Came Fifth?

Brendan, the saviour, was immaculately turned out in suit and tie and had absolutely no mud on him whatsoever. He'd been listening to the radio that morning and knew exactly what I was up to, and why I was doing what I was doing, which given my recent experiences, was more than I did.

He was a toiletries salesman from Northern Ireland who had recently gained clients down in the republic. He scored well on three fronts – he was charming, he was good company and he was heading for Cavan. As his windscreen wipers worked overtime clearing the now torrential rain, we talked about life, love, politics, religion, and the rising price of deodorants. All in the lovely dry interior of his car. Bloody hell, I'd been lucky.

Before he got to Cavan, Brendan said he needed to make a couple of business calls and he asked me if I minded. Of course not, he was my saviour. He could have asked for anything and I would have obliged. Almost. And so we sped through the rain as far as Cootehill where he sold some toiletries and I took coffee in the quaint tea-rooms. Taking coffee in a tea-room always brings me a certain amount of extra pleasure in that I feel I'm beating the system. It's like having spaghetti in a pizza house, chicken in a steak house, or having a neck massage in a Bangkok massage parlour. We headed north to Clones, in County Monaghan, which Brendan explained was republican 'bandit country'. I wasn't sure how to tailor my behaviour for this area but I decided that if we were stopped by a man in a balaclava wielding a shotgun, I'd cut the light-hearted banter right down and try not to get chatting about my days in the Combined Cadet Force at school. When we got to Clones, I waited in the car whilst Brendan did his stuff in a moderately-sized convenience store. He was quite a while, which surprised me, because I figured that the one place where toiletries would be easy to sell would be a convenience store. He must have started to feel guilty because after a quarter of an hour he brought me out an ice cream, apologised and said he wouldn't be much longer. I liked this. It was like being eight years old again. Forty minutes later we were in Cavan, my destination for the day. I was feeling rather pleased with myself as we drew close to an area where Brendan knew there were guest houses. It was only five o'clock or so, but the next part of my journey, zipping in and out of Northern Ireland, could be the most hazardous, and I didn't want to find myself wandering into a paramilitary training camp at dusk and asking directions to reasonably priced bed and breakfast accommodation. In a bleak residential road we stopped outside an unwelcoming hostelry, and I got out and began unloading. I was sorry to leave Brendan, it was like he'd been on my side when the others had been ganging up on me. And he had bought me an ice cream.

I kicked off the playful goodbye stuff, 'If ever I see you with a fridge by the side of the road in England, I'll definitely stop for you.'

'If ever you see me with a fridge by the side of the road in England, you will have just taken hallucinogenic drugs.'

'Have a good journey back to Northern Ireland.'

'What?'

'Have a good journey home.'

'I'm not going home.'

'Where are you going then?'

'Donegal Town.'

'What for?'

'I've got some business there in the morning.'

We'd got on so well with each other so quickly that we'd forgotten to do the smalltalk establishing these kind of essential details. I felt it was worth pointing one out now.

'Well, I'm headed for Donegal.'

'Not Cavan?'

'Cavan was only a stopping off point for Donegal.'

'Right. Well, you'd better jump back in again.'

And jump back in again I did, with some delight.

The day had been an exhausting maelstrom of emotions, but now as we drove through the breathtaking lakeside scenery of County Fermanagh, along the banks of the beautiful Lough Erne, I allowed myself to indulge in a new one – triumph. The sun even broke through for five minutes and the freshly doused countryside glistened much in the same way as I did, only with a touch less smugness. I proudly traced our progress on the map and pointed out the absurdity of Lower Lough Erne actually being above Upper Lough Erne. Brendan explained that according to my perspective as a North-South map reader it was above, but the physical reality was that it was nearer sea level and therefore most definitely the lower of the two Lough Ernes.

Triumph was immediately usurped by shame. History had delivered enough cartographical colonial incompetence in this part of the world without my own ignorant contribution. We were, after all, in Northern Ireland. We only had to pass a police station with all its preposterous fortification to remind us of that.

Soon we were in the capital of County Fermanagh, Enniskillen. Enniskillen. The name itself was enough to trigger TV memories of one of the all too frequent atrocities of the Troubles, but here before me was a real town, not a news story viewed from the comfort of England. I had grown up with Northern Ireland always in the headlines, but had built up an immunity to it, never really registering that the people there shopped in high streets like ours, used British Telecom phoneboxes and voted MPs into our government. I mean their government – well, whatever – therein lies the crux of the problem, methinks. The apparently peaceful border town of Belleek behind us, we slipped through one final deserted checkpoint and re-entered the Republic. I had been disorientated by a part of the United Kingdom that I couldn't recognise or understand but now, as Donegal Town grew ever closer, once again I was filled with a sense of achievement. I know it was only the first day, but I'd covered a lot of miles, and proved to myself that I wasn't attempting the impossible.

In reaching Donegal Town I had arrived at a point which would be both the beginning and end of a circular tour of Donegal County, and which would therefore have the privilege, along with Dublin, of being the only place in Ireland which I would visit twice. The entrance to the town was marked by a small harbour and delightful views across Donegal bay.

Brendan dropped me outside a B&B displaying a 'Vacancies' sign and we arranged to meet for a pint at his hotel later on. There was no need for directions; it was in Donegal Town and given the size of the place, that was sufficient information. There were probably vacancies at his hotel but I felt, and I think there was tacit agreement from Brendan on this, that we were starting to spend so much time together that the taking of different lodgings was somehow an important affirmation of our heterosexuality.

I was greeted by the lady who ran the B&B as if greeting Englishmen with rucksacks and fridges was quite the norm. She had a wavering voice and spoke at a frustratingly dawdling pace in the manner of one who had only just got the hang of this talking business the previous week. In one agonisingly long sentence she explained how I could leave the fridge by the front door, how the shower worked and how she'd prefer it if I paid her in advance. By the time she'd finished it was nearly time to meet Brendan for that drink. I holed up in my tiny room and thought about my amazing day, what I would attempt tomorrow, and whether I'd ever been in a bedroom with less floor space.

I only had time to do a quick circuit of the town before meeting Brendan. It was a shame I didn't have a little longer because I could have done it twice. Donegal Town is tiny, with not much to see other than the castle, which appeared to be a nice old house with some fortifications thrown in just to get 'Castle' status.

Brendan and I drank in three pubs, the last being far and away my favourite. From the exterior there had been very little about it to suggest it was a pub; net curtains, an old lamp and a faded old sign with a surname on it. In much of Ireland they don't go in for grand pub names like 'The Coach And Horses' or 'The Prince Of Wales'; they simply name it after the proprietor – 'Daly's' or 'McCarthy's', the first indication of the more personal experience that awaits you within. I came to call these establishments the old boys' pubs, where everybody talks to everybody else regardless of who they are, partly because the clientele are very friendly and partly because the clientele are very pissed.

Just like an orchestra will have a Lead Violinist, most pubs will have a Lead Drunk. Or Drunk in Residence. He must have some arrangement with the landlord that he doesn't have to pay for any drinks which he can't say. His main role seems to be to welcome newcomers with the emission of a loud wailing noise and by flailing his arms about like a drowning man, until his already precarious hold on his own centre of gravity is upset to the point of liberating him totally from his bar stool. This is where the Second Drunk instinctively reaches out with his left hand to stop him falling to the ground and continues drinking with his right, as if the whole manoeuvre has been carefully rehearsed. Which of course it has. Every night for decades.

It wasn't long before Brendan and I were embroiled in a conversation with the regulars, the theme of which was prompted by highlights of today's Grand Prix on the TV screen behind the bar. I took a back seat in the discussion, largely due to an ignorance of motor racing and an inability to understand anything that was being said. As far as I could make out, the main thrust of it was the establishment of who came first, second and third.

The Lead Drunk was now almost comatose, the exertions of his initial greeting for us having taken their toll. Many names were put forward and rejected but after ten minutes of animated debate, the fact that Schumacher had won and Eddie Irvine had come third was settled upon and those present seemed content with what had been achieved. Suddenly, and out of nowhere the Lead Drunk blurted out, 'Who came fifth?'

Everyone turned to him in shock. Where had this come from? This, from a man who had been folded up on top of his bar stool for the past quarter of an hour. Three questions troubled all of us. How had he followed what was going on, how had he managed his first intelligible sentence of the evening, and why did he care who came fifth?

'Who came fifth?' He repeated his extraordinary question but this time he felt it would be better bellowed. For the first time that night, (and I suspect for a number of years) the bar's customers were completely silent. No one knew what crossing of wires in the drunk's brain had caused this enquiry, when 'Who came second?' had been the more relevant and 'Help' the most suitable. More importantly there was silence because no one actually knew who came fifth. When discussions finally got under way to solve this mystery Brendan and I decided it was a signal to turn in for the night. Our 'one for the road' had turned into 'three for the road' and there was a danger of granting the road too much respect.

In the morning, I successfully completed a shower in a much quicker time than that taken for the previous day's explanation of how to use it, and got dressed with extreme difficulty standing on the narrow stretch of carpet between bed and door. This was quite literally a bedroom. Just room for a bed. Any additional space was there simply to accommodate the opening of the door. As I headed on to the landing, the sudden introduction to wide open spaces frightened me as it would an agoraphobic.

At the foot of the stairs I was a little taken aback to see that the fridge had gone, but it hadn't been stolen, as the lady of the house painstakingly explained at breakfast.

'I. . . . . . . put it. . . . . in. . . . . the. . . . . shop. . . . . for. . . . . safety.'

I wasn't sure what this meant but decided that I would find out sooner by not asking. I was joined at my table by the only other guest, a travelling salesman who had one eye which looked at you and one which didn't. The trick was deciding which one to focus on. Whilst eating my cereal I plumped for the left eye but by the time I was on to my toast I had switched allegiance to the right, although I was starting to have doubts about that. In the end I gave up and focused on his nose, which was quite an unnatural thing to do and had an adverse effect on my appetite. The man was a souvenir salesman and he spent most of breakfast moaning about how souvenirs were hard to sell when it was rainy and cold, as it was at the moment. I felt that it was more likely to be an ocular thing which was frustrating sales.

The previous night Brendan had offered to take me the forty miles or so to Letterkenny after he'd done his morning's business in Donegal Town, but after that he would be heading back to Northern Ireland, and once again I would have to subject myself to the uncertainties of the roadside. Whilst he made his morning calls I had enough time to visit the tourist office and establish the best method of getting out to Tory Island. I was told that a mail boat left every evening at 9.00 am from a place called Bunbeg, and so reaching there became my goal for the day.

As it turned out, my fridge had been placed 'for safety' in the butcher's shop next door. Why, I don't know, because when I went round to collect it I found that 'safety' had involved it being set down on the customer's side of the counter in a totally unmanned shop. I coughed to gain attention in the hope that the butcher might appear in anticipation of a major pork chop sale, but to no avail. So I lifted the fridge on to its trolley and headed out of the shop, at which point the butcher emerged, 'Is that your fridge?'

'Yes.'

'Oh. Very good.'

My God, security was sophisticated here. If the fridge hadn't been mine and I hadn't been able to come up with that clever answer, my life of crime would have been over.

'How much did you pay for that?' the butcher added.

'A hundred and thirty pounds.'

'Ah, we paid roughly the same. We have one like that upstairs in the flat.'

'Are you happy with it?'

'Oh Jesus, yeah. They're great for a wee place.'

Before we could become involved in the kind of conversation about fridges that motorcycle enthusiasts have about motorcycles, I bad him farewell and he wished me luck, happily reassured that the Donegal branch of Fridges 'R Us hadn't ripped him off. I hoped that this knowledge would give him the extra tonic he'd need to make it through another stressful day as Donegal Town's premier butcher, and watched him as he disappeared out the back to carry on doing whatever butchers do when they're not out the front.

Brendan, brilliant Brendan, waited patiently in his car whilst, from a phonebox in the square, I gave *The Gerry Ryan Show* a quick update on my first day. He was most impressed by my progress so far and declared that Donegal Town by the end of Day One was 'absolutely bloody marvellous'. I explained my plans to reach Bunbeg and then Tory Island and he told drivers to look out for me just north of Letterkenny in around an hour's time. This really was most kind of him, and given the threatening rain clouds above, could make the difference between good health and a lengthy hospital stay for pneumonia. At the end of our interview, I was told that someone had called in whilst we'd been on air and offered me free accommodation in Bunbeg, and I took down the details, staggered that my quest was being greeted with such a positive response. I hung up the phone and looked nonplussed, but with underlying gratification. It was a difficult face to do.

I read somewhere that Letterkenny has the only set of traffic lights in the county of Donegal, which is either a measure of the remoteness and tranquillity of this province or yet another example of the denial of basic human rights to people in side roads. If it was the former, which could be more likely, then hitching around these parts mightn't be that easy. When Brendan dropped me on the roadside just north of Letterkenny, I was mightily relieved that it coincided with a temporary respite in the continuous heavy rain which had accompanied the drive there. Having already rehearsed the goodbyes once, they were performed proficiently, and Brendan said he'd come back to see if I was still stranded there after he'd finished his business in town. Quite what he was going to do if I was still there other than offer commiserations, I didn't know.

Fortunately I never found out. I had just arranged myself in an appropriate position for hitching and was considering what course of action to take in the event of the next imminent downpour, when a huge truck, and I *mean* huge, slammed on its brakes and came to a standstill forty yards ahead. Leaving my stuff, I ran ahead to see if it was stopping for me or to avoid running something over. The truck was so big, I could only just reach the handle of the cabin door. I opened it and the driver said, 'Are you Tony?'

'Yes.'

'Well, go and get your fridge.'

Things were going rather well.

6
Bunbeg

It was a long way up into that truck, and the cabin was surprisingly small, its crampedness compounded by a fridge wedged behind my seat. The lack of space seemed a little ironic given that we were pulling a forty-five-foot trailer behind us.

After formal introductions (well, as formal as they could be in this situation), I learned that I was in the company of Jason, a man beaming with excitement, in his early twenties who wasted no time in peppering me with questions.

'What are you doing with that fridge anyways?'

'Well, I'm travelling with it to win a bet with someone.'

'You're mad. I was listening to you on the radio this morning and I was in stretches.'

I wasn't sure what stretches were, but Jason was smiling so I assumed they were good.

'I was just on the way down to Donegal Town when you were saying you were going to be starting in Letterkenny, so I've been keeping an eye out for you.'

'Brilliant. That's very kind of you.'

'I didn't know who you were until I saw that fridge, and then I thought . . .'

Laughter took him over for a while, before he managed, 'Ah, it's all a good laugh.'

Good, he understands.

I took a moment to digest all that was happening. The fridge, far from being a hindrance, had become a positive boon, and the protagonist in an excursion which was growing ever more surreal.

From the haven of the truck's cabin I watched the driving rain pelt against the windscreen and felt somehow invincible, especially when Jason announced that he was going to my chosen destination – Bunbeg. All right, I'd have to wait while he did some deliveries but I didn't mind that. Why should I? Yesterday I'd done toiletry sales – today groceries, deliveries thereof. And I was seeing at first hand what makes the world tick over – good honest labour.

Our first stop was McGinleys in Dunfanaghy, and watching Jason struggling with boxes and crates, I felt as heartened by the sight of his dogged industry as I was reassured by my own lack of involvement in it. It looked hard. Some people are born for this kind of work and others are born to watch it. I had no difficulties in identifying to which of these two categories I belonged. For many years I had measured success in my chosen career in terms of how little heavy lifting I had to do. Heavy lifting is good for the soul but bad for the back, and tends to interfere with lolling about.

The Mace supermarket in Dunfanaghy suitably replenished with groceries, we embarked on a journey through some of Ireland's more wild, unkempt and windswept scenery. Austere grey mountains towered over dark tranquil loughs, boglands and streams bordered the apology for a road, and stubborn sheep blocked the route wherever and whenever they felt the urge. Never mind that there was a bloody great lorry hurtling towards them, they were going to move as and when they were ready, and not a moment before. As far as I could see, there were miles and miles and miles of open spaces all around these sheep offering excellent grazing facilities and yet they still chose to congregate in the middle of the road. You're not telling me they don't take some perverse pleasure in the inconvenience that this causes. Sheep aren't stupid. They're petty, spiteful and bloody minded. 'Well, fuck ewe' I thought as the truck was forced to a standstill for the umpteenth time, deciding there was a case for popping mutton on the menu that night.

Somehow we left the sheep 'conference area' behind us and Jason made headway through the ten gears of his giant lorry until we started to experience something like its top speed. A lot of European Commission money has gone into the improvement of the roads in Ireland but there was exiguous evidence of any of it having been lavished on the road surfaces of Northern Donegal. Jason had his own particular method for dealing with the road's over plentiful relief, his policy being to accelerate into the bumps.

When we crashed over the bigger ones, I took off, my arse momentarily liberated from all things solid, and I was rewarded with an all too brief taster of unassisted flight. The uncomfortable downside came a fraction of a second later in the form of landing, and was immediately followed by the sharp top left-hand corner of a small fridge impacting at force with my defenceless shoulderblade. On each occasion this happened, which regrettably was about every twenty seconds, I tried not to recoil in pain and instead smiled at the unflinching Jason, unflinching because he had the advantage of knowing where the bumps were, and was spared the 'fridge slamming into shoulderblade' pain which I had to endure.

'That fridge all right behind you?' said Jason.

'Yes, fine,' I lied.

I didn't want to make a scene.

Naturally by the time Jason let me off in what he called Bunbeg and what most of us would call a stretch of road, it had stopped raining completely. Around me there was a hotel, a couple of houses, a lot of open space and a lovely view of a sandy bay. My free accommodation had been offered at Bunbeg House which the radio people had told me was down by the harbour. Enquiries in the hotel produced directions and my first piece of bad news. In polite conversation I had allowed it to become known that I was headed for Tory Island and this was greeted with a shake of the head and, 'But you won't be able to get out there until Friday.'

It turned out that once a year the ferry was taken down to Killybegs for a complete refurbishment, and it had gone for this year's earlier that morning.

The ferry was out of action for three days. Oh dear. Oh dear, oh dear. A setback of substantial proportions. Getting to Tory Island was a condition of the bet and just at this moment, spending three days in a stretch of road seemed a bit too long. So I did what everyone should do when their nerves are tested, I sat down and had a good meal. Given the absence of mutton from the hotel's lunch menu, I had pie and chips and followed it with jelly and ice cream, which was comforting in that it was the kind of treat my mother would have produced in a time of crisis. Jelly. I hadn't had jelly since Mark Evershed's party. A strange thing to find at a fortieth birthday bash, but life's full of surprises. Not least the non-running ferry.

The twenty-minute walk down a narrow tortuous lane to the harbour was to be the stiffest test so far for the fridge's trolley. Until now it had coped adequately enough with everything that had been asked of it, but this was over a mile and hardly similar terrain to a station platform for which it had been designed. We set off, me and the team of rucksack, fridge and trolley, and soon created an intriguing and not altogether pleasant rattling sound as the wheels of the trolley rolled over the uneven surface of Bunbeg's Highway #1. The fridge acted like a soundbox, amplifying the noise so as to draw more attention to someone, who without this extra assistance, was already quite a conspicuous figure. It prompted a reaction from an American tourist outside the hotel. At least I assumed he was an American tourist because he was wearing those check clothes that say to you 'I'm an American tourist'.

'You got your own fridge with you?' he said in an accent which confirmed the accuracy of my assumption.

'Yes, I have.'

'That's the way to travel.'

'It is.'

'I hadn't thought of that. That's real cool.'

I trundled on, unmoved by his facetious approbation, and five minutes down the road reached a spot where the view of the bay to my right demanded a photo. I perched my camera on a fence and began organising myself for a self-timer photograph. This should have been straightforward given that the camera I have is a idiot-proof one on which everything is automatic. However, in the commercial marketplace, the need to produce a camera which is small and simple has run concomitantly with the need to provide extra features. Extra features mean extra knobs and buttons. Consequently the best model on the market is the smallest, easiest camera to use with the most number of buttons and knobs on it. The one I have. So, when I pressed what I thought was the button for the self timer, the film rewound itself back to the beginning and in the ensuing confusion I managed to do something which erased all the photos I had taken so far. Since I'd just had a good meal and therefore had done what everyone should do when their nerves are tested, I did the next best thing and swore.

'Bollocks!' I shouted, at just enough volume for the distant American tourist to look over, to whom I responded rather ungenerously, 'And bollocks to you too!'

There had been no need for that, but the camera cock-up had been my fault and I knew it, so I'd had to look around for someone else to blame and American tourists are ideal for this.

Bloody camera. As with all new purchases I had completely ignored the accompanying booklet with 'Please read these instructions carefully' boldly written on it, and had jumped in at the deep end, confident that common sense and a healthy slice of good fortune would be enough to ensure a long and fruitful relationship with this particular piece of Japanese shite.

'Bollocks, bollocks, bollocks!'

The American tourist was beginning to feel relieved that he hadn't pursued our relationship beyond a light-hearted exchange. I sat down on my fridge, angry with myself, the camera, and the world's desire to make things smaller, failing to appreciate that it was the world's desire to make things smaller which had afforded me the very luxury of sitting on a fridge.

A car pulled up and a window was wound down. 'Whereabouts are you headed?'

Oh no, the driver thought I was hitching. He must have registered my look of disconsolate despair and perceived it to be that of a marooned hitch-hiker. I tried to let him down gently.

'Well, I'm not really hitching, I was—'

'You're the guy who's bringing a fridge round Ireland, aren't you?' I could only manage a nod. 'I heard you on the radio yesterday, now where are you heading?'

'Bunbeg.'

The man, in his forties and a smart suit, hesitated for a moment. 'But this is Bunbeg.'

'Is it? Splendid, I'm done for the day then.'

'What are you doing in Bunbeg? There's nothing here.'

'I'm going to get the ferry out to Tory Island.'

'I don't think it's running. Isn't it in Killybegs being re—'

'—furbished, yes. I think it is.'

It suddenly occurred to me that there might be little point in my staying here, Tory Island was inaccessible and that was that. It wasn't as if Kevin was going to hold me to the very letter of the bet. I elected to find out whether this fellow, who looked like another travelling salesman, could be any help to me.

'Where are you headed?'

'I'm heading down to Dungloe and then I'll be going on to Donegal Town. Jump in, I'll give you a lift.'

My journey was a celebration of the ridiculous, and I the champion of it, but even given that proviso, I couldn't accept the absurdity of having spent an entire day hitch-hiking only to end up by nightfall at exactly the same spot where I'd started in the morning. It was for this reason, and this reason alone, that I decided to hang on here and see if there was any other way of getting out to Tory Island. I thanked the driver and he drove off looking at me much in the same way as the Cavan bus driver had. I felt surprisingly free of guilt. My goodness, life on the road was making me pretty damn hard, I just didn't mind who I rubbed up the wrong way.

The sun almost came out as I hauled my load down a small hill and made a right after a pub, admirably shunning its hospitality. I was now on a particularly quiet lane, the reverberations of a fridge in transit echoing through the surrounding hills in an audio tribute to incongruity. I turned a corner and there in the distance was a derelict house with what looked like two ladies stood painting at easels in front of it. I drew ever closer becoming more and more fascinated by what their reaction might be to the bizarre spectre with which they were about to be confronted. They looked up, startled by the distant rattling sound and, as I edged closer, their interest in the subject of their paintings became secondary. Finally I drew up alongside them, one elderly and a younger attractive lady.

'Good afternoon,' I said. The more senior of the two looked at me in disbelief.

'My, oh my, a gentleman travelling with a refrigerator,' she said in an American accent.

'Not so. I am just part of a surreal dream you're both having.'

'I can believe it,' said the younger one in an accent which sounded distinctly more local. She had beautiful eyes.

I caught a glimpse of their canvases and witnessed their interpretations of the derelict house before them. Oh. Now I don't know much about art but I know what I don't like.

'I'm trying to find the harbour,' I said, astutely not mentioning how much I didn't like their work.

'Just round the corner and go to the bottom of the hill and you're there. It's lovely.'

And lovely it was. But it was hardly a harbour. It was no more than a narrow inlet with five fishing boats, three in the water and two in dry dock being painted. The quay was flanked by two buildings, one a hostel which was closed and the other Bunbeg House, a bed and breakfast guesthouse and the reason for my being there. I rang the bell and went through the motions of adjusting my clothes and generally preparing myself, but then gave up when I realised that I didn't know what I was preparing myself for. It didn't matter anyway because no one was there, which was a novel approach to running a guesthouse but not one that was altogether unexpected. I then noticed a hand written note in the window saying 'BACK SOON', which suggested to me that I was dealing with people who had their fingers on the very pulse of entrepreneurial commerce. 'Back soon' had an ambiguity about it which worried me a touch though. 'Soon', by any reasonable interpretation, would be a couple of hours, but this was Bunbeg, County Donegal, and there was no guarantee that this didn't mean somebody would be with me by mid October. I was in the middle of nowhere with no accommodation, no reason for being there, and no bright ideas.

I decided to forget about my agenda and allow myself to wind right down to 'local speed', so I dumped my rucksack and fridge outside the front door and embarked on the twenty-minute walk to the pub. If the proprietors of Bunbeg House were 'BACK SOON' they would see the fridge and be in no doubt as to who was going to be their extra guest for the night. As calling cards go it was effective, if a little bulky.

On the way back I passed my two lady painters and the younger one called out 'Where's your fridge?' and I went over and explained. Naturally enough they wanted to know more about why I had a fridge with me; in fact, I suspected that they had talked of little else for the past ten minutes. I tried to make the explanation quick but they kept firing questions at me like 'What sort of people are stopping for you?' and 'Do you keep food in the fridge?' and before we knew it we'd been chatting for half an hour.

Both women had a groomed scruffiness about them which seems to me to be the trade mark of artists. Lois was a distinguished woman of mature years who I was surprised to learn had a gallery on New York's 57th Street. I realised she must be an artist of some renown because I knew you didn't get a gallery automatically on leaving art school. Elizabeth, who was much younger, was married and lived in New York, although she was originally from West Cork. I guessed that she was less successful but may have been Lois's protégé, perhaps a budding star for the future. I learned that for the last two days it had been chucking it down with rain and that the ladies had decided to sketch a barn which they had discovered at the end of a mudtrack on some farmland. They were sat in their cars with sketchpads on their laps drawing this barn when they saw, in one of the wing mirrors, an old farmer standing very still and watching them from a distance. To him it must have appeared that two women were sat in a car directly in front of his barn, staring at it. Elizabeth and Lois explained that he would come back every two hours or so to see if they were still there – the women who were staring at his barn. Continuing rain the next day meant a return for completion of the sketches, and the farmer was even more perplexed by the women's decision to put in another full day's staring. 'Who are they? And why are they staring at my barn?' These were obvious questions which he chose not to ask. Instead he just built a two-hourly check on the 'starers' into his day. He never found out why these two women had come from nowhere to stare at his barn from a stationary vehicle and I expect he probably never even spoke to anyone about it. Therein lies the difference between elderly farmers from Donegal and . . . well, everyone else.

In the course of our conversation I must have demonstrated my complete ignorance of the area because Elizabeth and Lois announced that they would cut short their painting for the day in order to take me on an informative sightseeing tour. There was clearly something about travelling with a fridge which brought out the best in people.

Elizabeth, who was doing the driving, pointed out a brochure of Lois's work on the back seat which I quickly flicked through. The paintings were superb and I censured myself for my initial cursory dismissal of her work. It just goes to show – you should never judge work in progress. I wanted to articulate what I liked about her style but was unable to, so I glanced at the brochure's text to see if its writers had managed any better: 'Lois's art, in its engagement with the question of realism, fits into larger debates about the privileging of abstraction and its viability for a world in conflict.'

Exactly what I had thought although I probably wouldn't have put it like that. Instead I said that it was 'great', shut the brochure quickly and steered the conversation round to an area where I had much more to offer.

'So Lois, the weather has improved a good deal, hasn't it?'

'Believe it or not, this is the best day we've had,' she replied. 'You know what they say up here, "If you can see the mountains it's going to rain, if you can't see the mountains it's raining already."'

'Either that or you haven't opened the curtains,' I said.

They laughed. My God, I was great company. I felt vindicated in my decision not to discuss the privileging of abstraction and its viability for a world in conflict. After all, you can do that anytime and it's harder to get laughs.

The ladies explained we were in Gweedore which was a Gaelic speaking region, or 'Gaeltacht'. The terrain was rocky and sparsely covered with gorse, and it was peppered with little white houses dotted around as if a giant had dropped them like confetti from the sky. We came to Bloody Foreland, an expanse of coastland at the northern tip of Donegal, so called because of the vivid red hues the gaunt rock face took on when lit up at sunset, and not as I had assumed, because its discoverer had grazed a knee here. There was a very clear view of the remote Tory Island and I couldn't help but wonder whether it was going to be a case of 'so near and yet so far'.

When I was dropped at Bunbeg House, the fridge and rucksack were gone, so they had either been taken inside by the proprietors or stolen by an eccentric opportunist. I took a chance on it being the former and said goodbye to my delightful tour guides. As they drove away and I waited an alarmingly long time for anyone to respond to the doorbell, I started to imagine the awkward conversation I would have to have with the Garda if my stuff *had* been stolen.

'I'd like to report the theft of a rucksack and a fridge.'

'A fridge?'

'Yes, I'm travelling with it.'

'Very funny. What are you, some kind of comedian?'

'Well . . . yes.'

'Get out and stop wasting our time.'

Then I began to wonder what I might have let myself in for by coming here. What kind of person rings into a radio station and offers free accommodation to someone who is travelling with a fridge? A broad-minded philanthropist? A demented psychopath? Or – the door opened, '''Ello mate, 'ow are ya?' – a cockney.

Yes, a *cockney*. Andy from Bermondsey, and now a resident of Bunbeg. And bloody hell, was he excited to meet me. He invited me into the lounge area. 'Come in and sit down. Tell us about what you're up to. I was doing breakfast this morning and I 'eard you talkin' about you and yer fridge and I thought, well I just gotta phone up and offer free accommodation – anyone who's travellin' round wiv a fridge bloody deserves it.'

Quite right too. He continued, still giving me no time to respond.

'I thought what a brilliant idea – a fridge. You must be pickin' up lifts real easy like, what wiv *The Gerry Ryan Show* behind you. He's a good man Gerry, what d'you reckon on Gerry – do you get on with him? Sit down, sit down – wow this is great. A fridge. I told my wife Jean about it, she couldn't believe it, she's pregnant, you know.'

It was as if pregnancy was being presented as a reason for her surprise. Well, it can do strange things to the system.

'Do you wanna cuppa tea?'

It would give me something to do whilst he was talking.

'Yes, that would be nice.'

'I'm sorry we weren't here earlier, I 'ad to take Jean up the 'ospital. It's all all right though – no problems.' He looked at me and shook his head in amazement. 'The fridge man. The man with the fridge. I can't believe it. Sit down.'

I had sat down some time ago. We talked on in a similar vein with Andy occasionally allowing a question to be answered, but with no sign of an abatement in enthusiasm, or a cup of tea. It seemed his earlier question 'do you wanna cuppa tea?' was just to establish whether or not I was desirous of a cup, rather than an indication of any serious intent actually to produce one.

'I'll show you yer room, you get yerself a shower, clean yerself up and relax – perhaps we'll have a pint in the local together later?'

'Yes, that would be nice.'

Exactly what I'd said in answer to the offer of a cup of tea, but somehow I had a sneaky suspicion the pint in the local was more likely to materialise than the tea had been.

The room was first rate. It made up part of a modern extension which Andy had added to an already quite substantial building and it was a much more comfortable and sizeable proposition than I had expected to find. It was the nicest room I'd stayed in so far and probably would be for the whole trip. Certainly at the price. But in spite of its picturesque setting by the 'harbour' and its commodious rooms, Bunbeg House was far from full. I suppose in the tourist season it was packed, but just at the moment there was a man and his fridge, and one other couple in residence.

'There you go, mate,' said Andy as he led me into the room. 'Twin beds. One for you and one for yer fridge.'

Andy was around forty I suppose, of quite slender build, and with an impish angular face and a hairline that had just recently embarked on a new policy of receding. At first his initial excitement had rendered him somewhat overbearing, but once he had arrived at the dubious conclusion that someone travelling with a fridge was pretty much the same as the next man, he was much better company, and I was beginning to warm to him now he was telling me to 'sit down' less often. He recommended the pub for my evening meal and arranged to join me there after I'd eaten.

I showered in water which alternated between unpleasantly hot and unpleasantly cold, and then I took advantage of the best feature of the room – its tea- and coffee-making facilities. There is something soothing and reassuring about tea- and coffee-making facilities in a room. I delight in all the intricate packaging of the tea, coffee, sugar and milk, and draw enormous pleasure from the ritual of filling the lightweight kettle, struggling to find the power point, and being unsure of whether pushing the button in at the back of the kettle has turned it on or off. For me, once I've made a cup of tea I *belong* somehow. It's like I'm marking out my territory, and anyone attempting to come and make a cup of tea on my patch will be dealt with most severely, more likely than not with a counter attack into their territory and the seizure of their milk cartons and shortbread biscuits.

Before I left for the pub, I rang and left a message on *The Gerry Ryan Show* answerphone letting them know where I could be contacted if Gerry wanted to talk to me in the morning, well aware how much these chats were driving proceedings along. When I arrived at Hudi-Beags (the strangely titled local pub) it was around eight and still very quiet, but by the time I'd finished my pub grub it had filled up with a surprisingly young crowd. When Andy got there my anonymity had already been relinquished. Two girls had approached me at the bar and asked me if I was the man who was travelling with the fridge. This I couldn't believe. I had left the fridge back at Bunbeg House and was beginning to worry that there was something in my general demeanour which suggested to people that I was of unsound mind. It turned out that one of them reckoned they had seen me earlier in the day as I had made my heroic journey down Highway #1. I was soon surrounded by all their friends and bombarded with questions. Once my predicament with regard to getting out to Tory Island had been discovered, the whole pub seemed to mobilise in search of a solution.

I soon had the phone numbers of five fishermen who might be going out to Tory Island in the morning, and 20p coins were thrust into my hand as I was dispatched to the payphone to follow up these leads. But alas, nothing. I kept hearing a polite and regretful 'No, I can't help you'. The fishing must have been poor out that way because no one, but no one, was going there.

'Why doesn't he try Patsy Dan?' someone said.

'Who's Patsy Dan?' I asked.

'He's the King of Tory.'

'What?'

'Patsy Dan Rogers – he's the King of Tory.'

I had heard right. Tory Island has a long tradition of having its own monarch, and the present incumbent was Patsy Dan.

I was given his phone number. This was unusual in itself. I imagine that most of the time the personal phone numbers of Kings aren't readily handed out in pubs as a normal matter of course.

'Well, what use is ringing him?' I enquired.

'He might be able to organise something from his end.'

And so I found myself making my way to a pub payphone, urged on by a pubload of locals, to phone a King and explain that I needed to get myself and a fridge out to his island as a matter of some urgency. It was Tuesday night. I had set off on Monday morning. I couldn't have expected things to have developed thus far in such a short period of time.

'Hello, is that Patsy Dan?' I said, with a small group of my more fervent followers standing near the telephone in support.

'It is.' He had a deep, gravelly voice.

'Are you the King of Tory?'

'That I am, yes.'

'Good. I was wondering if you could help. I'm travelling around Ireland with a fridge to win a bet and I need to get out to Tory Island to complete the first part of that bet, but as you probably know, the ferry isn't running . . .' and so I went on. Patsy listened intently and seemed to find nothing unusual in my quest.

'Of course we would love you to come to Tory, and so I shall be happy to greet you on your arrival, so I shall give you the following numbers that you can ring to find if anyone is coming out to the island.'

He spoke at great length in a deliberate manner and proceeded to give me the names and numbers of all the fishermen that I had already telephoned. I resisted the temptation of saying 'Thanks for nothing' or asking if the Royal Yacht was available.

So, we had drawn another blank. My legion of helpers weren't defeated but instead returned to the collective drawing board.

On his arrival Andy was suitably impressed. 'Blimey Tone, you don't waste time in making new friends, do ya?'

I suppose not. It wasn't long before he had joined the 'Get Tony to Tory Island' committee, in fact he assumed the role of Chairman despite his tardy arrival at the meeting. The pints were being downed at an alarming rate and the suggestions were becoming more and more ridiculous, when a girl came through from the public bar and told us that she had been talking with a load of guys from the Air Corps who were stationed nearby. A voice piped up, 'Bejaysus, that's it! We'll get yer man out by helicopter!'

There was a split second of silence followed by overwhelming approval. That was it, the mob had their hearts on my reaching Tory Island by helicopter. There wasn't one dissenter.

'Come on Tone, let's go and 'ave a word wiv 'em,' said Andy, his accent a reminder of home, and a more rational world I had left behind. And off we went to the public bar where I was encouraged to stand before a group of servicemen and make my 'pitch' for a helicopter. I wasn't sure about this at all. I made a poor start which deteriorated rapidly when I attempted to casually throw in the involvement of a fridge in all this, and I could see the expressions of the servicemen change from curious to baffled. I lost my way and Andy took over, 'Now boys, we're not being silly 'ere, this man has got to get out to Tory Island, he's got national coverage on the radio and if we can get him out there, it'll be good for tourism – both for Tory Island and for us round here. Now I know it's not for you to worry about and that you're not from round here yerselves, but think of the good press you'd get if you 'elp out on this one and all the good feeling you'll get in the community.'

He was doing well. He went on, 'Now come on, one of you must have a chopper for him.'

All that good work undone in one careless turn of phrase.

We emerged from the bar unsuccessful, in spite of Andy's glib sales pitch having eventually fallen on sympathetic ears. The pilots said they were up for helping out and gave us the name of a woman from the Ministry of Defence in Dublin who we would have to ask to authorise such a 'mercy mission'. We returned to the main bar fairly confident that she would; 'She will, won't she?' 'Course she will.'

A common enough conversation between two men in a bar but usually with reference to less noble matters.

We allowed drink to inflate a moderate success into a magnificent triumph. It was taken as read by all and sundry that in the morning I would be flying to Tory Island by helicopter. Any doubts I may have still had were soon vanquished by the constant flow of pints which continued into the night.

'You see what you can do when you put your mind to it?' said Andy.

We could. The vision might be getting a bit blurred, but we could see all right. The landlord was waiting by the door in his pyjamas rattling his keys, which we took to be some kind of subtle signal that he might like us to call it a night, and so we did. As we made our way out I was offered one final piece of advice: 'When you get to Tory Island you should take that fridge to the top of a steep hill and then push it off the edge and let it roll all the way down and create a Tory landslide.'

It was a measure of how much had been drunk that a comment such as this should have been met with such universally enthusiastic laughter. If the landlord's loitering presence in nightclothes hadn't been confirmation that it was time to turn in, then this was. We made loud and clumsy goodbyes, reiterated promises which we wouldn't remember, let alone keep, and stumbled off into the night.

When Andy and I got back to Bunbeg House he opened up his bar and we made the ghastly error of having a nightcap. This is the point where one turns what might be a moderately bad head in the morning into a violently throbbing one. Freedom of choice. Whiskey in hand, we toasted each other, two Englishmen in a remote backwater of rural Ireland talking bullshit and slurring into the night. We were proud though, proud of what we had achieved. Andy struggled to his feet, wobbled, raised his glass and delivered as earnestly as he could, the same words he had uttered some time earlier, 'You see what you can do when you put your mind to it?'

I could. When you put your mind to it, you could get very very pissed. It was time to say goodnight.

'Gernye.'

'Gonnye, Caw blesya.'

We knew what we meant.

7

Tory Island, Here I Come

I woke in the morning with a dry tongue, throbbing temples and a severe ache in my right shoulderblade. I was ready to take on the world, provided the world wasn't in tip-top condition either.

I struggled to my feet, made my way tentatively to the window and, with the trepidation of someone about to dive into extremely cold water, I threw open the curtains. I winced, but not as markedly as the fisherman painting a boat just outside my window who was the unwelcome recipient of an eyeful of ungroomed male nudity. His wounded expression suggested that this unsavoury spectacle had deeply unsettled him and that he would be giving breakfast a miss this morning.

Once again the shower subjected my body to the extremes of ice cold and scalding hot water, but this time I suffered it with considerably less stoicism, instead choosing to scream and shout at it. If no one gave it a good talking to it would just carry on with the same sloppy attitude.

At breakfast I was joined by the only other guests staying in Bunbeg House, Cait and Rolf, a couple who were on a canoeing holiday. Their marriage was unusual in that Cait was from Ireland and Rolf from Germany, countries which seemed at opposite ends of the spectrum. Germany, a nation bonded by precision and determination; and Ireland, a nation held together by a relaxed attitude and extremely flexible drinking hours. Rolf's accent was eccentric to say the least – German with twenty years of Irish influence at play. He sounded like someone doing a poor impression of Manchester United's goalkeeper, Peter Schmeichel. Andy advanced from the other end of the dining room and hustled me over to the phone. He looked like a man who had spent a day and a half under a machine which had the opposite effect of a sunbed.

'It's *The Gerry Ryan Show* for you, Tone, now don't forget to tell him that we're tryin' to get an 'elicopter. He could be a big help.'

Oh God yes, the helicopter. I'd forgotten about that.

The Gerry Ryan Show put me on hold and said they'd come to me directly after the nine o'clock news. I stood there, phone against my ear, worried that I had killed so many brain cells the previous night that a piece of cheese would give a better interview than I was about to. Andy approached me again. What did he want this time?

'Tone, can you take it in the bar, cos then I can turn the radio on here in the dining room so that Cait and Rolf can listen. It's just that the speakers will cause feedback if you talk to him in here.'

'Are you sure? They're coming to me any second.'

'It'll be all right, I've set it all up, it's a new system we've 'ad put in, just hang up in here and then pick up the phone in the bar and press four.'

So, I hung up, picked up the phone in the bar, and pressed four. The line went dead. So far the new system had been a disappointment. In the other room though, clearly and with absolutely no feedback, Cait and Rolf could hear Gerry Ryan floundering on the radio:

'Tony? Are you there Tony Hawks? . . . Well that's funny, we had him a moment ago and now we've totally lost him . . .'

I looked at Andy, who looked at his shoes, and then back at me sheepishly. 'They'll ring again, don't worry.'

'Perhaps I won't take it in the bar and press four this time.'

'Fair enough Tone, fair enough. My mistake last time round, I think it might be six you have to press.'

'If it's all the same, I'd rather not risk it.'

'Are you sure, Tone? It's just that if it isn't four, then it's definitely six. If you take it in here Cait and Rolf will have to listen on headphones.'

As far as I could work out Cait and Rolf could listen with their ears, after all they were in the same room as me. But Andy's warped priority was that they should hear this radio interview exactly as the rest of the country would, even at the expense of the interview actually taking place.

The phone rang and I picked it up quickly, before Andy could pack me off into another room to press four, six or any other random number which might activate the 'new system'. In the receiver I heard an anxious voice.

'Tony?'

'Yes.'

'I'm putting you through to Gerry now.'

And so my third interview on national radio was conducted against a backdrop of complete mayhem, as Andy, Cait and Rolf attempted to share one set of headphones. As I endeavoured to chat naturally to Gerry, I could see six hands desperately unravelling one very tangled wire, and ears being thrust and manoeuvred into positions within range of the tiny headphone speakers. The scene resembled that of three spoilt children fighting over a present which they all badly wanted and, do you know, I found it a tad disconcerting. However I got the necessary information across, remembering to mention all the helicopter business, and Gerry made the relevant appeal over the airwaves: 'So the challenge has been laid down before us, we have to get Tony and his fridge out to Tory Island. So come on, if you have access to a helicopter, a submarine, a hot air balloon, a hovercraft, a flying boat, a yacht or indeed even a humble fishing vessel – phone us now, 1850 85 22 22, the Ryan Line is open.'

From a delighted table in the dining room, at the end of three intertwined arms, three thumbs went up from my devoted listeners, the general consensus being that the interview should have done enough to secure the helicopter. The phone would ring any minute with the Ministry of Defence offering a 'return ticket to Tory Island' with the Air Corps. And why not? It was only five minutes by helicopter and they just sit on their arses all day waiting to rescue people.

Cait and Rolf delayed their departure by fifteen minutes so they could hear the good news when it came through, but when it wasn't forthcoming they wished me luck and headed off canoeing for the day. Three pots of tea later, the phone still hadn't rung and Andy and I were beginning to pace anxiously in the dining room. Andy, for whom this mission had taken precedent over caring for a pregnant wife, was convinced that we needed to call in to Gerry Ryan's office to see if any offers of help had been received. I was less sure, not wishing to appear pushy, but I was swayed by Andy's convincing argument.

'If they've drawn a blank, we can start following up the contacts we made last night – but if we start doing that now, and Gerry's people are already talking to them, we're treading on their toes – so we need to know, Tone.'

Sometimes the outbreak of war can release a heroic side to a person's nature. It was Andy's personal tragedy that his had been released by the arrival of a man and a fridge. For when the bad news was received that *The Gerry Ryan Show* had taken *no* calls with regard to the Tory Island appeal, Andy defied his deathly white complexion and sprang to life, making phonecall after phonecall and declaring, 'Don't worry, Tone, we'll get you out there.'

The name we had been given last night meant nothing to anyone in the Ministry of Defence, so he called the Air Corps direct, rang local press, contacted the local TD (MP) for the area, and after forty-five minutes of almost continuous bullshit he eventually acquired the telephone number of the top nob in the Ministry of Defence in Dublin. We just needed him to give clearance for the Air Corps to fly me out. Andy's 'moment' had arrived. He had already demonstrated that he could talk persuasive nonsense but it had all been a rehearsal for this call. He was fantastic. I listened in wonder as he managed to convince a Dublin bureaucrat that it was vitally important to get a man and a fridge airlifted out to a tiny, sparsely populated Atlantic island.

'. . . you see he's from England, and they're following the story over there and I've been inundated with phonecalls this morning with press wanting to know how he's getting on. It's a big disaster for us up here because this is one of the biggest chances we've got to promote Donegal and Tory Island – and we're all in complete shock because the last thing we expected was this ferry to be broke down and everyone is gutted because everyone put so much work into this . . . this is a big bombshell, everyone was running round last night trying to 'elp . . . yeah . . . yeah . . . I understand that . . . right. It's just I don't want to be the one going back to the committee saying that we failed on this one. If we let Tone down, we let Ireland down and we lose out on millions of pounds of tourist revenue.'

I blushed a little. Andy hung up and turned to me.

'This is it – the end of the road. They've promised that they're going to ring me back in twenty minutes and let me know one way or the other.'

'What do you think the chances are?'

'Good. Pretty good. He really did seem like he wanted to 'elp.'

I was getting quite excited. I'd never been in a helicopter before.

Hang on though, hadn't I read somewhere that the helicopter is the single most dangerous form of air transport? I became jittery and tried to calm myself down with self assurances that it was only the take off and landing which were hazardous. Then I realised that given the short nature of this flight, taking off and landing was virtually *all* we were going to do. Jitters became full-blown fear.

I needn't have worried because twenty minutes later the Ministry of Defence rang to say they were sorry but they couldn't help.

We felt what a tennis player must feel after losing a match having held matchpoints. Okay, the matchpoints had been on our opponent's serve, and he was a big server, but all we'd needed was a bit of luck – a net cord or a streaky mishit return which went for a winner, and we would have been there. The adrenaline had been pumping, and victory – the moment of triumph had been within reach. It was close to midday but our day felt like it was over.

We consoled ourselves with meaningless platitudes like 'maybe it's for the best this way', 'well, at least we tried', and unsurprisingly it did little to ease the pain. Andy looked most dejected. After all, he had spent hours on what many would have described as a pointless mission, and all his efforts had been futile. It appeared that the thought of spending the rest of the day involved in things which were altogether less futile didn't inspire him. He left, presumably to renew his acquaintance with his wife and family, and to run some errands which should have already been run. I wandered down to the quayside to check out the possibilities of finding a fishing boat which might be making the journey the next day. If that failed, I might have to throw in the towel as far as Tory Island was concerned.

Outside the sudden subjection to bright light provided each flank of my forehead with a new and freshly throbbing temple, reminding me that in future I should make more resolute efforts to treat my body like one. A few yards from Bunbeg House I could see a rugged looking fisherman on his hands and knees messing about with tackle, and as I approached him I was relieved to see that he wasn't the one who had been privy to mine. I coughed self-consciously to get his attention.

'Hello, I don't know whether you'll be able to help, I'm trying to get out to Tory Island, the ferry won't be running till Friday, and I'm trying to find out if you know of any boats which might be going out there at all.'

He regarded me with some surprise.

'Rory McClafferty was away an hour ago.'

'What?'

'Rory McClafferty is just after leaving. Around an hour ago, I'd say. He left with a load of blocks he's taking out there.'

'You mean, he left in a boat, from this quayside, to go to Tory Island?' I couldn't believe what I was hearing.

'Ah yes, he was away about an hour ago. You say you wanted to get out to Tory?'

'You could say that.' I pointed to the dining room of Bunbeg House. 'We've been in there all morning organising appeals over the air on national radio and trying to get the Ministry of Defence to clear a helicopter to get me out to Tory Island.'

'Oh, you'll get nothing in there,' he said, pointing into the dining room. I had to admire the terse accuracy of this remark.

'Will anyone else be going out there today do you think?'

'Not now, not with the tide the way it is.' He looked up from his nets and eyed me quizzically. 'Were you not down at the pier this morning?'

'Er . . . no.'

'Well, if you'd been down at the pier this morning, someone would have told you about Rory and you'd be on the island now.'

Of course I would. I had made a terrible mistake. I had trusted in the local knowledge of Andy, a man who came from Bermondsey. His awareness of what was going on amongst the boats outside his very door was on a par with his understanding of his new telephone system. Whilst he had valiantly embarked on the fruitless endeavour of securing a helicopter, a friendly fishing boat had left for the desired destination literally a matter of yards away. Telephoning fishermen the night before had proved to be no substitute for wandering down to the quayside and asking. As I walked the five or six yards back to Bunbeg House I was struck by the lesson there was to be learned here. Be ambitious, strive for great heights and don't give up without a fight – but don't do so without first exploring the simple option. I decided to spare Andy the news until later, thinking it might spoil his day still further. Besides, our failure had produced the bonus of a free afternoon which I intended to spend reading and relaxing.

I was being naively optimistic. People knew where I was, and I was in demand. All afternoon the phone didn't stop ringing for me, and Andy's dining room turned into my office. RTE television were the first callers. An afternoon show called *Live At Three* had heard about me on the radio and were keen to send a presenter and a mobile unit to film me hitching by the roadside. They wanted to know where I would be on Friday. So did I. I tried to explain this, but it was a difficult concept to grasp for someone in the Filofax 'let's do lunch' world of television.

'But you must know where you're going to be. Do you not have a gameplan?'

'My gameplan is not to have a gameplan,' I said, being deliberately nebulous.

Antoinette, to whom I was talking, was torn between being genuinely amused by the whole notion of 'fridge hitch-hiking', and being frustrated by the guaranteed uncertainties which appeared to be a part of it. She seemed to be the producer, researcher *and* presenter on *Live At Three*, and I half expected our conversation to be cut short at any minute because she had to go and do some make-up or operate Camera 4. She called three more times in the space of an hour with more questions to which I could offer no satisfactory answers. I wasn't making her life easy with my 'I don't knows', 'maybes' and 'probablys', and I could have been more helpful, but there was a certain power afforded to me as a result of my not really caring whether I did this programme or not, and I wasn't going to squander it.

'Look Tony, you mad eejit, I'll ring you later – but this is how we'll leave it for now. My intention is to get someone to drive you to wherever the mobile unit are going to be on Friday and then drive you back to wherever you would have got to if you'd spent that day doing an ordinary day's hitch-hiking.'

Apparently it made sense to her.

The local press were next – *The Derry People*, *The Donegal Democrat* and the national gaelic newspaper *Foinse*, which I assumed meant 'easily excitable', because they were planning on putting me and my fridge on its front page. Donohoe, who was freelancing for them, was my third and final photographer on this, my afternoon of relaxation. He was an affable and erudite man who had initially assumed that the job to go and photograph a man who was travelling around Ireland with a fridge, had been colleagues winding him up. He approached the photoshoot with considerably more artistic integrity than the previous two photographers, who were happy enough with a handful of snaps and the correct spelling of Hawks. Donohoe was interested in me, what I was doing, and where he could get the most imaginative photos of me and my fridge.

'We've just *got* to get one of you and your fridge walking past the wreck.'

'What's the wreck?'

The wreck was the well preserved shell of a wooden boat which was seeing out its days on the expansive sandy shores of the bay I had so convincingly failed to photograph the day before. We headed up there and spent an engaging hour in this most beautiful of spots, creating arty fridge shots and discussing the history of the gaelic language. I learned the interesting piece of trivia that England and Portugal are the only two countries in the European Union which don't have minority languages. (Unless you count Cornish as a language instead of a type of ice cream.) With some satisfaction I logged this information away in the recesses of my brain, knowing that if I divulged it at the right moment to the right person, I could make an enormous impression. I continued to ply Donohoe with highbrow questions.

'What's the gaelic for "my fridge"?' I asked, smiling for his camera, with one foot on the fridge and an arm resting on the wreck.

'Mo Chuisneoir,' came the reply.

'Mo Kushnar?'

'That's right, Mo Chuisneoir.'

'I think I should put "Mo Kushnar" on the front of the fridge in veneration of the gaelic language.'

'Good idea. If we go up my office we can print it out on the computer and you can stick it on.'

And so it was that when I arrived back at Bunbeg House, the fridge was admirably adorned with the words

MO CHUISNEOIR

'What's that mean?' said Andy.

'It means "Always explore the simple option".'

'Eh?'

I explained whilst waiting for a cup of tea which never materialised.

8
The Poorest King On Earth

The next morning I woke and made exactly the same mistake with the curtains as I'd made the previous morning, revealing myself once again as 'nude at window' to the painting fisherman. It appeared that a day's experience had hardened him and he took it all in his stride, or rather his brushstroke, even managing the semblance of a good morning nod.

The previous night had been a quiet one by my standards so far. I had met Elizabeth and Lois for a meal, avoiding the overwhelming hospitality of Hudi-Beags in the interests of self preservation. (I'd come up with my own nickname for Hudi-Beags which was 'Houdini's', because you had to be an escapologist to get out of it.) So this morning I felt pretty good.

Before breakfast I did what I should have done the previous morning and strolled down to the pier to find out if anyone was going out to Tory Island later. I called out to a fisherman who was squatting knee deep in nets with his back to me.

'Excuse me–'

He turned and looked startled. It was the fisherman who had twice seen my genitalia. Neither of us had the social skills to deal with this situation.

'Oh hi,' I continued, feeling it somehow necessary to acknowledge that we knew each other. 'You don't happen to know if there are any fishermen going out to Tory Island today?'

He just looked at me and froze. I don't think his life's experiences had required him to converse with anyone he'd seen naked before, and I elected to move on before he needed to call on the attentions of the Bunbeg cardio-vascular unit. (Presumably a postman who had the apparatus in his front room.)

The other fishermen on the quay, who hadn't seen me with my clothes off, were more forthcoming. I was told that Rory McClafferty had said he was leaving to deliver another load of bricks out to Tory Island at eleven o'clock this morning, and that he would be happy to take me out there. This was good news indeed and there was a spring in my step as I returned to base.

Nine miles of water known as Tory Sound separates Tory Island from the shore, the last few miles of which are notoriously treacherous, being exposed to strong winds and dangerous currents. In the winter months the island can be isolated from the mainland for up to a month at a time, and it's quite common for no boats to be able to get in or out of it for three consecutive days. There was a fair breeze today but thankfully it was blowing off the land and the infamous swells would be considerably smaller than if we had been cursed with a Northwesterly. According to Donohoe, the island had been inhabited since prehistoric times and was desolate, rocky and barren, with now a population of around a hundred and thirty living off the fishing, and a few had sidelines as artists, painting landscapes with a naivety which had won them acclaim. I hadn't seen any of their work but doubted very much whether it fitted into larger debates about the privileging of abstraction and its viability for a world in conflict. I decided I wasn't going to bother raising this though, unless conversations were floundering very badly.

'Phonecall for you, Tone,' said a patient Andy, who at times was in danger of turning into my secretary.

It was Antoinette from *Live At Three*, and on this occasion she was far less tolerant of my abiding indecisiveness, making it clear that they had a programme to make the following day and they could do without ditherers like me.

'Look, don't you commit to anything in your life?' she said, her words a chilling echo of accusations fired at me by at least two past girl-friends.

Thrown off balance by the resonance of this last remark I thoughtlessly agreed to do the show, not realising that by so doing I had put in jeopardy the romantic ideal of spending at least one night on an isolated island. The plans to which I had agreed involved a bloke called Gary picking me up at 10.30 the following morning and driving me to wherever the mobile unit was going to be. And so the new and very important question was – how and when was I going to get *back* from Tory Island? And would I be able to get back in time?

There was nothing for it but to call a King.

'Hello, is that Patsy Dan?'

'It is.'

'Good morning, my name is Tony, I spoke to you the day before yesterday, I don't know whether you remember–'

'I do.'

'Well, I've found a boat to bring me out to your island this morning, but I need to get back by ten or so tomorrow morning – do you know of any boats that might be leaving first thing from your end?'

'That I do. We have had some Americans staying on the island and Patrick Robinson will be taking them back at around eight o'clock.'

'Will there be room for me?'

'They will make room.'

Perfect. After a day or two of things not going exactly to plan, I was back in 'falling on my feet' mode.

'I hope I get the chance to meet you – I've never met a King before, a Prince yes, but we didn't really hit it off.'

'I'm sure we'll meet, the island isn't too large, and I shall be happy to tell you all about Tory.'

'Will accommodation be a problem? I read there are no hotels on the island.'

'No, we have one now. And it will not be full at this time of the year. Will you be bringing your fridge?'

'Of course.'

'In that case we will make you both most welcome.'

As Kings go, he seemed to be a good one. I wondered if there was an opportunity of marrying into royalty.

'You don't happen to have an unmarried daughter do you?'

'As a matter of fact I do. Her name is Brida.'

'How old is she?'

'She is twenty years old.'

'Hmmmm. I shall look forward to meeting you both.'

The round trip to the local shop had taken forty minutes and had been quite tiring. Still, at least it had been productive. At breakfast, Rolf couldn't resist asking, 'Towny, vot iss the borkay off flars for?'

'I beg your pardon.'

Cait stepped in. 'What's the bouquet of flowers for?'

'Oh right, sorry Rolf – well it's for the King of Tory's daughter, I'm planning on marrying into royalty.'

This caused much more amusement than I thought it merited, Andy suggesting that I wasn't good enough for her, Cait proclaiming that romance wasn't dead, and Rolf rounding things off with, 'Iff she likes yer fridge then she iss yourss.'

I hoped he was right – I'd already committed forty minutes of free time into this courtship project and I was banking on that being enough to translate into results.

Soon the discussion had moved on to the maritime traditions of the local fisherfolk, aspects of which I found alarming. Many hundreds of years ago the fishing communities in these areas had settled on the quaint custom of *not saving anyone who fell into the water*. This wasn't based on an ungenerous '*You* fell in, *you* get yourself out' policy, but on the superstitious belief that any encounter with the sea was pre-ordained, and any act of rescue was an obstruction of fate's natural course which would only bring tragedy upon yourself and your family. So, if some unlucky fisherman slipped overboard, instead of rushing to his aid, colleagues would run to the side of the boat shouting 'Chuck us your watch' or 'Can I have your dining table?'

Adherence to these perilous conventions even involved embracing the tenet that *swimming* itself was meddling with the divine right of the sea to take your life and (according to Andy, Cait and Rolf anyway) the majority of the present day fishermen in this locality still couldn't swim. Instead of being fascinated by an intriguing piece of folklore, I took all this to be over-whelming evidence of the unworthiness of these people to be my escorts across a treacherous stretch of water. I wanted sailors who could swim, and hadn't been inculcated with a fanatical hatred of lifebuoys. Mine was a gentle adventure which was to involve at worst, a loss of dignity; the loss of life thing is for climbers and Antarctic explorers who do what they do because they can't mix at parties. If I had wanted to take unnecessary risks travelling, I would have got Mark Thatcher to drive me there.

Rather chastened by these revelations I returned to my room and packed, gathering together what few things I would need, opening the fridge door and chucking them in, turning the fridge into an overnight bag. On the way down to the quayside I was stopped by an intrigued fish-erman who had been watching my noisy advance with interest.

'Is that a fridge?' he said.

'Yes.'

'What are the flowers for?'

'They're for the King of Tory's daughter.'

He looked at me like I'd lost my mind. It was impossible to ascertain which of these two pieces of information had provoked his stunned visage. But I did have my fears.

Rory McClafferty and his boat left dead on eleven o'clock, the first time in over four hundred years that anyone in this part of the world had done anything at exactly the time when they said they were going to do it. There was a small party seeing me off – Cait, Rolf, and Andy and Jean and their three small children who up to now, in a favourable twist on the adage 'children should be seen and not heard', I had heard but not seen. The fridge and flowers were loaded by a puzzled crew member to cheers from my wellwishers. Both precious items were dumped unceremoniously on top of a load of breeze blocks, and left there looking as out of place as I was feeling. We wasted no time in slipping our moorings and heading off, one of the benefits of the fishermen's belief system being that there was no need for a delay whilst we were told where the lifejackets were stashed. There was tacit understanding of the emergency procedure: 'In the event of the ship going down – drown.'

The route out of Bunbeg harbour involved negotiating a narrow but exceptionally pretty series of channels before we hit the open sea. The sun beat down in earnest for the first time and London seemed aeons away. As I looked down the boat and saw my fridge and my bouquet of flowers alongside it, I felt good about myself and what I was doing with my life. I knew it bore no close scrutiny, but there was no one around to do any close scrutiny bearing, so in that regard I was lucky, and was able to enjoy the fact that everything was grand, and that I was 'getting away with it'.

The first forty-five minutes of our voyage was spent wending our way past small islands dotted with derelict houses. Rory informed me that no one had inhabited them for twenty years and that ironically the demise of these island communities had been due to their proximity to the shore. Because of the accessibility of the mainland, islanders would row ashore for a night out in their primitive rowing boats or 'currachs', and attempt to make the return journey completely inebriated. Now, a drunk has a considerable propensity for falling over even on terra firma, but add choppy waters, an inability to swim and a crew with a distinct lack of lifesaving medals, and you end up with the ultimate and somewhat terminal hangover cure. The death toll became so high that the Irish government insisted that the islanders resettle on the mainland, but out on Tory, where their drunks tumbled into ditches with relative impunity, island life survived.

With caution I stood by the boat's siderail and viewed the sea respectfully, a little confused by its jet black, inky colour and its refusal to reflect the blue sky above it. Perhaps it chose to present a hue more in keeping with its funereal past.

Soon enough the tiny dot which was Tory Island became visible on the horizon. As we drew closer, it grew larger and larger until eventually it was near enough to be identified as being really very small indeed. Three miles long and half a mile wide. From the helm Rory steered us in and I stood beside him looking over his shoulder at a map of the island. There was an 'East Town' and a 'West Town' clearly marked, although there couldn't have been more than a few hundred yards between them. I imagined the signs outside each of them:

EAST TOWN
(Twinned with West Town)
Please walk carefully

WEST TOWN
(Twinned with East Town)
West Town welcomes careful walkers

We docked at the end of a deserted pier and I was disappointed to see no royal welcoming party with a beautiful, sexually frustrated princess waiting to be wooed by her knight in shining armour. (Or man with fridge – whichever came first.) A couple of scruffy looking islanders eventually emerged from one of the four dwellings in the metropolis which surrounded us, and began speaking in Gaelic with Rory and his crew. One of them gave me a hand lifting the fridge ashore and I took the opportunity to garner some information.

'I'm looking for Patsy Dan, the King of Tory.'

'Oh yes.'

'I thought he might be here to welcome me.'

'Maybe he's suffering after last night's boozing.'

'He likes a drink, does he?'

'I didn't say it.'

He smiled and jumped aboard and started passing breeze blocks to his extremely scary looking colleague. I had absolutely no idea if inbreeding took place on this island but if you were going to bring a case that it did, then you would produce this fellow as your most convincing piece of circumstantial evidence. I continued to address the one with whom I had already spoken, assuming that of the two, he was the least likely to have killed a man.

'What time is Patrick Robinson leaving with the Americans?'

'Oh, he left an hour ago.'

'What?'

'I'd say it was around an hour, anyway.'

'I thought he wasn't going until tomorrow morning.'

'Well, the Americans decided they wanted to go today.'

I looked around at this tiny bleak outpost of civilisation, and saw how the Americans might have arrived at the sudden change of mind. There is obviously a fine line between peaceful and desolate, and small and downright boring, and the Americans had clearly crossed it.

'So, no one's going back to the mainland today?'

'The first boat back will be the mail ferry tomorrow at midday – if it's running.'

Damn. So either I went straight back with Rory after the bricks had been unloaded, or I stayed over and blew out Antoinette and her colleagues at RTE. I called out to Rory, 'Rory, how long is it going to take you to unload the bricks?'

'Oh, around half an hour, I'd say.'

Was that all? After all the trouble I had gone to getting out to Tory Island, was I really only going to stay here for thirty minutes? That would be ridiculous. And then there was the other issue. Princess Brida. Would it really be possible to secure her hand in marriage in that time? I doubted it. I looked at my watch and saw it was one o'clock. Once again I called to Rory who was busy unloading and really didn't need these distractions.

'Rory! Patrick Robinson has already gone, so I'd like to come back with you if I may, but if I'm not back here by half past one that means I'm not coming.'

He nodded, doing his best to look like he gave a shit.

The inhabitants of this tiny isolated island must have seen a great number of strange things in their time, but had they ever seen anything so odd as the arrival of a man pulling a fridge on a trolley and carrying a bouquet of flowers? The few people who were around the quayside stopped what they were doing and stared, completely unable to deduce what sequence of events could have led to these two particular items being transported in tandem.

I had to find Patsy Dan, and the flowers had to reach their princess. My load and I rumbled to a halt before an old man who was gaping as if weights had been hung from his jaw.

'Do you know where yer man Patsy Dan is?' I asked, my use of 'yer man' a recent affectation intended as an affectionate nod to the vernacular.

He surveyed me and my belongings and then slowly winched his jaw up to join the rest of his face.

'Patsy Dan? Oh aye, he won't be far away.'

This is the one thing you could be sure about saying of anyone who was on the island. It hadn't helped much.

'Will he be at home?'

'Oh aye, I imagine he will.'

'Where does he live?'

The old man proceeded to give detailed directions, all the time guardedly eyeing my fridge and bouquet of flowers, but not feeling able to broach a questioning of their presence here.

'How long will it take to get there?' I enquired.

'Oh, I'd say about six or seven minutes.'

I assumed he'd taken into account that I would be slowed up a little by the fact that I was pulling a fridge behind me. Six or seven minutes there, and six or seven minutes back. That left under a quarter of an hour to win the hand of a princess and I didn't hold out much hope. Even if her name had been Princess Slapper I still would have had my work cut out. Then again, I could stay over . . .

As I pulled the fridge up the hilly dirt track which led to the King's residence, I decided that unless I fancied the princess something rotten, I was going to take the boat back with Rory McClafferty. The sun was still shining brightly but even so there was a bleakness about the place which said anything but 'Come, stay, and enjoy'.

A man in a pair of dungarees, resembling an extra from the Waltons, confirmed that I had followed the old man's directions correctly.

'That's right. He lives right there,' he said proudly.

If there were any perks for being the King of this island, then superior accommodation wasn't one of them. I was now looking at a white bungalow which fell some way short of being a palace. I knocked on the door and seconds later there appeared a stocky, rugged looking man with a fair moustache and a peaked cap where his crown ought to have been.

'Hello, are you Patsy?'

'Yes indeed.'

'Patsy, I'm Tony Hawks.'

'Ah – failte, failte!'

I took 'failte' to be the Gaelic for 'welcome' but it could just as easily have meant 'Get lost!'. If it did, Patsy must have been impressed with my riposte, 'Thank you.'

I had an answer for everything. Boldly, I went on, 'I've got some flowers for your daughter because she's a princess, and princesses merit flowers.'

'Oh dear. She's not on the island. She left this morning to go to the mainland for a couple of days.'

They say that timing is the secret of good comedy. It can be advantageous in other areas of life too.

'She would have been here,' Patsy explained, 'but she went with Patrick Robinson because the Americans wanted to leave early.'

That decided it, I was going back with Rory.

'Well, you can have the flowers then, Patsy – or give them to your wife, let the Queen have them.'

'My goodness, tank you. Tank you very much.'

'It's a shame about your daughter not being here, I was hoping to marry her and then become a prince.'

'Oh my goodness, well I don't know that it would be so easy but you would have to do a lot of talking and a number of meetings and so on. Would you like a cup of tea?'

It felt like this was being offered as the next best thing.

'I've just about got time for a very quick one, but then I've got to get down to the pier otherwise the boat will go without me.'

And so tea was taken in the palace's cramped kitchen and five cordial minutes were spent discussing the life of the islanders and their struggle to remain on Tory during the 1970s and 1980s when the Irish government was doing its best to get them to leave. Not so very long ago there had been open sewers running down the island's streets, and hot water and electricity had only been acquisitions of the last twenty years. We talked of how Patsy Dan came to be King, the story being that after the last King had died, his son had turned the job down on the grounds that there was too much responsibility, and Patsy had landed the position pretty much because no one else on the island could be bothered to do it. No protracted and bloody power struggle here, instead a plethora of forged sick notes and new versions of evergreen excuses used to get out of things at school, cleverly modified for the purposes of evading the throne.

'I'd love to become King but I have a verruca, and also my mother doesn't allow me to wear anything metal on my head like a crown, or else I get a migraine.'

On a couple of occasions Patsy leant in towards me to emphasise a point, and a whiff of his breath suggested to me that his predilection was for drink a little stronger than tea. I looked at my watch and was impressed that I could smell this much alcohol on his breath by only twenty past one. Twenty past one! I had to get going. I jumped to my feet and my stomach emitted a loud rumble almost by way of reminding an indolent brain that it would appreciate some food sooner rather than later. Realising there were two more hours at sea immediately ahead of me I scanned the work tops until my eyes alighted on a fruit bowl.

'I wonder if I could have one of your apples?' I asked the King. (I apologise for this last sentence sounding like an excerpt from a children's book, but it's what happened.)

'My goodness, oh aye, go ahead.'

I took an apple, which came to feel like the physical embodiment of all that I had achieved here. I made apologies for a ridiculously short sojourn and Patsy countered with his own for not having been at the pier to greet me when I had arrived. We quickly posed for a self-timer photo outside the palace, and goodbyes were postponed when Patsy insisted on coming to see me off, making it his business to pull the fridge for me so that I could, in his words, 'take a rest from it'. He was filled with admiration for my fridge journey mainly because he was convinced, despite my two attempts to persuade him otherwise, that I was *walking* round Ireland with it. As if I'd take on a project as stupid as that.

As the fridge rattled satisfactorily down the hill back to the sea, I felt pleased at the way the audience with the King had gone. It had been considerably more successful than my previous encounter with royalty, and I had an apple to boot. By Appointment. My only regret was that the parley with the King had come close to matching for brevity the one I had had with a Prince. At the quayside a huge pile of bricks signalled that the boat's departure was imminent.

Patsy shook my hand and uttered his most memorable words, 'You know Tony, I may be the poorest King on Earth, but I am a happy one.'

This had a nice ring to it, and a fair measure of profundity. Of course, it might just have been a line that rolled off the tongue for tourists, and the truth might have been altogether different, but as the boat pulled out of the harbour and he stood on the pier smiling and waving, I liked to think that he understood better than some, how to handle life, love and monarchy.

9

Bandit Country

Gary didn't seem to have much time for my desire to have an early night.

'Ah, don't be so silly, come and have a couple,' he said. 'I'll pick you up at nine.'

'But–'

It was too late, he'd gone, and he was sure to be back.

Gary lived in Dublin and was thin, around thirty years old and a TV sound engineer by trade. He had landed the job of my driver for the following morning as a result of having a good friend in this area and owing somebody at *Live At Three* a favour. Before he had arrived, ostensibly to say 'Hi' but in reality to offer to take me up the pub in the evening, Antoinette had phoned and told me that under no circumstances was I to allow Gary take me up the pub in the evening.

'Yes, she said the same to me,' said Gary in his strong Dublin accent as he sat down alongside me and popped two pints on one of Hudi-Beag's sturdy tables.

'What?'

'She said that under no circumstances was I to take you up the pub in the evening.'

'Oh right. Do you know, if she hadn't have said that I probably wouldn't have come. She just made me curious as to what havoc you could wreak.'

'Antoinette thinks I drink until I can't stand up, and insist on bringing people down with me.'

'And do you?'

'Oh yeah. But don't worry about that now, that's hours away.'

I had a feeling 'Houdini's' was going to live up to its name tonight.

We were joined by five or six of Gary's friends, a couple of whom I had met the other night when, over a quiet pint, we had tried to secure the use of a helicopter.

'Did you get out to Tory?' one of them said.

'Yes, thanks.'

'How was your flight?'

Their faces were pictures of incredulity when they heard that no offer of a helicopter had been forthcoming.

Another voice piped up, 'Did you have a good time out there?'

'Yes, I met the King and he gave me an apple.'

'Good. So it wasn't a waste of time.'

This last remark was delivered without any hint of sarcasm, the speaker simply not listening to my reply and automatically offering a response of anodyne approval. A few of the others looked a little bemused by the mention of an apple, but chose not to pursue the matter further.

Gary informed me that our destination for the TV interview was going to be by a roadside just south of Armagh in Northern Ireland. Apparently the RTE mobile unit were filming just outside Newry in the morning and so we were going to record an interview for Irish television in a province of the United Kingdom. It was definitely a little odd, and it meant my going back on myself, but I was learning to go with the flow and not question anything too fully. The subject of Northern Ireland being raised, it prompted a short discussion on 'the Troubles', with Gary revealing himself to have quite strong views. Although he wasn't candidly anti-British, I decided I didn't wish to cross him on the subject after several more pints had been downed.

The audio backdrop to our conversations was provided by Dave, a drunk whose intoxication had led him to believe that he could still remember his entire repertoire of traditional Irish songs, and that this was the time and the place to present them before the public. Fortunately for him, the public were good-natured and long suffering. Obviously it was only a question of time before Dave's musical 10,000 metres was over and he could be seen draped over a bar stool, but he wasn't ready for the finishing tape yet, not whilst this final, interminable lap was still causing others a modicum of discomfort. He was selfless in that regard.

I didn't want this evening to turn into an all-nighter, but Gary had other ideas, and at closing time declared as much.

'Let's all go down to Dodge's and get really pissed.'

'No, I really must go now,' I said, sensing that Dodge's wasn't going to offer a sophisticated finale to the night's proceedings. Naively, I looked to the others for support. It wasn't forthcoming, and I faced something of a barrage of viewpoints which weren't wholly in favour of my calling it a night.

'Tony, it's completely at odds for a man who travels round Ireland with a fridge just to go home to bed.'

'I know, I know, it's just that I'm really tired and–'

'Yeah, yawn, yawn, we know that, but we've got to do the "One for the Road" thing.'

'I've got to get some sleep, I really must.'

'So it's true that English people are wimps.'

'I'm sorry but I am tonight, I really am.'

I stood up, hoping this might help matters but Gary was quick; 'Sit the fuck down, cos you're not going home.'

I sat down. This was 'Houdini's', and my escapology skills fell some way short of what was required. In the end it was my own sozzled befuddlement which brought about my liberation. I stood up again, turned to Gary, and tried to look determined.

'I'm going to go now, I'll see you in the morning, James.'

James. I called him *James*. Oh, it was a reasonable enough mistake to make, getting someone's name wrong at the end of the evening, but of all the incorrect names available to me, I had to go for James. Gary's expression seemed to change and I became momentarily anxious that he had taken my error as a Freudian slip, and that I saw him as 'James', my subservient Irish underling and chauffeur for the morning. I felt conspicuous, the old English landlord figure, benevolent maybe, but still a symbol of centuries of injustice.

Tiredness had made me paranoid. Everyone was laughing, and although there may have been a hint of the riled in Gary's demeanour, his parting shot to me was delivered in a genial enough tone. It also bought me my freedom.

'Tony, after calling me James, you should *definitely* go home.'

The walk home was exactly the one I had made when I had first arrived in Bunbeg three days ago. It ought to have been easier now, without a fridge and rucksack, but somehow it seemed further, no doubt the meandering gait of a man in the trough of physical condition doubling the distance to be covered. Back at the harbour, I sat on the quay and looked up at the stars, and then down at the gently shimmering water, the green and red lights of the harbour entrance providing a dash of technicolour to this, the tableau for a black-and-white movie about idyllic rural life. I decided I liked it here, and I felt a fellowship with all those who had left Ireland for London, New York or wherever, but had still maintained an unfaltering devotion to this, their pure and precious motherland. I let out a loud belch which rather brought my romantic reverie to a vulgar conclusion, and reminded me that thinking was best done in the morning, and sleeping was always the best option at night.

At 8.30 am I woke with an erection. There was no call for this – I wasn't in the company of a beautiful woman, nor had my awakening interrupted an erotic dream, it was simply my body's chosen way of saluting the new day. This phenomenon of an unwanted, unnecessary and more often than not unsightly erection, is undoubtedly a design fault by God. God did pretty well all round, creating oceans, clouds, wind, snow, whales, tigers and obstinate sheep. He had a heavy workload and no one could deny that the Almighty turned in a top-notch performance. But in one particular area – the design and implementation of the workings of the human penis, his work was sloppy. God, bless him, was accountable to no one, but if he had been, what would his school report have been like?

GEOGRAPHY......10/10 Excellent. Especially well done with the Ox Bow lakes
HISTORY......10/10 Very well done. If you hadn't created 'Time', this would have been a free period.
MATHS......10/10 Everything seems to add up.
ENGLISH......9/10 Good, but you could have made them better at 'making a scene'.
RELIGIOUS INSTRUCTION......8/10 You could have been a bit clearer about which is the right way, but most humans seem to worship you anyway, so you've got away with it.
BIOLOGY......2/10 Design of the human penis, poor. See me.

After breakfast, *The Gerry Ryan Show* called and asked if I could give them a quick update on how I was getting on; presumably his listeners had been on tenterhooks as to whether I'd made it to Tory or not. I relayed all the news and told Gerry I was heading for County Sligo today, conveniently forgetting to mention the extraordinary route I was going to take to get there.

'Will you be watching the FA Cup final tomorrow?' he asked.

I'd forgotten about that.

'Well, yes I'd like to. Is it on TV over here?'

'It is. I'm sure you and your fridge will find a suitable pub to watch it in. Have a good weekend now, won't you?'

'Yes, and you, Gerry.'

I was pleasantly surprised when Gary turned up only half an hour late, proudly announcing that he had gone to bed at 6.30 am. My appearance on *Live At Three* had depended totally on Gary being 'Live at Ten Thirty', which at 6 am must have been an evens bet, at best. I looked at him, frail and gaunt, his blood vessels coursing with alcohol, and began to wish that I *did* have a driver called James, with boiled sweets by the dashboard, a flask of tea and a rug in the back seat. Instead I had a wild man who was about to turn me into a road accident statistic.

'Get hitching then!' he croaked, in a voice about an octave lower than I recalled.

The previous night we had agreed that it would be wrong for me to accept a lift from Gary without having 'worked' for it, in the form of hitching. So, as Andy assembled his family for a formal seeing-off ceremony, Gary drove off to turn the car around and I dumped myself by the side of the road and stuck the old thumb out.

Seconds later a car pulled up. The window was wound down, and a frail, gaunt man with alcohol coursing through his veins called out to me, 'Where are you going?'

'I'm headed for Northern Ireland, just south of Armagh.'

'That's lucky, so am I. Jump in.'

My goodness, what a lucky break.

I was sad to leave Andy, Jean and family, Bunbeg House having been home for an eventful three days and three nights. Andy had refused to let me pay for my accommodation, and only after a long struggle had he finally accepted some money towards a phone bill which I expected to have been doubled by the whole 'helicopter incident'. As Gary drove me away up the narrow lane with which I was now so familiar, we passed a van coming the other way with 'Donegal Plumbing Repairs' written on its side, and I felt proud that if nothing else, my legacy at Bunbeg House would be a better quality shower for those in Room Six.

Gary entrusted me with the map reading but was unforthcoming when I asked for our exact destination.

'Just get us to Armagh, and we'll worry about the rest after. I've got a fax somewhere with all the details on it.'

I proposed a route which Gary approved with a worrying insouciance.

He was only concerned with specialising on his half of the bargain – driving. I hoped he was up to it.

'Are you not knackered?' I asked.

'Ah no, I'm grand. I only need three and a half hours' sleep.'

Gary was a vigorous driver. He should have had a sign on his windscreen saying 'No Concessions', because he was uncompromising in pursuit of the shortest route between two points, and paid little heed to the discipline of driving on any particular side of the road, or to the well being of his passenger. What made things worse was that this was a hire car and Gary cared little about the future state of its suspension, and so I was bounced along Donegal's roads at excessive speed to meet my TV crew, or if it pre-empted it, my maker.

Even though the scenery was passing quicker than I would have liked, I was still able to observe its wild beauty. Be it the impressive Errigal Mountain, its quartzite cone almost making it appear snow-covered, or the dramatic cliffs and marshy valley of the darkly named 'Poisoned Glen'. As we hurtled past, Gary told me something about a vengeful British landlord who had deliberately poisoned the waters of the glen, but I failed to take in the finer details, finding it difficult to concentrate when each bend in the road threatened my very existence. We overtook on another blind corner and I felt my appearance on *Live At Three* was about to be usurped by a slot on *Dead At Noon*.

At Strabane the roadsigns changed and the distances were marked in miles instead of kilometres, marking my return into British Sovereign Territory. This was the province of Tyrone, and we were soon whizzing through its county town, Omagh, where the playwright Brian Friel was born. His play *Philadelphia Here I Come* was no doubt inspired by these surroundings, and might just as easily have been called *Anywhere Other Than Omagh, Here I Come*.

It was another sunny day, with a few clouds around, but threatening to turn into something of a scorcher. But I still couldn't understand why I was feeling so hot. Then I discovered the reason.

'Gary, do you know that the heater is on full?'

'Yeah, I can't work out how to turn the thing off.'

I gave it five minutes of my time and achieved very little other than the establishment of the fact that I too was unable to turn the thing off. I made use of the only piece of equipment in the car which I understood, and wound down the window.

At Aughnacloy we were back on the border again and Gary made a short detour to show me the staunchly loyalist estate where the citizens had seen fit to paint Union Jacks on the paving stones. It was almost as if they had felt the need to be literal about the word 'flagstones'. Not to be outdone, on their estate the nationalists had the Tricolour adorning their pavements. A battle for souls, under the soles. Would that the conflict had been fought entirely with the paintbrush.

I consulted the map and alerted Gary to the fact that Armagh wasn't that far off now and he instructed me to rummage in the back for the fax with the details of our rendezvous.

'Of course, the area south of Armagh is one of the few identifiable danger spots of the Troubles,' he said, the beginnings of a grin suggesting that he was going to relish what was to come. 'It's bandit country. We should see a lot of army activity round there, and there'll be choppers in the air and all that. Do you know about the sign they've put up near Crossmaglen?'

'No.'

'It's a picture of a gunman with the words "Sniper At Work" written underneath. When the nationalists first put it up, the British Army took it down. But then they made another one and put that up, and when that was taken down they made another, and so it went on until the British gave up and they just leave it there now.'

All rather sinister. I tried to lighten the mood by suggesting that the British Army should put their own sign up with a picture of a sniper crossed out. Who knows, it might do the trick; for the most part it works for 'No Right Turn'.

It must have looked odd, my arse being presented to oncoming traffic, but that was an unavoidable bi-product of my back-seat rummaging. I couldn't find the fax anywhere.

'It must be in the boot,' said Gary with confidence, and so we stopped the car just outside Armagh and did a joint boot rummage.

No fax.

'Have you looked under the fridge?' asked Gary.

'No, I haven't but–'

'Well, look under the fridge. I bet the bloody fax is under the bloody fridge.'

We looked, and it wasn't. It wasn't anywhere, because the man who only needed three and a half hours' sleep had failed to put it in the bloody car. He pretended to be unconcerned,

'It's all right, because I remember that Antoinette said that the meeting point was somewhere on the Armagh to Dundalk Road.'

I consulted the map.

'But Gary, as far as I can see, there are two roads to Dundalk, a big main one, and the B31, which is much smaller.

'The B31? I'm pretty sure the B31 was mentioned.'

Everything about Gary's countenance suggested that he was anything but 'pretty sure' of the B31's involvement in the day's plans. However that was the route we took until I realised what was going on here. I was being driven to an approximate area in Northern Ireland in the faint hope that we would casually run into a mobile TV unit, and the only reasons for suspecting that we might possibly be in the correct 'approximate area', were the vague recollections of an overtired man with a hangover. It made little sense and I insisted that we stop at a call box and phone the *Live At Three* office in Dublin.

From a British Telecom phonebox, I made an international call to the Republic of Ireland, and a flustered secretary at RTE gave me the address of our rendezvous and I took down the directions. I looked at my watch. It was 1.30 pm. At least we had time on our side, the crew couldn't be far away and we had an hour before everyone at RTE would start to panic.

'What we're looking for, Gary,' I explained, 'is the Silverbridge Harp GAA Club. Apparently we take the R177 five miles south of Armagh.'

Gary was now the chief map reader, his cavalier driving skills temporarily rendered surplus to requirements since we had ceased having anywhere to head for. He studied the map and shook his head in frustration.

'I can't see a feckin' R177 anywhere.'

Calmly I took the map from Gary, sure in the knowledge that I would be able to pat the page, point to a specific spot and in a patronising tone, say, 'There. The R177.'

And I surely would have done had I been able to see a feckin' R177 anywhere. Jeez, where was it? The reason for our failure to find this road was not discovered until much later, but it was a result of the numbers and letters of the roads changing when they left the Irish Republic and entered the United Kingdom. At some stage in the past, one government or other had decided that the cultural identity of a nation couldn't be preserved without it having its own letters and numbers for a road. And, to be fair, you can see their point of view, I mean I'm hardly going to feel British and proud of it if I'm driving down the R177, but if I'm on the A29, then I'm far more likely to be infused with a strong feeling of allegiance to the Crown, and be an altogether more rounded individual. Unfortunately Gary and I remained ignorant of this particular bureaucratic pearl of wisdom and became progressively more lost as a result.

We considered stopping and asking directions to be an admission of our own deficient orienteering skills, and so resisted it for as long as we felt it possible so to do. When we found that we were no longer on the B31 but instead on an industrial estate just outside Markethill, we made a U-turn both with this policy and the car. The arrival at an industrial estate is something which always seems to happen to me when lost in a motor vehicle and with alarming regularity. Usually I take the sight of these brightly coloured, pre-fab units as a cue either to become hysterical or tearful. On this occasion I showed great strength and did neither, believing that weeping openly or screaming might undermine Gary's confidence.

Having escaped the bleak world of industrial estates, we sought assistance just outside Markethill, where Gary pulled the car over to the side of the road and I wound down the window to ask for directions. I found myself facing a belligerent looking band of labourers, hard at tea break.

'Excuse me,' I said, suddenly very conscious of my English accent, 'but do any of you have any idea where the Silverbridge Harp GAA Club is?'

They looked at me, and then at each other. No one responded. Gary looked uneasy and leant over.

'Don't worry, fellas, sorry to trouble you.'

He pulled the car away quickly.

'What did you do that for?' I said.

'I think round here it's best that I do the talking.'

His reasoning turned out to be sound enough. Recent violence and alleged complicity in it by the RUC had left temperatures running high in the nationalist communities, and we were in the very heart of one here. Gary pointed out that since the Silverbridge GAA club was a Gaelic Football Club, and something of focal point for Republican unity, it might arouse suspicion if someone with an accent like mine should wish to make a visit.

'They are pretty tight knit communities around here, and they've got the wherewithal to have us followed.'

I didn't gulp, but I wanted to. Followed? And then what? Would we be 'dealt with'? In a pathetic attempt to appear unflustered I changed the subject and said something which confirmed, beyond all doubt, my country of origin.

'Is it hot, or is it me?'

'Course it's feckin' hot, the heater's on full, you tosser.'

James was being over familiar.

The sun won its battle with the clouds and beat down upon us with an uncustomary potency, and Gary and I, now potential targets, drove aimlessly around bandit country in a mobile sauna. This journey could have been going better.

I looked at my watch again. It was 2.25. I figured they would be starting to panic at RTE round about now. I was supposed to be the first interview on the show at around 3.05. Provided we found the B78, we were still confident that wouldn't be a problem. I consulted the map.

'I'm pretty certain the B78 is a right turn, off this road we're on now,' I said, with all the confidence of a condemned man.

'And how far to the turning?'

'About six miles.'

'Right, time to put the foot down.'

This new and frightening resolve left me nauseous with fear and had the effect of *losing* us valuable time, because as we overtook an Ulster Bus at around 95 mph, I thought I just caught a fleeting glimpse of the B78 on our right.

'We ate that bus for breakfast,' boasted Gary. It wasn't just the heater which was belting out hot air.

'Yes, well done. It's just that I think we may have passed the B78 as we were overtaking.'

'Shit! Are you sure?'

'I'm pretty certain I saw a sign.'

Gary slammed on the brakes and we screeched to a halt. We needed to turn around, but the bus which we had just overtaken, had now stopped to take on passengers, and cars were overtaking it at speed. Even the maniacal Gary knew it was suicidal to attempt any turning manoeuvre until the bus had moved off and we had a clear view of the road.

There seems to be some correlation between the amount of time it takes other people to do things and the extent to which *you* are in a hurry. This phenomenon (which is a variation on Sod's law – let us call it Arse's law) was clearly in evidence at the bus stop behind us. Each passenger seemed not only to have no change whatsoever, but must have been a relative of the driver, who felt the need to bring him up to date with all the family news over the past six months. I haven't seen a queue move so slowly since . . . well, the last time I was in a hurry. Gary and I fretted, cursed, and at least one of us smashed a fist down on to the controls of the car's heating system, shouting, 'Feckin' well leave it out with the feckin' heat, will ya?'

You had to hand it to the farmer. It was almost as if he had been laying in wait thinking to himself, 'Why, there's no point in getting my cattle to cross the B78 at the moment, far better to wait a couple of hours until somebody comes along who is in a desperate hurry.' His timing was impeccable or disastrous, depending on whether you wanted to do a TV interview or not.

And so we sat there, having scored a momentary victory in circumventing the bus, watching lackadaisical cows amble across a road, the malicious farmer looking on with a self-satisfied grin. With a stick, he gestured to his cows as if to say, 'You take your time today fellas, because these two look like they're most eager to get somewhere.' Time was ticking away. It was twenty to three.

'Antoinette will kill me,' said Gary, as the last cow dawdled past.

'There's plenty of time. No need to panic,' I said, panicking.

There had been, of course, no need to panic. It had been our panic which had allowed Arse's law to manifest itself, and it was only when we resigned ourselves to the fact that we probably weren't going to make it, that things began to proceed with some measure of normality. As it happened, we arrived in plenty of time. Well, from our perspective, five minutes before the show went on air was plenty of time. Antoinette didn't see it quite that way.

'Jeez, where in Christ have you been? We were just working out how to fill seven minutes of air time.'

She looked me up and down.

'Hello there. You must be Tony, the nutter with the fridge. I'll have to get to know you on air because we're on in five.'

Why the producer had chosen this location for a roadside interview was a mystery. Quite apart from it being in another country to the one I was hitching in, it was probably the noisiest stretch of road for miles around. No doubt the producer had his reasons, and no doubt they were crap.

The viewers of *Live At Three* must have been puzzled as to why its make-up department had thought I would look best in bright red. The flurry and fluster of the journey with its constant blast of roasting air had made me resemble a ripe tomato. I was certainly not looking my best and was unlikely to become the focus of the amorous attentions of the octogenarian ladies who chose this show for their afternoon's entertainment. Another missed opportunity. I chatted well enough though, my conversations with Gerry Ryan having left me adept in the patter required to explain all that I was about, and the interview went very smoothly. I stood by the roadside with my fridge, and Antoinette fired questions at me whilst I hitched. It couldn't have gone much better. Okay, the occasional juggernaut hurtled past drowning out everything that was being said, but this didn't seem to bother the producer who was more than happy. Gary stood by, smiling a proud smile which said, 'Against all odds, I got that guy here.'

At the end of the interview Antoinette presented me with three indelible marker pens, with which I was to get those who had given me lifts to sign my fridge. What a good idea. Then, as I had been asked to do, I announced that I was going to look for a better spot to hitch, and pulled my fridge up the road and away from the cameras, allowing Antoinette to do her final piece to camera. When we went off air, I stopped and looked up at a road sign which was now above me. It had a picture of a man in a balaclava, and below it were written the words

SNIPER AT WORK

Thank you RTE. They had brought me to one of the most dangerous locations in all of Ireland and had encouraged me to swan around with a fridge. All of this had probably been noted by one of the Republican paramilitary's intelligence units, who, as we showbiz types said our emotional goodbyes, were back at headquarters struggling with one of their more difficult reports.

'We discovered what the film crew were there for.'

'Yes? What exactly?'

'They were talking to a guy who stands by the road with a fridge, and then pulls it along a bit on a trolley.'

'Eamonn?'

'Yes?'

'When did you last have a holiday?'

10

Surf City

'This is brilliant, thanks very much,' I said to Antoinette as she drove us towards Sligo.

'Don't thank me, thank Kara, my series producer. She thought it would be a good idea if people could get hold of you, so she rang a mate at Eircell and they came through with the goods. The phone is yours, provided you mention them on the radio a couple of times and do a photocall with the fridge and the phone when you get to Dublin.'

This was quite something, a mobile phone. I was going up in the world.

'Have they given it to me for the duration of my trip?'

'Absolutely.'

'Why?'

'Because they were rather taken with the idea of a man hitching round with a fridge.'

I let it sink in. Then, 'I love this country.'

Antoinette was the new James. She had taken over from Gary as my personal chauffeur. The considerable improvement in the standard of driving was offset by the retrograde quality of the car. The Republic of Ireland's government doesn't require its vehicle owners to obtain the equivalent of MOT certificates, and Antoinette's car was testimony to the lack of wisdom of that policy. To call it a deathtrap would be to pay it a compliment. A trap is usually a device from which you can't get out, but the doors and windows on this car threatened to throw themselves open at any given moment, liberating the anxious passenger from the bare springs of the passenger seat.

'Sorry about the car,' Antoinette had said, 'it's a bit of a disaster area. The only thing which really works properly on it is the heater.'

Well, that was a relief.

Antoinette was charming, intelligent and a mother. She didn't look old enough to have a fourteen-year-old son, but she assured me that was the case. The destination of Sligo suited her because she had friends close by who she could stay with after she had dropped me off. It was agreed that it was a likely enough place for me to have reached in a day's hitching from Bunbeg, and my delivery to such a point had been the deal I had struck in exchange for my appearance. The mobile phone was something of a bonus.

The drive to Sligo through Monaghan, Fermanagh and County Leitrim was a pretty one, and even though I was becoming accustomed to that, the latter stages still prompted a drawing of breath, with Glencar Lake on one side and the imposing Dartry mountains rising above us on the other. We were in Yeats country, so called because Sligo was where W.B. and his famous family once resided. They were quite a talented lot, the Yeatses; his brother Jack and father John were both considered to be fine artists. W.B. Yeats himself always professed to have a deep affection for the countryside of his childhood and wrote, 'In a sense, Sligo has always been my home.' In what sense? In the sense that he chose to live almost anywhere else? Honestly, the stuff poets get away with, just because they've got a good turn of phrase. All right, he chose to be buried there, but it has always struck me as more of a compliment to a place to spend time there when you're alive, rather than dead. Like Yeats, I too would choose to see out my days on the French Riviera, but where we differ is that I don't give a toss where you bury me.

Antoinette was worried about where I was going to stay.

'Have you booked anywhere?'

'Nope.'

'Have you got a brochure with details of accommodation?'

'Nope. The right place will come along.'

'Tony, you're too laid back for your own good.'

'I'm not that laid back, I just have faith.'

'In what?'

A pause.

'That's the only bit I'm not sure of.'

When we got to Sligo, (the largest town in the northwest, with a population of 17,000) we parked in the main street and had a mosey around. I couldn't see anywhere I fancied staying and I wasn't sure whether I wanted to spend a Friday night in a town centre. Antoinette led me into a delicatessen hoping to buy a type of seaweed called 'dilisc', but unfortunately they had sold out. Never mind, the old man in the shop had a pleasing way about him which I instantly liked, and there was a huge egg on the counter which caught my attention.

'What's that?' I asked him.

'It's a duck egg.'

'How much is it?'

'What do you want a duck egg for?'

'I don't know, I just like the look of it. How much is it?'

'Don't be so silly, you don't want a duck egg.'

'I do, I want to buy this duck egg off you.'

'No, now come on, what would you want with a duck egg?'

Whatever happened to the aggressive hard sell? I couldn't buy this bloody duck egg off him until I could prove that I really needed it. And I couldn't, so the duck egg remained in the delicatessen until a more suitable home was found for it.

The one hotel I enquired in was full, but I didn't like the look of it much anyway. However, we needed refreshing after the drive so Antoinette and I had a quick drink in its dingy bar where I noticed a sign which read,

STRICTLY NO SINGING

Dave, the drunk from last night, must have been here recently. I had never seen a sign like this before, and it struck me as rather harsh. I mean, you may as well go the whole hog and have a sign up saying,

STRICTLY NO HAVING A GOOD TIME

The need for the sign reflected an admirable Irish character trait, and that is – when the Irish get drunk, they sing. I had already witnessed this in Hudi-Beags, and although it wasn't the most pleasant experience, it was tolerable enough. Signing is preferable to fighting, which is probably why the audio cassette of Ali versus Foreman has been comprehensively outsold by Frank Sinatra's *Greatest Hits*. It would certainly be a step in the right direction if pub drunks in England forced you into a corner and sang Elton John's 'Saturday Night's All Right For Fighting' instead of treating the lyrics as a set of instructions. Singing, however poor in quality, is always preferable to having the shit kicked out of you. (With the possible exception of Chris de Burgh.)

It hadn't escaped Antoinette's noticed that here in Sligo I had failed to fall on my feet.

'So, this "faith" of yours hasn't exactly come up trumps with accommodation.'

'Not yet, no.'

'Perhaps it would help if you knew what it was you had faith in?'

'Oh, one doesn't want to worry oneself with unnecessary details.'

Antoinette was still a sceptic, but there was time to convert her.

'You know, I think I *do* know what I have faith in. I have faith in the fridge.'

I sounded like a man who was becoming delirious. Maybe I was. Perhaps the excesses and surreal events of the last few days had taken their toll.

'You too can have faith in the fridge,' I said, each word edging me closer to committal. I wasn't an impressive proselytiser and you needed to be when you were asking someone to have faith in a fridge. During the car journey I had expounded the credo that wherever you go, good things will happen to you, provided that you truly believe they will. As we sat in this third-rate establishment where not even a natural expression of human joy like singing was permitted, it appeared the validity of my philosophy was in question. Then it came to me.

'We'll ask the man in the delicatessen.'

'What?'

'Come on, finish your drink, let's go and ask the man in the delicatessen.'

I was testing this poor girl's levels of tolerance to the very limit, but her protestations weren't vociferous enough to prevent a return to the delicatessen and a question for the elderly proprietor.

'If you could stay anywhere in the Sligo area, where would you stay?'

He wasn't remotely taken aback. I had thought he would be expecting me to have another crack at purchasing the duck egg.

'Expensive or not expensive?'

'Doesn't matter.'

'Have you got a car?'

'Yes.'

I rather boldly assumed that Antoinette wasn't going to tire of my indulgent behaviour and dump me and my fridge on the streets of Sligo.

'Well, Strandhill is very nice.'

'Is that where you would go and stay, given the choice?'

He thought for a moment. 'Yes, I think it is. You could try the Ocean View Hotel, or there are a couple of bed and breakfasts down on the front.'

And very nice they were too, overlooking a broad expanse of sandy beach complete with panorama of evening sun setting over the Atlantic Ocean. I resolved that this was the place for me, the presence of a nice looking pub within spitting distance having no bearing on my decision. Both B&Bs had vacancies, but I plumped for the one which had bathrooms en suite, deciding that it was worth the two extra pounds, if only to spare other guests the sight of a half-naked drunk struggling to the toilet in the middle of the night.

When Anne Marie, the lady of the house, had accepted me as a guest on her premises, she had been affable enough, but when I began to wheel my fridge up the front path, and she discovered the true nature of my identity, her demeanour altered and I was confronted with an insanely grinning woman.

'My God, it's *you*! They've been telling people to look out for you on North West Radio. Well done, you made it to Sligo then.'

Apparently so.

'Come in and have a cup of tea.'

I smiled at Antoinette who looked back at me resignedly.

'Okay, I have faith in the fridge,' she said, rather magnanimously.

The three of us took tea together in the living room and I offered my well versed replies to the string of questions which Anne Marie fired off at me. Why are you doing it? When did you start? Is it hard to get a lift? When she went to fetch more biscuits, Antoinette, who was now a devotee of the faith, demonstrated her new-found fervour.

'So, are you going to take the fridge out tonight?'

'What?'

'It's Friday night, you can hardly leave it on its own.'

'Are you suggesting that I take it out to the pub?'

'Yes I am. And if you do, I've just got to see it.'

'Haven't you got to get to your friends?'

'They can wait. It's not every day you see what happens when a man walks into a pub pulling a fridge behind him.'

I wasn't in a position to say the same.

And so Antoinette's friends had to wait, because their absent guest was taken up with the important business of laughing at a man pulling his *date* towards the Strand pub. In some parts of the world, a stranger pulling a fridge on a trolley into a bar on a Friday night might be a recipe for a good kicking, but here I felt it more likely that if set upon I would be held down, and sung to.

Antoinette opened the door and I proudly marched into the pub, the heads of those at the bar turning towards me in unison, as if following the flight of a tennis ball at Wimbledon. A man with a beard who was enjoying a quiet drink with his girlfriend, looked down at the fridge. His face lit up and his eyes sparkled like those of a child at Christmas.

'Well, if it isn't the man with the fridge?'

He offered his hand, and I duly shook it and said, 'Hello, my name's Tony. This is Antoinette.'

He nodded and turned to his lady friend. 'Mary, have you heard about this fella? He's bringing a fridge round Ireland.'

'Jeez, what an eejit. What's he drinking?'

It really was that easy. My new 'friends', Willy and Mary took us under their collective wing and introduced us to everyone they knew in the pub. With frightening predictability, I was involved in another 'session', with drinks, conversation, and hospitality flowing like flood water. Amongst the enthusiastic gathering who were now around me, I noticed a big man with blond hair tied in a ponytail, eyeing me with interest. He waited for the initial hubbub to subside and then approached me, full jug of lager held proudly aloft before him.

'I've heard about what you're up to and I just wanted to congratulate you.'

'Oh thanks.' I thought for a moment. 'What for?'

'Look around you. Everyone is having a damn good laugh about you and your fridge. You may not know it, but you're spreading joy.'

I was in the company of Peter, whose loose-fitting clothes of a predominately reddish pink hue led me to believe he was something of a buddhist. We talked, laughed, bought each other pints, and it soon became clear that we were coming at life from exactly the same direction. I knew as little about his faith as I did about my own, but he clearly *understood* what the fridge journey was all about, and gave it credit where I had never thought credit was due. It was nice to hear how you were 'transcending the material' from someone who had a full pint of lager and a fag on the go.

Antoinette came and joined us. She was either having the time of her life or she was trying to postpone contact with her 'friends' as long as possible.

'I'm having the time of my life,' she said, clearing that one up right away. 'I've just met Bingo. He's the manager of this place, and you'd never believe it, but I interviewed him for a TV show in 1988 after they had the storms up here. You'll meet him in a minute, he's insisting that we have meals on the house, so he'll be over with a menu.'

Bingo. A great name, and one that in my present circumstances it seemed appropriate to shout. My numbers were most definitely coming up.

Antoinette fell under Peter's spell.

'He's wise, isn't he?' I whispered to her, and as I did so he demonstrated his wisdom with a visit to the lavatories to create more space for lager.

'He's certainly got a calmness about him,' said Antoinette, 'and there are some questions about his philosophy which I want to ask.'

'But what about your friends–'

It was too late, she had fallen victim to a stealthy advance from Michael, and was now beginning the smiling and nodding that a conversation with him involved. Michael was *almost* the Strand pub's drunk in residence, fulfilling all the criteria required, but for the fact that he was mobile. Though shaky on his feet, he was still able to move freely about the pub and ensnare innocent drinkers, offering a long-winded, barely intelligible and uninformed opinion on absolutely any subject. Antoinette's eyes glazed over and, with laudable disloyalty, I sidled off, smirking.

Leaving it long enough to make it look like I wasn't copying Peter's idea, I set off for the toilets. It was a good forty minutes before I made it back, interest in my fridge adventure apparently having gripped the pub's clientele, and I felt obliged to offer each well-wisher a certain amount of time. It would have been churlish to have done otherwise, and I found I was now benefiting from what I had learned from Prince Charles, which I attempted to implement, only with less hand clasping. When I got back to Antoinette, Michael had been sidelined somehow, and Peter was in full flow.

'You see, life is little more than a dream, the world isn't a physical reality, but a three-dimensional illusion. Our left side knows this, but our right side takes the materialist view. Our left side knows that life is a chosen adventure in consciousness. We are conscious beings who have freely chosen to be physical. Consciousness didn't emerge from matter; matter emerged from consciousness.'

At this point the efficacy of his enlightened peroration was undermined by someone offering him a pint of lager. He gave the thumbs up and mouthed the word Carlsberg. Probably. He continued, 'You see everything is interconnected – all energy, all consciousness. There are no "separate" objects or "separate" beings. Time, space and separateness are illusions. So, nothing actually exists.'

As he said this, a pint of lager was passed to him, which for something which didn't exist, he looked far too pleased to see.

'My fridge exists,' I said defiantly.

'Ah well, I'll not argue with that.'

We all looked at it sitting happily by the door. It had grown tolerant of its master's excesses. Tonight its patience was going to be tested to the full.

'Are you sure you won't let us pay for those, Bingo?'

'Absolutely not. I hope you enjoyed your meals.'

'Oh yes, they were lovely.'

Bingo was a handsome man, probably in his early thirties, who seemed responsible and patient. Maybe he looked that way because he was working in an environment where almost everybody else was half cut. He put two liqueur glasses on the bar which were filled with a black drink with a tiny white head on top.

'They look like little pints of Guinness,' I said.

'Close. We call it a baby Guinness,' replied Bingo. 'It's a mix of Tia Maria and Baileys. Try it.'

I took a sip. 'Mmmmm. Lovely!'

'Tony had better have mine,' said Antoinette, pushing hers towards me, 'I can't drink any more if I'm going to drive, and I had really better be going, my friends were expecting me hours ago.'

'I was beginning to doubt if your friends existed,' I said.

'According to Peter, they don't. Still, I'd better go just in case. I'll see you tomorrow.'

'Will you?'

'Yeah, Peter is going to do some reflexology on me. So I'll call past your B&B and see how you're doing at around eleven. Don't drink too much.'

I already had, and as Antoinette fought her way out of the now crowded pub, another pint arrived from somewhere, and I now had three drinks in front of me. *And* Michael.

'Do you know what my cure for a hangover is?' he said, the sight of my immediate drink obligations obviously prompting the subject.

'No.'

'Well, I'll tell you.'

Yup. I had expected as much. What was it going to be? A pint of water before you go to sleep? Two aspirin as soon as you get home? Of course not. I was way off beam.

'One Drambuie just as you're on your way out to the door.'

'What?'

'A Drambuie just before you go home.'

I shook my head in disbelief. To prevent the ill effects caused by excessive alcohol, this man was earnestly promoting the taking of one more alcoholic drink.

'That's an interesting one.'

'It never fails.'

'I'll bear it in mind.'

The pub closed at around 1 am, but there seemed to be no effort on the part of the management to remove me. I had survived some kind of arbitrary selection process and was one of the drinkers privileged to be part of a 'lock in'. The net had been thrown quite wide, seeming to incorporate around half the pub's previous occupants, but those of us who remained, like golfers who had 'made the cut', felt the need to celebrate. Other survivors included Michael, naturally enough, and Peter, who had moved on from his earlier metaphysical conjecturing, and was discussing surfing with Bingo.

'I've never tried surfing, can you do it here in Strandhill?' I asked.

'The beach here in Strandhill is excellent for it,' said Peter. 'Bingo here is a champion surfer; if you ask him nicely, he'll take you out surfing tomorrow.'

Bingo didn't need to be asked nicely.

'Ah sure, Tony, we'll get you a wet suit and we'll have you up on a board within an hour.'

'Really?'

'I'll guarantee it.'

Michael had been observing all with some interest. Now was the moment for his contribution.

'Of course, you'll have to take the fridge.'

We all looked at him as if we hadn't just heard what we had just heard. But oh yes we had, because there was more.

'Tony, you can't go surfing and not let your fridge have a go. If you surf, the fridge has to surf – it would be unfair otherwise.'

There was a pause whilst this sank in. Then Peter looked at Bingo.

'Could you get a fridge on a board?'

He thought for a moment.

'Yes, I think it's possible.'

Suddenly everyone became animated on the subject of the plausibility of taking a fridge surfing. Methods for strapping it to the board, and techniques for getting it far enough out past the breakers were discussed with a totally unwarranted gravitas. I started to feel a little odd. My head began to swirl with a combination of all that I was hearing now, and all that Peter had said earlier on the subject of reality. The result was that I now had a less tangible hold on whether I actually existed. The continuation of discussions about the viability of getting a fridge on to a surfboard in the Atlantic Ocean brought me firmly to the conclusion that I most certainly didn't.

The arrival of another baby Guinness acted as proof. I should have left it because I had already consumed far too much alcohol, but unthinkingly I drank it. My lack of thought proved beyond all doubt that I didn't exist. 'I think therefore I am.' 'I do not think, therefore I am *not*.'

I certainly didn't think I was going to fall over. For anyone who existed it would have been most embarrassing. I was thankful that I didn't fall into that category. Only into an unsightly heap on the pub carpet.

Morning brought the disappointment of discovering that I did exist. I existed big time, with a throbbing head to prove it. It was my own fault, if I had remembered to take a Drambuie just before I had left the pub, then I wouldn't have been in this sorry state. I lay in bed trying to remember how I had got there, but failed. Suddenly I thought, 'God, the fridge!' but then saw it in the corner of my room looking back at me, almost admonishingly. I know that scientists will tell you that a fridge is incapable of feeling or expressing emotion, but what do they know? This fridge disapproved, and it wanted me to know it. It had no right to be reproachful, I should have been congratulated for getting it home at all, given that by the end of the night I was struggling to move myself about the place, never mind a domestic appliance on a trolley.

Sometimes you can lie in bed looking around the room, the dim light and your horizontal perspective bringing a totally different reality to objects that you see. A belt can resemble a snake, the folds of a jumper thrown on the floor might look like a small dog curled up and fast asleep. This morning I could see a small alien rocketship undergoing a mid-air re-fuelling. The more I looked at it, the more I became baffled as to its real identity. What could it be? I lay there trying to think of something I had in my luggage which could come to represent such an image, but I drew a blank. I remembered Peter's words, 'You see, life is little more than a dream, the world isn't a physical reality, but a three-dimensional illusion.'

I knew that to sit up and turn the light on was to accept defeat, but I needed confirmation fast that I wasn't part of a three-dimensional illusion.

No longer reclining, and with the bedside lamp on, I could see clearly that I had been looking at a lead coming from a plug half way up the wall, leading to my new mobile phone which had been charging up overnight. Of course. I had forgotten all about that – my own personal alien rocket-ship for use during my voyage of discovery. I thought of using it to call Anne Marie to ask her if she would come and help me down to breakfast, but it seemed to be an irresponsible use of space hardware.

Beside the mobile phone was a note written in my own drunken scrawl. 'Meet Bingo at 11.00.' Of course, the surfing. Last night anything had seemed possible, and now, just a few hours later, even breakfast was a challenge.

When Anne Marie graced the dining room with the tea and toast, she was quite blunt. 'You had a late one last night.'

'Yes, I think it was quite late.'

'Half past three.'

'I don't think so, it was closer to two.'

'No, it was half past three, because my husband and I looked at the clock.'

'Oh God, I'm sorry, did I wake you?'

'Ah no.'

I sighed with relief, but then she added, 'Your fridge did.'

'What?'

'The sound of your fridge falling off its trolley woke us up.'

'Oh. I'm so sorry.'

The tea and toast were deposited in front of me. Anne Marie was showing no sign of any anger, but it was as if she just had a need to *let me know*.

'My husband and I were wondering why you didn't leave the fridge downstairs – you know, in the hallway, where you left it before you went out.'

Oh no! They were thinking I had taken it to bed with me, that I was some kind of fridge pervert. I had to call on all the wit at my disposal to avert an embarrassing misunderstanding.

'Err, well . . . that's a good question Anne Marie, and I . . . well . . . I don't really have an answer for it.'

Unfortunately I had absolutely no wit at my disposal. I simply had a headache and that was all.

The local commercial radio station, North West Radio, was my only company during breakfast, and at ten o'clock I found myself listening to a phenomenon called the Death Notices. An announcer, doing his best to sound sombre and respectful, read out a long list of people who had died recently. North West Radio were clearly of the view that their listeners would be able to make it through today a lot better if they were provided with a comprehensive list of those who had failed to make it through yesterday. It wasn't so much the late news, but news of the late.

'Declan O'Leary from Sligo died at his home after a long illness yesterday afternoon, and the funeral is next Tuesday. Margaret Mary O'Dowd from Inishcrone passed away peacefully in her sleep at half past six yesterday morning. The funeral will be at St Meredith's Cathedral, Ballina. And that concludes our death notices. A reminder that our next bulletin will be at five o'clock this evening. North West Radio extends sympathy to the deceased. May the souls of the departed rest in peace.'

The mournful mood was then brutally punctured by a lively advert jingle and a chirpy voice declaring, 'Right now at McDonagh's it's time to get your new home in order with a vast range of home appliances to choose from . . .'

Was it just a coincidence or were we witnessing McDonagh's, at lightning speed, attempting to secure the business of those who were inheriting the properties of the deceased?

I was fascinated by the inclusion of these death notices in the radio station's scheduling. How necessary were they? Did it matter that much if you were blissfully unaware that the man who once sold you a pair of shoes in Drumcliff had passed on? Surely you were only really interested in the deaths of those with whom you were reasonably close. Had inter-familial communication in this part of the world faltered to such a degree that the radio had to be relied on as the bearer of such news?

'Hello darling, Grandad's died, you know.'

'Really? How do you know that?'

'Heard it on North West Radio this morning – the death notices.'

'Oh right. When's the funeral?'

'I don't know, the lads at work were talking and I missed that bit.'

'Never mind, we'll catch it on the five o'clock bulletin.'

This is why it was so important to have the two bulletins a day. Plus of course, the listener would be kept up to speed with any additions to the ten o'clock total. The way I was feeling, I was tempted to call North West Radio and tell them to put me down as a definite for the later bulletin, promising that I would have the good manners to call if for some reason I hadn't actually died by five o'clock.

Anne Marie brought in a plate piled high with a full Irish breakfast which looked a touch too much for a fragile stomach to handle.

'You'll have to eat this in a minute because there's a phonecall for you. Very odd. I answered the phone and they said "Have you got the man with the fridge staying with you?" It's North West Radio.'

'How did they know I was here?'

'Search me. Word must be out.'

Anne Marie led me to the hall where I took the call and listened as a secretary explained to me that the manager of Abrakebabra in Sligo had called the radio station to say that if I turned up at their restaurant today, with my fridge, then I could have a free lunch.

'That's nice,' I said, almost patronisingly. 'I tell you what, I've got a mobile phone now – let me give you the number in case any more exciting offers come through.'

Abrakebabra. What a truly awful name for a restaurant. Still, bang went the 'there's no such thing as a free lunch' theory.

'Do you want a coffee?' said Bingo from his familiar position behind the bar.

'Thanks, that would be nice.'

'I've sorted you out with a wet suit.'

'What?'

'Well, you'll need a wet suit in there, it's pretty cold you know.'

'Do you mean to tell me Bingo, that we're really going to have a go at taking the fridge surfing?'

'Of course.'

'But I thought that was all just drunken high spirits.'

'You were drunk. I wasn't. We'll do it all right.'

Surely not. But I looked at Bingo and saw that he wasn't joking. Then I heard a female voice behind me.

'Ah, there you are!' It was Antoinette, perky and alert, a picture of abstemious freshness. She eyed me cannily, 'Tony Hawks, I hope you have left this establishment since I last saw you.'

'Oh, I had a couple of hours over the road.'

'So, what are you up to this morning?'

I looked at her, and saw a woman who had been in the company of friends. Sane, sensible, balanced individuals.

'I think you had better sit down.'

God, it was a struggle. A wet suit is possibly the last thing you want to try and put on when you have a severe hangover, especially a wet suit which is a size too small. Back at Anne Marie's, I grappled with it in my room, cursing and stumbling and banging into things, and generally creating sounds consistent with the theory that I was a pervert. Fifteen minutes of physical exertion resulted in both legs being 'in', but then came the disappointment of discovering that it was on the wrong way round. I let out a wailing sound which might have suggested to anyone within earshot that whatever deviant activity I had been participating in had reached a successful climax. Twenty minutes of further tussling later, and I had succeeded in getting the wet suit on. It wasn't a comfortable feeling, there being absolutely no doubt in my crotch that this wet suit was too small for me.

I opened the bedroom door to see Anne Marie facing me at the other end of the landing. I don't know why, but I felt strangely self conscious emerging from my bedroom pulling a fridge on a trolley and dressed in a wet suit. Anne Marie wasn't someone with a ruddy complexion but the little colour she did have in her cheeks had vanished, leaving a pallid ghost-like figure before me, appearing to be in need of resuscitation. I had never, even at the most inspired moments in my life, had the amount of wit at my disposal that this situation demanded, so I chose to smile inanely as I pulled the fridge gingerly down the landing.

As I shut the front door behind me, I was fairly confident that Anne Marie's next action would be to call the police. I didn't worry though, knowing that by the time the Garda arrived, I would be surfing with the fridge, and everything would make sense.

Antoinette and Bingo were sat on the beach wall giggling as I advanced towards them, the loud rattling vibrations of the fridge on its trolley compounding the intensity of an already well established headache. It was a Saturday morning and those who had chosen to spend it enjoying a pleasant beachside walk were understandably bemused by the unusual sight before them.

Surfing is a glamorous sport. Mention surfers to most of the girls I know and they will make a funny kind of grunting sound which I have always taken to mean that they expect hunky, healthy and sexy men to be involved. And rightly so. Most of the TV footage of this sport that I have seen, has involved hunky, healthy and sexy men in abundance. But there are two simple ways to take the glamour out of surfing. The first is to wear a wet suit which is a size too small for you, and the second is to bring a fridge along. To be fair to Bingo, he looked the part, but he suffered by association. There was no doubting that he was *with* the bloke who looked very stupid and was carrying a fridge, and it was difficult to be truly sexy if you kept that kind of company. When girls buy 'sexy', they buy the whole deal, and unfortunately for Bingo he was part of a double action package in which one half was incontrovertibly sub-standard.

We set off from the beach wall on our journey to the sea's edge. This involved a short walk along the promenade and then clambering over some rocks before reaching the vast expanses of open sandy beach. The wet suit was getting tighter and tighter around me, and I was finding it increasingly difficult to bend my limbs. The effect of this was to diminish still further my overall sexiness. I was moving like a monster from a 1930s horror movie, the only clue for observers that I wasn't such a creature being the presence of a brilliant white kitchen appliance, which was clearly one of the more recent models on the market.

When I nearly fell over, Bingo, in a big-hearted gesture, gave me his surf-board and took over the burden of the fridge, thus relinquishing any 'beach cred' he may have still had. I was now able to see for myself just how ridiculous a man in a wet suit carrying a refrigerator really looked. As we started clambering, I could see a small crowd gathering by the beach wall in wonderment.

The conditions were by no means ideal for surfing, the sea being altogether too calm, but this probably favoured the fridge which was new to all this and hadn't been designed with this kind of activity in mind.

'What's the plan then?' I said to Bingo as we began wading out to sea.

'I think what we'll do is balance the fridge on the board, and then I'll try and jump on with it and ride in on a wave.'

To think the previous evening I had taken him to be responsible.

'Good idea,' I lied, and held the board steady as he lifted the fridge on to it.

It looked surprisingly stable on the board, a fridge's centre of gravity being one of its strong points. However its ability to adjust it in the face of a wave is not, and unfortunately the first wave to come its way was quite large in stature. Despite his prowess in the realm of surfboarding, Bingo had no experience in the art of keeping a fridge balanced on one, and as the wave suddenly forced the board upwards, he lost his grip on the fridge and it slid sideways into the sea. Fortunately, it just remained afloat long enough for Bingo and I to dive towards it and reinstate its position above the salt water. That had been a close one. If it fell in again and we failed to get to it quickly enough, it might fill with water and sink, and the weight of the water within it would make it difficult or even impossible to raise without professional underwater lifting equipment. Foolishly, I hadn't packed any professional underwater lifting equipment.

If I was to lose the fridge in such a way as this, it would make for a difficult explanation as a reason for failure to win my bet: 'Well, it all went very smoothly indeed until I reached Strandhill and I had a touch of bad fortune when the fridge sank just off the coast, and we were unable to raise it.'

If the fridge did sink, it would also be a considerable inconvenience to bathers who would have to learn the exact position of the wrecked fridge or risk the agony of their toes ramming into its rusting metal shell. In the future, it might even appear on naval charts of these waters, novitiate navigators baffled by the small white cuboid marked as a hazard just off the shore.

We lifted the fridge back on to the board and Bingo pushed the two of them further out to sea, this time paying more attention to oncoming waves. I watched him as he waded out a good distance, my camera poised ready to capture this lunacy on film. He turned and waited, watching each wave in anticipation of his moment. Suddenly a bigger wave appeared and Bingo leapt on his board to join the fridge. The most extraordinary sight followed. A man and a fridge riding the waves in perfect harmony. For a few glorious yards the two of them coasted in with such ease that Bingo looked to have time to open the fridge door and take out a refreshing drink. The onlookers on the promenade broke into a spontaneous round of applause, and from the water's edge Antoinette cheered gamely. It had been done, the fridge had surfed, and what is more I had photographic evidence, provided I didn't screw up with the film again. Okay, the surfers hadn't exactly covered a huge distance, and it hadn't been long before Bingo had needed to leap off the board quickly and save the fridge from another drenching, but nonetheless for a matter of seconds it had been a magnificent victory for Man and Domestic Appliance over the turbulent and untamed sea.

'Congratulations, Bingo, I think that's a first,' I said.

'Thanks. The trick now is to get the thing coming in on its own.'

'Eh?'

'We've got to get the fridge to surf on its own.'

Have we? Why? Honestly, with these people if it wasn't one thing, it was another. Here was me, innocently trying to hitch round Ireland with a fridge, and I kept running into people who wanted to find all kinds of new and exciting things for the fridge to do.

'Oh, all right,' I said cravenly. 'What's the best way to do that then?'

'Well, what I propose is that you wait about here and I'll wade a bit further out, and when I see a wave that looks suitable, I'll give the board a shove and with any luck the fridge will ride in on the board until you catch it.'

What could be simpler?

The whoops, hollers and applause we received from the shore were entirely deserved.

'We'd better not do it again,' I said. 'It would never go as well as that again. Ever.'

It had gone like a dream, exactly as Bingo had planned, the solitary fridge riding in on the wave and the surf board arriving on cue before my outstretched arms as if guided there by remote control. And what a sight it had been. Surreal, funny and somehow inspiring. For the benefit of a crowd of about fifteen people who wouldn't be believed when they got home, the kind of stunt you might expect to see in a big-budget movie, had been carried out for nothing by a couple of jokers. The euphoria even served to clear my head. Compared to a single Drambuie before leaving the pub, it was an immensely complicated hangover cure, but most efficacious.

'You guys are something else,' said Antoinette as we came ashore, delivering a line which could have been lifted directly from the movie in which our stunt belonged.

She had hit the nail on the head. We were, undoubtedly, something else. But more likely than not, in the pejorative sense.

11

Eat Your Heart Out, Michael Flatley

'Well, it's ringing for me all right,' said Antoinette, coffee in one hand, mobile phone proudly held aloft in the other. Obviously I hadn't consulted the instructions, and consequently had been unable to make any kind of progress with my new toy, but Antoinette experienced no problems and was straight through to whoever she had phoned.

'Hello, Peter? . . . Oh I'm fine, you'll never guess what we've just done . . . shit, how did you know that? . . . Oh . . . listen are you still on for this reflexology? . . . yes . . . right . . . well I'll tell him.'

'Was that "Wise Peter?"' I said, studying the phone as Antoinette handed it back to me.

'Yes, he says he'll see you directly after me, probably around 2.30.'

'Right.' I waited for a moment, not knowing what I had said 'right' to, hoping for an explanation which was not forthcoming. 'Er . . . what exactly is he going to see me for?'

'Well, reflexology, obviously. He said that last night you were really keen that he fitted you in.'

'Oh I was, I was.' Frightening. I honestly had absolutely no recollection of that. 'It's just that . . . well . . .'

'What?'

'Well, it's just that the cup final starts at three.'

Antoinette pulled a face that only girls can pull when they are fed up with boys and football.

'Tony, at worst you'll miss the first quarter of an hour. You need to relax down after all that you're going through. Are you really going to turn your back on a potentially profitable new experience for *football*?'

How is that done? How is so much venom incorporated in the articulation of one word? *Football*.

Of course she was absolutely right, cup finals come and go and are habitually disappointing, and here was an opportunity to discover something new. I'd never had the soles of my feet massaged before. Certainly not by a bloke who I'd met in the pub the night before.

'Before you do all that, you've got to see the Glen,' said Bingo. 'You can't leave here without seeing the Glen.'

'What's the Glen?'

'You'll see. You've got a car, haven't you? It'll only take us half an hour.'

And so the relentless programme of events continued with a visit to the Glen. Neither Antoinette or I had any idea what it was, but we had been assured that we shouldn't leave this place without seeing it, and for two followers of the 'faith', we knew it would be wrong to let the opportunity pass.

Bingo must have had second thoughts when he saw Antoinette's car. He said nothing but his expression suggested that his thought was, 'And you want me to get *in* it?'

In the past, Bingo had given detailed directions to holidaymakers but none of them had managed to find the Glen. It was like a secret place, not in any guidebooks and accessible only to a select few who were in the know. After ten minutes of driving, the road started to carve its way round a hill, giving us views across the beautiful bays and inlets of the coast on our right hand side, and steep grassy banks on the other.

'Right, just pull over on the left here,' said Bingo.

He led us across the road where there was a tiny gate almost completely hidden by overgrown bushes and long grass.

'This is it.'

A short walk down a narrow path and we were in a place which was truly special. Just like three children on an adventure, we found ourselves descending into a narrow passage at the foot of two huge walls of stone. There were two theories as to what had caused this vast fault in the limestone rock around the time of the Ice Age, either an earthquake, or the top collapsing in on an underground river. We were now the fortunate witnesses to the spectacular result. Vegetation growing over the rock face and water trickling over limestone stalactites had created in microcosm, Sligo's very own tropical rain forest. The narrow shafts of light battling through the overhanging branches and leaves above us, the sound of running water, and the echoes of our voices, gave the place a mystical quality which required us to stop talking and just listen. Listen to the voice of Nature.

I walked on ahead, sat down on a tree stump and looked up at the huge limestone walls which encased and sheltered us. As I watched the youthful water of a mini waterfall cascading over a narrow strip of stone, I allowed its gentle sounds to waft me into a faintly meditative state. A rare moment of peace in a journey which had become a hectic and clamorous celebration of the absurd. I felt suddenly grateful for all that had happened to me and I looked up and gently whispered 'Thank You'. This was directed to no one and no thing in particular, but to anyone or anything who was listening and fancied taking the credit. I looked around me and saw that both Bingo and Antoinette had found their own private locations for a moment's quiet contemplation, and I felt deeply privileged to be here in this unique and spiritual place.

But if I had attained some momentary balance, inner calm and enlightenment here in the 'Glen', then my next action served as a reminder that I had undergone no lasting conversion to a spiritual path. I looked at my watch and noted that the cup final started in just under an hour.

With the unwelcoming piercing sharpness of a car alarm, my voice punctured the tranquil atmosphere, 'We'd better go if I'm going to catch the cup final.'

The others turned, initially startled by this intrusion into their solitary reflections, but then became suddenly aware of who they were, where they were and, above all, who they were with. And unfortunately for them, they were with the bloke who wanted to go and watch the cup final.

'Oh right, no problem,' said Bingo accommodatingly. Antoinette said nothing, but didn't need to.

On the walk back to the car we noticed the evidence of trees having been cut down and used as firewood.

'This has become a popular spot for the occasional rave party, and unfortunately the kids don't always treat the place with the respect it deserves,' explained Bingo.

'Is there much of a drug problem in this part of Ireland?' I enquired.

'The police don't admit that there is, but it's there all right.'

He went on to explain that an unpopular Chief Superintendent had proudly boasted the absence of any kind of drug problem in Sligo in a quote which the local newspaper had lifted for a banner headline,

WE DON'T HAVE A PROBLEM WITH DRUGS

The wind was somewhat taken out of his sails by the opportunist who cut out the headline and used it as the first line for a poster which was duplicated and then plastered all over the town.

WE DON'T HAVE A PROBLEM WITH DRUGS
WE CAN GET THEM ANYWHERE

Whatever your views on drugs, it was clear who had won that particular battle.

Time was running short but 'Bingo Tours' included another brief stop at a derelict old landlord's house which a local businessman was restoring to its former extravagant grandeur, with the intention of soon opening it as a hotel. The countryside of Ireland is littered with roofless derelict houses, each of which mark an isolated moment in its troubled history. A government tax on roofs had meant that landlords in England had arranged for the roofs to be destroyed on their Irish properties which they could no longer afford to run or be bothered to visit. Britain had seen its own idiosyncratic and unsightly physical manifestation of man's obsession with tax evasion when the introduction of a 'Window Tax' resulted in the owners of many large houses in England having their windows bricked up. It seems that the more privileged in society you are, the more convoluted, devious and determined your efforts became in the evasion of putting a penny back into it. Certainly the scars on the Irish landscape of these old and roofless landlords' houses are monuments to the human weakness for accumulating personal wealth at the expense of social justice. Just at a moment in history when the basic human right of a 'roof over your head' was being denied to large numbers of the Irish population, roofs were actively being destroyed in order to preserve healthy bank balances on an island across the Irish Sea.

A pivotal moment in my own personal history was marked by the mobile phone ringing for the first time. It was North West Radio giving me the name and address of a woman who ran a bed and breakfast in Ballina, and had offered me free accommodation if I turned up there. A roof over my head.

Antoinette shook her head in disbelief. 'Honestly, the doors that are opening to you! I've got to get myself a toaster and travel round Ireland.'

'Ballina? Is that where you're headed next then?' asked Bingo.

'It is now.'

I'm not proud of having missed my reflexology appointment with Peter. To choose watching a game of football in a noisy Sligo pub ahead of a relaxing massage from one of life's natural healers was shallow and immature, but an FA Cup final is an FA Cup final, and if you miss one there is a gap in your personal experience which could put you at a serious disadvantage in a pub conversation at some time in the future.

The honour of being the first person to sign the fridge was bestowed upon Bingo when we had dropped him back at the Strand pub. With a green marker pen, the words 'Cheers! Love Bingo' heralded the process of transforming an ordinary household fridge into a personalised oddity.

The irrational need to watch a game of football had left me with a deadline, and I had been forced into the unusual position of needing a game plan.

'I thought you didn't have game plans,' said Antoinette, as I outlined it to her.

'I don't, but today is different.'

It wasn't actually. It was exactly the same as the previous day, in that I had to be somewhere by three o'clock.

By rushing away from the beauty and peace of the Glen, and denying the soles of my feet the luxury of a good massage, I had freed up enough time to grab a quick bite to eat before the match. So when we reached the centre of Sligo and I got out of Antoinette's car for the last time, my intention was to find Abrakebabra, claim my free lunch, dump my fridge with them, and go and watch the game in the nearest pub. It was a good plan, although I was the only person in the car who thought so.

Antoinette and I hugged and wished each other good luck.

'Thank you for the most surreal weekend of my life,' she said and then drove off back to Dublin and relative normality. In stark contrast, I turned, hauled my rucksack on to my back and wheeled my fridge through the hordes of hurried shoppers in Sligo's city centre.

Abrakebabra turned out to be a fast food restaurant, and although it wasn't quite what I had imagined, the 'fast' element of its service was going to be crucial, since time was ticking away. The boss, who had come up with the magnificent marketing ploy of donating a free lunch to anyone who wheeled a fridge into his establishment, wasn't there, but a confused lady called Mary honoured the agreement and allowed me to leave my fridge and rucksack around the back.

At two minutes to three I rushed out on to the street, steak sandwich in hand, and went into the first pub I saw. It was empty, and the reason soon became apparent. It wasn't showing the match. Time was running out. I dashed outside and there were no pubs in sight. What was it to be, left or right? I went left.

Turning left was a mistake, and led me into the only populated square mile in the whole of this country which had no pubs, but I ran my heart out and made it to one in a time which, had it been in a formal athletics event, would undoubtedly have been a personal best. It had a big black-board outside advertising 'Chelsea v Middlesburgh'. I looked at my watch and saw that it was one minute past three. Not bad. Not bad at all.

Well, that is in normal circumstances. In normal circumstances both teams cancel each other out for the first forty-five minutes in a dull and nervy first half, the game coming alive in an enthralling last twenty minutes which makes the whole experience worthwhile. On the day when I was one minute late – one miserly minute late, Chelsea scored after thirty-five seconds. Thirty-five seconds! That never happens, not in a cup final. I was furious. I badly needed some reflexology to calm me down. Instead, I chose a far less healthy relaxant, and sat back, occasionally sipping at it, hoping that the early strike might open the game up and we might be on for a goal fest.

The pub was large and it looked like three separate rooms had all been knocked through to create an open-plan effect. Two large screens at each end provided the focus for everyone's attention. Everyone that is, except for the resident drunk. Actually, I think this man was a guest drunk, possibly on loan from another pub, with a transfer fee under negotiation. Confetti in his hair and a smartish suit suggested that he had come straight from a wedding reception. Presumably he had drunk the free bar dry, and his hand had been forced into carrying on his good work elsewhere. At this precise moment this man was the most drunk man in Ireland, and the lead he held over his rivals was a substantial one. Using his tie as a microphone he stood at one end of the pub, just below the TV screen and sang his interpretation of Bob Geldof's 'I Don't Like Mondays'. It was tuneless, loud, and unpleasant. Too close to the original for my taste. He then began jumping around as if someone had put five thousand volts through his body. If it hadn't been for his exclamation, none of us in that pub would have had the faintest idea what he was doing.

'EAT YOUR HEART OUT MICHAEL FLATLEY!!' he bellowed at the top of his voice.

Ah, that was it then. He was doing *River Dance*. His exertions were such that I thought he was going to have a heart attack there and then. Instead he took a huge swig from his pint mug and distributed an equal share of the beer within it, between his mouth and his suit.

This man was creating an enormous distraction for the majority of those, like me, who were in the pub primarily to watch a game of football. But there wasn't a sign of any antagonism towards him. The drinkers simply smiled, laughed or shook their heads good-humouredly. This hadn't been my natural reaction, but I soon realised that the best way to diffuse my irritation was to smile along with the rest. If you can't beat them or join them, laugh at them.

I was grateful to him really. He was more entertaining than the football and his 'songs' helped to drown out the commentators' bland analysis. I could just make out the distinctly nasal tones of Trevor Brooking.

'That's five times that Ravanelli's been offside, and it hasn't even been marginal – he's comfortably off.'

I should say he's comfortably off, I heard he was getting £20,000 a week.

Chelsea won 2-0. They scored their second goal when I was in the toilet. I felt a little for Middlesborough; after all, their season had involved them getting to two cup finals, losing them both and being relegated from the Premier league. What does a manager say to his players after a string of such devastating failures? I'm not aware of there being a satisfactory euphemism for 'you are a bunch of losers'.

I bet it wasn't as bad for the players as the fans. Most of the players would be transferred to another club within the week, but the fans would continue to live in Middlesborough with their shattered dreams. It's probably just as well they don't have the Death Notices on local radio up there.

As I sat in this Sligo pub I momentarily forgot what I was doing here in Ireland, such was my empathy with the Middlesborough fans. I knew the pain. I had been there. The last team to lose an FA Cup final and be relegated in the same season had been Brighton and Hove Albion. I had been to Wembley and seen my side lose 4-0 to Manchester United, the largest margin of defeat for any club since the second world war. Frankly it had been an embarrassment. Still, at least I hadn't taken along a toy machinegun.

When I left the pub, the most drunk man in Ireland was increasing his lead over any potential rivals, having just lost a head to head race to down a pint of beer, and was now shouting at the bar staff, demanding two large brandies. He must have had a strong constitution – but few would deny that it was in need of some reform.

At Abrakebabra, I collected my stuff, said I had enjoyed the football even though I hadn't really, and ordered a taxi on my mobile phone.

'Could you drop me on the road to Ballina?' I had said.

'No problem, it will be about five minutes,' they rep*lied*.

I waited outside Abrakebabra for twenty minutes. Eventually a thick-set man in his twenties, who I had seen eyeing my fridge with interest, approached me.

'Were you on the television yesterday afternoon?'

'I was.'

'I thought I recognised y–... well, the fridge. Where are you headed?'

'I'm waiting for a taxi to take me out to the road to Ballina where I'm going to start hitching.'

'Wait here, I'll go and get my van. I'll take you out there.'

Excellent. I had mastered my art to such a degree that I could get lifts now without even hitching.

Kieran made fruit and veg deliveries. (But in his busy daily schedule he obviously found time to watch daytime television.)

'I was just on the way home when I saw you. I had packed up for the day but then I realised I had forgotten to deliver six cucumbers, so I had to get the van back out again.'

All part of the stresses that go with the job. So, I owed this lift entirely to six cucumbers. Tick that one off – another first.

'It's very kind of you to drive me out here like this.'

'Ah it's a pleasure. You don't meet an eejit like you every day.'

Fair point.

Kieran drove me about five miles out of Sligo past the beautiful Ballysadare Bay.

'Look at that,' he said, 'God's television.'

We arrived at a fork in the road where the smaller N59 branched off to Ballina, and it was time for me to get out and set myself up on the road-side. It was just after five thirty, and I was on the road again. Literally. I didn't know what was coming next. I was getting hooked on the unpre-dictability of this whole fridge experience. There was only one thing I could be sure of, and that was that it wouldn't be long before one of the agreeable drivers in this agreeable country plucked me from the road-side and bore me ever onwards.

12

Roisin

An hour and a half later I was still waiting, and I was beginning to feel rather low. With an over-confidence bordering on arrogance, I had thought that I could just leave a town whenever I felt like it and pick up a lift with great ease, but the reality was that in another hour it would be dark and I would have to give up and get a taxi back to Sligo. Could my liver handle another night in the Strand? I slumped down on to the fridge, tired and despairing.

Two very young children, a little boy and a little girl, walked past. The boy viewed me with some interest and asked, 'What are you doing?'

It was a question I had begun to ask myself.

'I'm hitch-hiking.'

He nodded. He seemed satisfied even though he clearly didn't know what 'hitch-hiking' was.

'Are you just after coming from school?' the little girl asked.

I shook my head, more in disbelief than in answer to the question. What cross circuit of wires in her brain had caused her to arrive at a question like that? A complete absence of the application of any logic whatsoever. She would have a great future in this country.

Finally a car stopped. But the driver got out and crossed the road to the Convenience Store.

Tease.

For the next ten minutes all the drivers seemed to be solitary lady drivers, and for obvious reasons, solitary lady drivers don't stop. Especially on a Saturday night and when the hitcher has a fridge. A priest went by, but he made a signal with his hand, pointing to the left, meaning that he was turning off very shortly. Quite a few drivers had done this and I respected it as a courteous gesture, even if nine times out of ten it was probably a downright lie.

Another twenty minutes dragged by. Clutching at straws, I decided what I was lacking was a card to hold up with my destination written on it. Up until now I hadn't bothered with this hitch-hiking accessory since I had no real need for one. It didn't matter particularly where I ended up, any kind of lift, provided it was in roughly the right direction, was good enough for me. The nice lady in the Convenience Store provided me with a piece of cardboard, and after a little creative work with the marker pen, I went back to my hitching with renewed vigour, and with a 'BALLINA' sign held proudly aloft.

It didn't make a scrap of difference. Well it did actually, now the drivers knew exactly where it was that they weren't going to take me. It was almost half past seven. I decided twenty more minutes and then I would give up and call for a taxi to take me back to Anne Marie's. Three unsavoury looking youths turned the corner and headed towards me. For the first time on my trip I felt a little uneasy. It was Saturday night, they looked a tough lot, and I was something of a target for those in search of alternative amusement. Would they say anything? Worse still, would they do anything? I held my breath and closed my eyes, but they passed by without a word. Quite whether I was all too confusing a proposition for them, or whether they were simply law abiding, upstanding citizens, I do not know. Perhaps the fridge made me look hard.

I was about to give up, and had just started to gather my irregular belongings together when a Vauxhall Cavalier pulled up. I watched it suspiciously, expecting the driver to get out and go across to the store, but he remained in his seat and looked over his shoulder at me. I ran to the car window.

'Are you going to Ballina?'

'I am too.'

I had lucked out again.

Chris had been at a goat fair earlier that day, and afterwards had made a brief visit to friends in Sligo for early evening drinks. He had seen me on the way into town and identified me as the strange fellow he had heard talking about his fridge journey earlier in the week. He hadn't been surprised when I was still by the roadside as he headed out of town again. He had hitched around Ireland himself many years ago and had found that one of the longest waits he had endured was when he was trying to leave Sligo. He reckoned that Limerick was another difficult place to get out of, so I logged that useful information away in my foggy, weary brain.

One of the more tiring aspects of hitching is a need to be sociable and make conversation with whoever is driving you. It would be considered poor form to accept a ride, hop into the passenger seat and then simply to crash out until you reached your destination. How I longed to do just that, but instead I chatted merrily away, energy ebbing from me with each sentence, until Chris dropped me at the address of the lady who had offered me free B&B.

One of the more tiring aspects of accepting an offer of free accommodation is a need to be sociable and make conversation with whoever has offered it to you. It would be considered poor form to turn up, dump your bags, crawl into your bedroom and order an early morning alarm call. How I longed to do just that, but instead I chatted merrily away to Marjorie, energy ebbing from me with each sentence, until the tea was drunk, the cake was eaten and I finally plucked up the courage to mention just how exhausted I was. I apologised and said that I simply had to grab a couple of hours sleep, and Marjorie understandingly showed me to my room.

It was a beautiful room too, with splendid views over the River Moy, thanks to the elevated position of the guest house at the top of a steep bank. I thanked Marjorie again for her kindness.

'Think nothing on it, Tony. When I heard what you were doing I just had to ring the radio station and offer you a room. I think it's a great idea.'

Of course it was. I had never doubted it.

It was close to 8.30 when I got my head down for a couple of hours' nap.

When I awoke from the deepest of sleeps it was only 8.45. I got up to go to the toilet and looked out of the bathroom window, and saw the sun shining on the river. From the east. It was morning. I had napped for twelve and a quarter hours. And I felt rather good for it.

'Did you sleep all right?' asked Marjorie, at breakfast.

'You could say that.'

Having taken note of my choice of breakfast, Marjorie shuffled off leaving me to admire the view of the river and chat to the other guests. I surveyed them and elected not to bother. There were three of them, a young married couple, and a lone obese German man, and they were all sat at one table together and clearly not having a very comfortable time. They were saying absolutely nothing to each other and their silence seemed to have a terrible stranglehold over them. The sound of their cutlery clinking on their crockery echoed round the dining room and seemed to be amplified tenfold. It became apparent that for all of them, the task of introducing words into the proceedings was becoming increasingly hard with each passing minute. They hung their heads over their plates with grim determination and resolve, knowing that the sooner their food was eaten, the sooner the whole unpleasant experience would be over. I was glad I wasn't sat at their table.

Marjorie's voice seemed deafening when she arrived with the most wonderful plate of breakfast. Over tea, the previous day, she had told me that she had written two cookbooks, and even with as simple a meal as breakfast, she clearly wanted to demonstrate her skill in the culinary field. I had no objections, smoked salmon, tomato, and beautiful fluffy scrambled egg suited me just fine. As far as I was concerned, she fully deserved the Michelin One Star she had told me she craved. But what's the big deal there? I have never understood the need to have one's cuisine endorsed by Michelin. Who cares what they think? No one is looking for food which corners well.

Marjorie was knocking on the door of middle age, but had the impressive zeal for life of a much younger woman. After the young couple, and the now even more obese German had fled the dining room for the sanctuary of their rooms, she explained how she and her husband had separated, and how she felt she was undergoing a new start and was more positive than ever about the future.

'I'm going for it!' she said. 'I think that's why I knew I had to make contact with you, because with what you're doing, you're going for it too.'

'Right.'

I knew what she meant, but I had never expected my fridge journey to be used in comparison with a marriage break-up.

'So, are you taking that fridge back out on the road today, Tony?'

'Well, Sunday is traditionally a day of rest, and I think I may have been overdoing it a little, so would you mind if I stayed here one more night – I fully expect to pay.'

'You'll do no such thing, you'll stay here for nothing and there'll be no argument about it. So, what are you going to do with your day today then?'

'Oh, I think I'll just take it easy, do some reading and writing, maybe take a walk down by the river.'

'Oh. My friend Elsie is coming over at one o'clock. She's a character – you just *have* to meet her. I'll warn you though, you might need a valium.'

Marjorie hadn't exaggerated. Elsie, an effervescent and voluble woman, cut short my leisure time when she arrived an hour early, and marked midday by planting a big wet smacker full on my lips.

'You'll have to excuse me, Tony, but that's the way I do things,' she spluttered as I reeled back in shock. 'Did I come too early?'

She may have done, but I certainly hadn't.

'No, you're fine, I'd nearly finished reading.'

Elsie wasn't slow in coming forward. Within two minutes of our having met, she showed me a poem she had written and asked me to read it. As I endeavoured to do so, she continued to talk, telling me how she wrote and sang songs too and was making a CD soon. Unfortunately Elsie's incessant spoken word meant that concentration on her written word was impossible.

'It's very good,' I said, handing the poem back and hoping that she wouldn't wish me to comment on its subject matter.

After a delicious lunch, which I could only fault in its alarming proximity to breakfast, the two ladies took me on a tour of the sights of Ballina. The fridge had to come too, and at all points along the way, at Elsie's and Marjorie's insistence, the fridge was to be paraded as a celebrity for all to see.

We visited Kilcullen's Seaweed Baths in Enniscrone where I had the privilege of having seaweed draped all over me whilst immersed in an enormous bath full of hot sea water. It seemed a ludicrous idea but was surprisingly relaxing. We dropped in at Belleek Castle, a stately home set in a thousand acres of woodland and forestry on the banks of the River Moy, but we couldn't look round it because viewings of the castle were by appointment only. That's what estate agents say, isn't it? We were hardly going to buy the place.

On the way back, a drink was taken in the clubhouse of the golf club where the ladies had begun taking lessons. I was to learn a lesson here too. As I wheeled the fridge into the bar on its trolley, Elsie announced at the top of her voice, 'THIS IS TONY HAWKS FROM ENGLAND! HE'S BRINGING A FRIDGE ROUND IRELAND! YOU'VE PROBABLY HEARD HIM ON *THE GERRY RYAN SHOW*.'

Elsie's announcement was greeted with silence. The relaxing golfers eyed me with suspicion and returned to their conversations. Marjorie, Elsie and myself drank our drinks without one person coming over to talk to us or have a joke about the fridge. I felt sure that this wasn't the customary frostiness of golf clubs we were experiencing here, but more of an example of 'Irish Begrudgery'. I remembered someone in Hudi-Beags announcing this alleged national trait, and I understood it to mean that people would have little time for you if you forced yourself upon them or announced your greatness, instead of allowing them their own time and space to discover it for themselves. This was something else to log away in my now-crowded brain, but I found room just beside 'Limerick being a difficult city to hitch out of', and 'England and Portugal being the only EC countries without minority languages'.

Throughout the afternoon Elsie kept up a constant stream of jokes and ribald remarks, each of the latter followed by the apology, 'I am sorry about that, but that's the way I am.'

In fact, she said, 'I am sorry about that, but that's the way I am' so many times that I began to wonder whether that wasn't the way she was, at all. Whatever she was, she was a good friend to Marjorie.

'A while ago now when I was low,' said Marjorie, when Elsie was out of earshot, 'I called Elsie eight times in one day. And when I called the eighth time, she behaved just like it was the first. Now *that's* a friend.'

Or someone with a very poor memory.

It was a beautiful evening, the mile or so walk to the pub hugging the bank of the River Moy, with the setting sun casting its soft final rays over the river's steadily flowing waters. I felt inspired by Marjorie and Elsie. Two women in their fifties who were going for it. Marjorie with her cook-books, and Elsie with her poems and songs. I had no idea whether either of their efforts were of a high quality, but that didn't seem to be the point. Far more pertinent was the joy it was bringing to them.

Sometimes in life you've got to dance like nobody's watching.

The pub was called Murphys, a newly and tastefully refurbished bar which was packed full of young people. Young attractive people. Young attractive girls. I ordered a pint and allowed myself to get a little excited. I leant against the bar and scanned the room for my favourite. She wasn't hard to find. She was sat at a table in a slightly elevated section of the pub, talking with two guys. She had dark hair, big sparkling eyes and a mouth which I felt needed to be kissed. I was considering how pleasurable an experience this might be, when she looked up and saw me looking at her. I didn't look away. She gave me a kind of half smile and went back to talking with her friends. Good. The half smile was a good sign.

Perhaps at this point I should take a moment to explain how, in the area of the pursuit of women, I have always demonstrated an exceptional adeptness for deluding myself. I have always been able to convince myself that I'm doing much better than I really am. With an assured grace and on gossamer wings, I fly in the face of reality, never seeing the crash landing that awaits me. On this occasion, for example, I had completely dismissed from my mind the fact that the object of my interest was in the company of two males who, no doubt, were just as aware of the kissability of her mouth as I was.

When she left her friends (for in my eyes that was clearly all they were) she came to the bar to order a drink, and was almost alongside me, presenting me with an opportunity I couldn't afford to miss. However, I made the mistake of thinking too much about the opening line. By far and away the best option in this situation is to say the first thing that comes into your head and not worry about its quality – the thinking being that if the girl likes the general look of you, she will be moderately forgiving in the first few minutes of your advances.

On this occasion it was just unfortunate that the only line which kept forcing its way to the brink of being spoken was, 'Are you aware that of all the countries in the EC, England and Portugal are the only ones with no minority languages?'

After hearing a line like that, not many females, however much they like the look of you, would think 'Hey, he sounds like the kind of guy I'd like to spend some more time with', and the ones that did were probably best avoided.

Her transaction at the bar was nearly completed and I knew that I had to say something, and fast.

'Is there a pub quiz on tonight?' I blurted, averting my eyes from the sign saying 'Pub Quiz Tonight', which was up on the wall directly in front of both of us.

'Yes,' she replied warmly. 'You can come and be in our team if you like.'

Inwardly I punched the air, whilst on the cool exterior I attempted to give the impression of being rather blasé about the whole idea.

'If you like,' I said, and then, thinking I'd overdone it, added, 'Thanks, that would be nice.'

Her name was Rosheen (which I later learned was spelt 'Roisin'), and she wasn't with the two guys at the table, but with a crowd of friends who were further up the bar to my left. With great politeness, not normally afforded to a stranger who had just asked you a stupid question, she introduced me to all her friends, one by one, but their names were just sounds which I failed to absorb, such was my fixation with her, the mistress of ceremonies. It mattered only that it was her name I remembered. Roisin.

'A totally purposeless idea, but a damn fine one…'

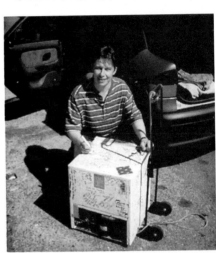

A man becomes the embodiment of his obsession...

…and a kitchen appliance becomes a new folk hero.

An 'arty fridge shot' for the
Donegal Democrat.

Andy and me in Bunbeg – masters of
misguided enthusiasm.

Patsy Dan. The poorest King on Earth.

'I hereby christen this fridge Saiorse,
meaning "Freedom"…'

Fridge and Drunk In Residence.
A meeting of great minds.

The Resident Drunk suddenly produced a pair of spoons and proceeded to play them with great skill.

he fridge and me on an unexpected tour of Kinsale harbour.

The flooring boys, hard at work.

The Great Gerry Ryan. One phone call after breakfast and the country was mobilised in my support.

In the doghouse.

'Caesar enters Rome, ladies and gentlemen…'

'Tony, Ireland now pronounces you its Fridge Man…'

Lovely Roisin. With the kissable mouth.

Annoyingly, Roisin began talking to two girlfriends and I fell into conversation with Declan. I had nothing against Declan other than the fact that he wasn't Roisin, and therefore had a mouth which I had no desire to kiss. He asked what I was doing in Ireland. I had hoped I wouldn't have to answer that question for some time, and tried to cope with it without mentioning the fridge.

'So you're just travelling around for a month then, are you?'

'Yes.'

'Grand.' A beat, then, 'So what made you decide to do that then?'

The questions went on until the truth, the ridiculous truth, was inveigled out of me.

To my relief, the pub quiz began before word of the fridge could reach Roisin, for although I wasn't ashamed of what I was doing, I wanted to break the news to her myself. An explanation of what I was up to could sound silly if it wasn't handled sensitively.

The quiz was about pop trivia and I was a useful addition to their team. I knew the answers to the first four questions and it wasn't long before everyone turned to me for either the answer, or confirmation of someone else's. In the second section of the quiz, the quizmaster played the first few bars of a record, and we had to name the artist. I was good at this too, definitely on top form tonight, but I was aware that when it came to pop trivia there was a fine line between impressive and tragic. I crossed that line on the fifth song in, when after only three or four notes I called out, 'That's "The Time Of Our Lives" by Bill Medley and Jennifer Warnes!'

I did it excitedly and with too much gusto, and at a volume which readily offered the information to our rival teams.

Throughout the proceedings I kept a close eye on Roisin, secretly hoping that when it came to pop quizzes, she had a yen for men who could get ten out of ten. She had looked over on a couple of occasions and rewarded me with a half smile, and this had given me enough encouragement to move over to her,

'How are you enjoying it?' I said, without inspiration.

'Oh, it's a craic. You're a bit good, aren't you? I think we might win this.'

'What's the prize?'

'Well, all the names of the winning team go into a hat, and the name drawn out wins a champagne dinner for two at the restaurant upstairs.'

Another half smile. God, she was beautiful. I suddenly realised that we had to win this, and that the way my luck was going, mine would be the name drawn out of the hat, and she would be my date for the champagne dinner. The quizmaster fired the final question, 'What was Neil Diamond's first number one hit as a writer?'

The team turned and looked at me. The difference between outright victory and second place probably hinged on this one question. Brilliantly, I knew the answer.

'UB40 – "Red Red Wine".'

We had done it! All the questions right. Now all we had to do was wait for fate to decide who got the sexy dinner.

Ten minutes later (to my chagrin, all of which had been spent chatting to Declan) the quizmaster's PA clumsily halted our conversations.

'We have one team with all the questions right tonight, so good going there.' He then read out the answers,

'. . . and that one was of course one of the toughest questions of the night but the answer was . . . Bill Medley and Jennifer Warnes.'

I looked at Roisin. She smiled back. A full smile this time, none of that half smile business. She saved that for losers.

'. . . and so we come to the final question of the night. What was Neil Diamond's first number-one hit as a writer? And the answer of course is "I'm A Believer" by The Monkees.'

I didn't look at Roisin, but apologised to the rest of my team.

'I'm sorry, I thought it was "Red Red Wine",' I mumbled to the floor.

'Ah, who cares?' said Declan, generously.

I was born into the wrong generation. How I would have loved to have been a dashing young man in the 1930s and 1940s when dance bands and orchestras played at dancehalls, and you could hold your partner close and whisper sweet nothings as you waltzed her into your heart.

I have never liked discos. I have never understood why, in a place specifically designed for people to meet each other, an environment has been created in which you can't be heard unless you shout. Shouting is unattractive. It's certainly not my style, and I doubt that it brings out the best in most of us. Why have we put together a twilight entertainment world which is tailor made for the Reverend Ian Paisley? For my own part I have always preferred a gentler approach to courtship, and there is no doubt about it, dry remarks lose something when bellowed

These places are great levellers intellectually, the sharpest mind reduced to the level of the lowest common denominator – that of being understood. At one of these 'Nitespots' (and that's another irritation – spell 'night' correctly or don't spell it at all) a typical exchange might be:

TONY: (Shouting at a girl) *Would you like to dance?*

GIRL: (Shouting back) *What?*

TONY: (Shouting louder) *Would you like to dance?*

GIRL: (Shouting) *Yes, I have. but just on a school trip to Calais.*

TONY: (Shouting a bit louder still, directly into the girl's ear) *Not, have you been to France? – Would you like to dance?*

GIRL: (Shouting) *Yes please, I'll have a large gin and tonic.*

TONY: (Under his breath) *Greedy cow.*

GIRL: *I heard that.*

The club we were now in, which was in the basement of Murphys, had all the unpleasant features that I had come to associate with these places – overcrowded dancefloor, booming bass, strobe lighting and mindless remarks from the DJ. Perfect for making me feel uncomfortable. I felt I had gone back in time and was reliving one of countless unsatisfactory teenage evenings. It was a nightmare, but most of all because I had completely lost Roisin.

She was here, at least she had said she was coming, but I couldn't see her anywhere in this crowded sweaty hellhole. Naturally, were I to bump into Roisin and find myself marching off hand in hand with her to the dancefloor, I would have found the whole ambience entirely more agreeable. As it was, I was reduced to drinking beer and watching girls dancing. Man at his most atavistic.

I engaged in a brief social shouting match with an English girl from Finchley. Thinking how awful it would be if Roisin was somewhere in the club and just saw me standing around like somebody's Dad, I asked the Finchley girl to dance.

She replied that she *had* been to France, having made two visits to a penfriend in Lyons. I took this as a cue to return to my solitary position by the dancefloor and resume my role as a steady drinker.

It must have been quite close to the end of the evening when I put my pint down, marched on to the dancefloor, and did my little jig with as much dignity as I could muster. Nobody had asked me to dance and no one was dancing with me. I suppose this is the one advantage of the modern discotheque. Had I been doing this on my own at the 1930s dancehall I would have been thrown out. A girl suddenly grabbed me and started swinging me about by my arms. It wasn't clear whether she was dancing with me or trying to soften me up for interrogation. Had an interrogation followed, I surely would have spilled the beans. She continued to swing me around until I was close to exhaustion. I wouldn't have minded but I hadn't even asked her if she'd been to France. When the record finished, the lights came up, and that was it, the night was over.

Except of course that no one was in a hurry to leave. Why should they be? With the music no longer blaring, here was the first opportunity for people to talk to each other.

On my way out, I bumped into Roisin who was in the queue for the cloakroom.

'Where have you been? I've been looking for you,' I said.

'I've been talking to Paul.'

'Who's Paul?'

'Paul is who asked me out this evening. This is our second date.'

'Oh.' I felt two hours of drink swell inside me. 'I think you're lovely, you know.'

'Do you? That's nice.' She seemed genuinely chuffed, although presumably she could spot '3 am drunken boy at disco' talk, when she heard it. The thing is, I really meant it.

'Do you like him?' I said.

'Who?'

'Paul – second-date man.'

She hesitated and, like a politician, chose her words carefully. 'He's a lot more local than you are.'

She had a point.

In the brief conversation that followed I broke the fridge news to her, which she assimilated with surprising ease, and then I took her address promising to send her flowers in the morning.

'You won't. You're just saying that,' she insisted.

'You'll see. You'll get the flowers. You're my princess and princesses merit flowers.'

I don't know whether Paul heard these last words as he arrived at his date's side, but he didn't look too pleased with me. I gave him an apologetic shrug, kissed Roisin on the hand, and set off on the long walk back to my lodgings. I fell into bed, and with a ringing in my ears and a spinning of the room, wondered how long it would be before the next time I didn't sleep alone. It was like being nineteen all over again.

13

Freedom

Westport was next. At breakfast Marjorie had said it was a lovely little town, and that I should go to Matt Molloy's pub and get Mick Levell to sing the 'Lotto Song'. This had made absolutely no sense to me, and for that reason alone it seemed an apposite destination.

Outside the florists, Martin the taxi driver had waited patiently in his taxi as I had collected my second bouquet of the trip, and he was doing the same now as I nervously walked up the path to Roisin's front door. Even though he was clearly amused by my decision to deliver these flowers, he had agreed that it was the right thing to do.

'Ah, if you said you'd bring her flowers, then bring her flowers. What harm can it do?'

She lived in a small residential estate, at number twenty-four. As I rang the bell, I felt more nerves than I had before performing at the Royal Gala. I didn't know what to expect. The door opened and there was lovely Roisin, not wearing any make-up, unlike the night before, but somehow looking fresher for it. I smiled and brandished the flowers.

'Hello, remember me?'

She looked absolutely horrified. Then she put her forefinger over her mouth indicating to me to be quiet and did something which I thought only happened in poor situation comedies. For the benefit of someone inside the house, she announced to me in a loud voice, 'NO THANK YOU, NOT TODAY – WE DON'T NEED ANY.'

Oh no! Somebody was inside who shouldn't know about me. I began to panic. God, what had I done? Perhaps last night things between her and second-date Paul had moved on a pace and he was in there, having stayed the night. Perhaps he had a vicious temper, a criminal record, and a penchant for brandishing things less benign than flowers. Was Martin's question on the subject of the flowers – 'What harm can they do?' – about to be comprehensively answered?

Roisin leant forward and whispered to me. Even in these uneasy circumstances, it felt good to be close to her.

'My aunt's in the house.'

Her aunt? So what? What's so special about her aunt? This was a new one on me. A jealous aunt?

Roisin must have known from the look of disbelief on my face that I was in need of elucidation.

'Look, I didn't tell you this last night, but I'm recently separated from my husband, and the family don't know about Paul, let alone . . .'

'The idiot with the flowers.'

'Yes. I mean no. Not at all. You're not an eejit.'

I bloody was. What if the husband were to turn up now? The jealous, violent psychopath of a husband.

'YES, WELL THANK YOU. TRY AGAIN NEXT WEEK,' announced Roisin for the benefit of the Aunt.

'I'd better go.'

'I'm sorry.'

This had all been rather disappointing. I handed her the flowers.

'Thank you, Tony. That's sweet.'

'Look, I've got a mobile phone, I'll give you the number, if you ever feel like giving me a call.'

'Thanks.'

'Although you're hardly likely to.'

'No, I will.' She looked me in the eye. 'I *will* call.'

Something about that look led me to believe that Roisin would call. She wasn't out of my life forever. Not just yet, anyway.

I got back into the taxi of the gently smirking Martin, leaving Roisin to explain to her Aunt why a tradesman had brought her a bouquet of flowers.

'I've done a receipt for you,' said Martin as he helped unload me and my stuff by the roadside. He handed it to me. It read:

DATE: 19th May
TO: Dublin Road, Ballina
FROM: Marjorie's
DRIVER'S NAME: Martin McGurty
FARE: £0.00.

'Thanks, that's really so kind Martin.'

Especially given the amount of his time I had taken up with florists and doorstep dramas.

'I couldn't take money off "the Fridge Man" now, could I?'

I couldn't argue with the logic, and was extremely grateful that this sentiment seemed to be shared by quite so many of his countrymen.

*

It was a beautiful day, and the sun shone down on me as I stuck out the thumb of destiny once more. By way of a coincidence, the best spot for my hitching turned out to be just round the corner from Roisin's house, and I could actually see her frontdoor from the roadside. It occurred to me that I could see when the aunt left, and if she did, I could make my way back to the house and Roisin and I could spend a blissful afternoon making love.

Twenty minutes later, the chances of that were ruined when Michael pulled his red Toyota over to the side of the road and invited me on board.

Killjoy.

Michael was a self-employed builder who was headed for Swinford. He had heard nothing about my trip but thought it seemed a fun project. As we talked, the subject turned to the forthcoming general election, and I made the mistake of asking how the electoral system worked. As Michael explained it, I discovered that it wasn't that simple.

'The system we have works on the basis of a single transferable vote. You've only got one vote, but you may vote for everybody on the ballot paper.'

Already I was lost. He went on.

'You vote with your choice, one through six, or ten, or however many people is on the ballet paper. If the person you vote number one for is eliminated then your number two vote becomes a number one vote for the second person that you chose.'

Ah, it's all falling into place now.

'. . . and thus your votes may be distributed until the fourth or fifth or sixth count until somebody is finally elected.'

No, you've lost me again.

'It seems very complex, but it's not actually.'

Come off it Michael, it is.

'It was devised by the British so that a plethora of small parties would be elected and it would lead to division and a lack of cohesion. However the system works very well in Ireland in that it reflects the exact wishes of the electorate.'

As our conversation developed, Michael impressed me with not only his extensive knowledge of Ireland's electoral system but also by the way he articulated it.

'You know your stuff,' I said.

'Well, I'm interested. Not in a party political sense but in a general sense. The philosophy of "consent to be governed" is something that interests me. Over here we consent to be governed in such a way, and where you come from, you consent to be governed in another. The problem in Northern Ireland is that there is no broad consent to be governed, and that is what distorts their society.'

I was finding that it wasn't uncommon to run into someone with Michael's eloquent self expression. The people here liked to talk, and they did it very well.

He dropped me at a T junction where an arterial road from Swinford joined the main N5 road, which he told me had been built with the help of an EC grant. When he turned around to the back seat to sign the fridge, he laughed heartily when he saw the words 'Mo Chuisneoir' taped to its front.

'That means "My fridge" doesn't it?' he said.

'Yes.'

'I've seen it all now.'

About half a mile up the road I could see another hitcher. I had little choice but to start hitching where Michael had dropped me, but effectively by doing so, I was pushing in front of this other fellow. That didn't seem right, and it made me feel uncomfortable. No doubt I was experiencing some kind of inherited British need to play fair with regard to queuing. I think its roots are in the colonial thing. Shooting hordes of insubordinate natives was acceptable when 'needs must', but jumping a queue was *always* quite intolerable. The whole *raison d'être* for a vast British Empire had been a desire to teach the ignorant peoples of the world how to queue correctly. We British lead the world in queuing. (Well, we used to, until a few other countries pushed in front of us.) And here was I flouting my responsibility as a good British Citizen to respect this most basic of all human rights.

But what could I do? It was too far for me to drag my fridge and bags beyond this other hitch-hiker, and surely the onus was on him to rectify the situation. He must have been rather peeved that this other chap had pushed in front of him, but he showed no signs of marching down in my direction to protest.

This N5 was by far the best stretch of road I had come across since I had been in Ireland, but it certainly wasn't over-used. Cars and lorries came along at the rate of about one a minute. This was a frustrating length interval between vehicles, in that it was just long enough to feel that there wasn't going to be another along for a while, and to sit down on the fridge and relax, only to find that the moment I had done so I had to jump to my feet and begin hitching again.

The N5 was disappointing on another front too. Faced with the rare sight of a relatively smooth stretch of road before them, the Irish drivers clearly felt the urge to discover the maximum speed of their chosen mode of transport. This meant that the poor hitcher was only noticed at the very last minute as the driver hurtled past, and was all too quickly an afterthought. Perhaps this is why the hitcher ahead hadn't protested at my arrival in front of him, calculating that the breaking distance for any car that stopped for me, would be such that it would draw to a halt exactly where he was standing. Clever bastard.

I looked at my watch and saw that I had been there for over an hour. I didn't mind one bit. I was enjoying some precious time on my own. As a lone traveller I had expected a good deal more of it, but the way things were turning out, these roadside vigils were my only oases of peace.

Jack screeched to a halt. An emergency stop. Of course. If you saw the man with the fridge by the side of the road, what else was there for it? Boy, Jack was excited. He was a big fan of *The Gerry Ryan Show* and said that he had been charting my progress since day one. I climbed into the lorry's cabin which was packed full of boxes. There was only just room to squeeze in. I looked further up the road and saw that the other hitcher was still there. He can't have been that happy, but was probably consoling himself with the fact that I would be decent enough to implore the driver to stop for him too. I would have done had there been enough room.

As we drove past him I tried to do a kind of apologetic wave, which probably backfired and looked like I was rubbing salt in the wound. She waved back. She? I looked again and saw that, yes, it was a girl. Oh no! This offended my hereditary colonial sensibilities even more. For this, I would surely be hauled before the Viceroy of the Raj.

'Now Hawks, as you well know, we take a pretty dim view of anyone who pushes in front of the next man – but there is only one thing good enough for a man who stoops so low as to push in front of a woman. Perkins! Take him away, and have him shot.'

Jack was going to Westport, and was delivering fire extinguishers. I had never thought of fire extinguishers being delivered, but I was discovering that everything got to be where it was by being delivered.

Deliveries made the world go around. They were certainly getting me around.

'Elaine?' said Jack on his mobile phone. 'You'll never guess who I've got in the cabin with me.'

Elaine didn't guess, but Jack told her, and the phone was handed over for me to have a chat with her. It was an unusual conversation which hardly flowed, but the reason why it was taking place was an endearing one. Jack was excited to have the fridge man in his lorry, and he was excited to have Elaine as his girlfriend. I was reminded of something Gerry Ryan had said about my journey after I had spoken to him on my first morning.

'It's a totally purposeless idea, but a damn fine one.'

The same could be said of this phonecall.

Jack dropped me in the main street of Westport. I called out to a girl in the chemists, 'Do you know where Mat Molloy's pub is?'

'It's behind you,' she said, seven months too early for panto season.

I turned round and there it was, a simple semi-detached two-storey property decorated in red and black. It was odd to think that Marjorie's one mention of this neat little pub had been my reason for coming here to Westport, but that was the way I was allowing my journey to unfold. I was trusting my intuition. I elected to go in for a quick pint and then head for the tourist information office to sort out my night's lodgings.

It was mid afternoon and there were only six or seven customers in the pub. However it wasn't long before the winning combination of fridge and rucksack had everyone discussing the merits and drawbacks of this kind of travel.

'How much was the bet for?' said Niamh, who was working behind the bar for the summer.

'A hundred pounds.'

'And how much was the fridge?' enquired an interested bystander called John.

'A hundred and thirty pounds.'

'Jeez, you're an eejit,' added Seamus, the pub manager.

'Niamh, get this man a pint,' concluded Geraldine, the boss and wife of the eponymous Matt, plus mother of Niamh.

I was beginning to understand how the Irish mentality worked. The more foolish, illogical or surreal one's actions were perceived to be (and mine surely fell into one of these categories), the wider the arms of hospitality were opened in salutation. I now found myself surrounded by inquisitive customers and staff. Brendan appeared from behind the bar where he had been stacking bottles.

'Has the fridge got a name?'

'Well, no it hasn't.'

'Well you've got to give the fridge a name. You can't be travelling around with a nameless fridge.'

A chorus of approval greeted Brendan's sentiments.

'What sex is it?' asked Etain.

Things were moving too fast for me.

'I hadn't given it much thought.'

'There must be a way of telling.'

Amidst much amusement, a series of implausible methods were put forward, the most universally approved of which was proposed by John.

'What you have to do is you have to put it between two donkeys of either sex and see which one of the donkeys makes a move for the fridge.'

I was happy to accept this method as incontestable proof of the fridge's sex, but a distinct lack of donkeys restricted further progress down this particular scientific avenue.

'Why don't you give it a name which covers both sexes?' said Geraldine. 'You know, like Kim, Lesley or Val.'

'That's a good idea,' agreed Brendan, 'but you can't call a feckin' fridge Val!'

I concurred. No fridge of mine was going to be called Val.

'How about Saiorse?' suggested Seamus.

'Seersha?'

'Yes, Saiorse. It can be a boy or a girl's name, and it's Gaelic for "freedom". And you wont get many fridges experience more freedom than that one!' He had a point.

'Full name Saiorse Molloy,' said Geraldine.

'Sounds good to me,' I said, to cheers from the group. 'I hereby name this fridge Seersha Molloy.'

Geraldine was clearly moved by this new addition to the family, because she asked, 'Where are you staying Tony?'

'Oh, I haven't sorted it yet, I was going to find a bed and breakfast.'

'You can stay in the flat above the pub if you want.'

'Really?'

'Niamh, go and get the keys. Let's put him and Saiorse upstairs for the night.'

'Are you sure? That's very kind.'

A good portion of my time on this trip was spent thanking people for their kindness.

I couldn't have expected that a brief mention of the fridge's surfing activity would cause such a furore. The response was immediate, and it was as if the gauntlet had been thrown down. My new-found friends took it upon themselves to rise to the challenge of coming up with something whacky for me and the fridge to do. The suggestion that Seamus should take it water skiing was gaining in popularity, but Seamus, an apparently practical man, seemed to have some difficulty with this notion, although the rest of us couldn't see what the problem might be. Attach a rope, start the speed boat, and let Saiorse do the rest.

Geraldine introduced me to a couple called Tony and Nora, friends of hers and Matt, who had been visiting for a long weekend.

'If you're ever down in Ennistymon, we'll take Saiorse scuba diving,' said Tony, thrusting a piece of paper into my hand. 'Here's our address – you've no need to bother with hotels and the rest – you come and stay with us.'

'Are you sure that's not just the drink talking?' I joked.

'I don't drink,' he said, holding his orange juice proudly aloft.

This trip was full of surprises.

It was early evening before I got a chance to look around Westport. It would have been shameful if all I had got to see of the place was the inside of Matt Molloy's pub. Westport had been a prosperous landlord town, designed by architect James Wyatt in the eighteenth century. It only took me ten minutes or so to do a full circuit, and discover that its streets radiate from a focal point, the Octagon. There was a monument here with St Patrick on the top, proudly having taken the place of a British dignitary after the demise of British supremacy. The words beneath him made interesting reading:

I AM PATRICK

A SINNER MOST UNLEARNED

THE LEAST OF ALL THE FAITHFUL

AND UTTERLY DESPISED BY ALL

Now that guy had a self esteem problem, no two ways about it.

I saw a signpost saying Westport Quay, and since it was a nice evening I decided to walk there. It turned out to be further than I had thought, but worth it. I was lucky enough now to be experiencing weather for which the west coast of Ireland is most definitely not renowned. Clear blue skies and a gently setting sun hung over Clew Bay as I headed up a dusty path towards a grand-looking house I had seen in the distance. It was quite magnificent, and in a wonderful location, with stunning views across the bay. It was clearly the landlord's home around which the entire town of Westport had been built, to house the estate workers. I climbed through a hole in the perimeter fence of the grounds and indulged in a little trespassing. This was too special a house not to merit further investigation. Subsequently, I discovered that it was Westport House, and that by the following month it would be a commercialised tourist trap, but at the moment it was closed to the public and I genuinely believed that I was getting a privileged glimpse of some palatial splendour which was off limits to the hoi polloi.

On the walk back to Westport, out of nowhere some storm clouds appeared, and the heavens opened. I tried to hitch back, but the irony was that without my fridge, no one was remotely interested in stopping. By the time I got back to the pub, I was completely drenched. There was no one around from the afternoon's 'naming committee' so I took the opportunity to sneak upstairs, dry off, and profit from an early night.

As I lay in bed, the sounds of the pub below reminded me of times when, as a child, I was trying to get to sleep when my parents were entertaining downstairs. There even seemed to be someone down below with the same booming laugh as my father's, but presumably this man's raucous guffaws greeted other people's jokes rather than his own. But once I had nodded off, not even the traditional Irish music emanating from just beneath the floorboards could keep me from eight solid, sound, substantial hours of sleep.

Roisin hadn't called.

14

One Baptism And A Blessing

I woke, washed, decided to fix myself breakfast, and soon found myself in somebody else's kitchen. An awful place to be, especially if you need to make use of its facilities. There is no such thing as a simple operation, even something as modest as I was taking on – a pot of tea and a couple of pieces of toast – becomes a Gargantuan task and a severe test of patience. In somebody else's kitchen.

I started well. I located the kettle and even managed to work out how to turn it on. The hunt for the tea bags didn't go to plan, but after two or three minutes of slightly irritated opening and shutting of cupboard doors, they turned up in the one on the left just below the sink. Silly place for them, but I didn't let that get to me, and at this point I was still relatively calm. The hunt for the teapot was futile. It had been naive even to consider attempting to locate it. Those of you who are experienced in other people's kitchens will know that the teapot is always placed in the most idiosyncratic of locations, known only to close family members and passed down from generation to generation by oral tradition.

It got worse. They had no mugs. How could anyone have a kitchen with no mugs? This was a first. I looked everywhere. I covered every square inch of cupboard space, but there was not a mug anywhere. Except for me, the searcher, who for five full minutes was mug enough not to look in the dishwasher. Fifteen minutes later I was on the verge of doing something very silly with a sharp kitchen knife.

Fortunately I couldn't find one.

'That was very nice, thank you,' I said to the waitress as she took away my plate, on which were the scant vestiges of a full Irish breakfast.

I was just heading on out of the café when an elderly grey-haired woman approached me.

'Excuse me,' she said, 'you're not the window cleaning company are you?'

'No.'

'It's just that I'm meeting someone from the window cleaning company in here, and I don't know them.'

I shrugged and left the café, not at all envious of the morning that lay ahead for her – routinely addressing strangers and enquiring as to whether they were from the window cleaning company or not. Quite why the rendezvous had been set up at a café and not at a suitable address, or why a little old lady should require a meeting with a representative from the window cleaning company, I couldn't fathom. It didn't matter, in fact it fitted nicely into the ludicrous design of things.

By lunchtime I was back in the bar, having finished with Westport's launderette, and I was ready to say my goodbyes.

'Are you sure you have to leave today, Tony?' said Geraldine.

'Well, I think it's right to keep on moving.'

'That's a shame, because my husband Matt is back from Dublin tomorrow and I spoke to him on the phone and he's dying to meet you.'

'Another time, Geraldine, another time.'

'Well, will you have a quick pint before you go?'

This was dangerous. I had been here before. I had to be careful.

'Go on then,' I succumbed. Immediate surrender on the willpower front.

'Frank should be here in a minute,' said Niamh.

'Frank?'

'Yes, Frank. From the local paper, *The Mayo News*.'

'Local paper? What for?'

'He's going to get some photos of the baptism ceremony.'

'Oh. I didn't know about that.'

Brendan's head popped up from below the level of the bar.

'We christened Saiorse yesterday,' he said, 'today we baptise her.' Clearly this had all been decided in my absence, and who was I to stand in the way of a group of people who were set on baptising my fridge?

Just as Geraldine delivered me a pint of the black stuff, a young guy called Brian called into the pub, complaining of a hangover of epic proportions after having been on an enormous binge the previous day. He was pale and extremely shaky on his feet, and as he took hold of his pint, his hands were trembling. Shortly after he had been introduced to me, I announced to the group, 'Well, I'll just go upstairs and get my stuff, and then we'll get on with baptising the fridge.'

Brian looked at me in utter disbelief at what he had just heard. He glanced at the others and was even more perplexed by a set of expressions which showed no signs of having heard anything remotely out of the ordinary. He turned to me again, and was about to say something.

'Don't even ask,' I said.

He nodded obediently. He wasn't ready yet. We all knew he needed to finish that pint first.

The baptism ceremony took place on the pavement just outside the pub and was a humble affair. It constituted myself, Geraldine, Niamh, Brendan, Etain and Brian (who was now in the know), all gathering in deference round the fridge. Brendan held a small bottle of Babycham which was to be used in place of champagne, and the rest of us stood around wondering quite what was expected of us, whilst Frank enthusiastically took photos. Slowly a crowd of well-wishers gathered, some out of curiosity but I suspect most out of a complete absence of anything else to do.

Suddenly I seized the initiative. I cleared my throat, took a step forward and declared, 'We hereby name this fridge Saiorse Molloy. God bless all she rides in.'

It was a short, but few would deny, quite brilliant speech. Brendan poured some Babycham over the fridge and everyone cheered. One of the more nonconformist religious ceremonies was over.

Etain had disappeared up the road immediately after the formal service, but now she returned, proudly clutching a large blue certificate which she handed to me. It read:

SAIORSE
From Saiorse, a name of Irish origin,
Meaning 'freedom'
Faces problems head on
Admired for its originality, dedicated to worthy causes
A kind and generous fridge
It always stands firm for its principles
It does not have to get its own way always
Others think it is an extremely clever fridge
From Matt Molloys Pub
May 20th 1997

I was quite touched. I hadn't been given a certificate since I had passed Grade Six piano, and this one meant a great deal more.

As I stood and waited on a narrow band of road just outside Westport, it suddenly dawned on me that I had hardly seen any two-door cars. All four-door. Of course. One of the benefits of being in a good Catholic country. Fridge hitch-hiking is made easier by the fact that people have large families and therefore buy four-door cars. The neat little Fiat Punto that pulled up in front of me fifteen minutes later had been the first two-door I had seen.

'We heard you at breakfast, didn't we, Jane?' said Billy, from behind the wheel of the hire car.

'Yes, they had the radio on the hotel dining room and we started listening more closely when we heard your English accent.'

'So, when we saw the fridge, we knew it was you.'

'This is the first time we've stopped for a hitcher. I keep telling him to stop but he won't – will you, Billy?'

'Well, I have now.'

It was unusual to get a lift from a couple, especially with geordie accents. Well, almost.

'Technically we're not geordies, we're from Middlesborough,' Billy had explained.

'Oh. I'm sorry about the cup final.'

'Oh God, Tony. What a day. Thank goodness we're not back home. Course, we've lost Ravanelli, Juninho and Fester already.'

And so my first foray into the wilds of Connemara was complemented by a detailed analysis of Middlesborough's tragic season. Maybe it took the edge off my enjoyment of the bracken browns and soft violets of the mountains, but Billy and Jane had been decent enough to stop and give me and my fridge a lift, and they needed to get this football stuff out of their system. Better out than in, and I knew I was performing a necessary service by being the ears for their pain.

Just between 'Where the team really went wrong' and 'How the manager should build for the future', I had enough time to look out of the window and recall the snapshot of my new-found friends from Matt Molloy's waving me goodbye. Hey, I thought, they were more than friends now, they were family. Well, the fridge's family. In less than twenty-four hours we had achieved a genuine bond of affection which we had unwittingly formalised and cemented in our own childlike baptism ceremony. I reckoned I'd miss them.

Billy and Jane were on holiday touring around the west of Ireland and they absolutely loved the place. Jane was adamant that she wanted to uproot and settle there.

'It's great now, but maybe you should have a look what it's like in the middle of winter,' I said, offering creditable circumspection.

'Can't be a lot worse than Middlesborough,' said Billy, suggesting that he mightn't need too much arm twisting on the subject.

'So what exactly is Kylemore Abbey then, Tony?' asked Jane.

'It's a convent of Benedictine nuns.'

'And you're *sure* you want us to drop you there?'

'To be honest, I'm not sure if I'm sure of anything, but it feels like the right place to go next.'

There was a pause, before Billy asked, 'Do you mind if we ask why?'

'Not at all. It's just that this guy Brendan said that I ought to get the fridge blessed by the Mother Superior.'

Another pause. This time Jane broke the silence. 'Well you can't say fairer than that.'

And you couldn't. It may have been nonsensical, and whimsy bordering on the cavalier, but it certainly wasn't unfair.

You first see the abbey when you turn a corner in the road and the imposing turreted building becomes visible across a reedy lake, on whose shores it sits, sheltered by the wooded slopes of the hillside climbing steeply behind it.

'Wow!' gasped Billy. His exclamation, though not eloquent, couldn't have better summed up the sight that was before us.

In the abbey car park, Jane stooped over Saiorse to add her signature, and I noticed that the space available for such scribbles was filling up rather quickly. All the gang at Matt Molloy's had signed, plus a good proportion of the well-wishers outside the pub. Not having any connection whatsoever with the fridge or its owner had proved no disincentive for the shouting of 'Give me that marker pen so I can sign the feckin' thing!'

As I wheeled the fridge into the reception area of the abbey craft shop, in the corner of my eye I could see Billy and Jane watching me in amazement. It occurred to me that the reaction I was eliciting from people was almost becoming the fuel on which I was running. The more extraordinary my behaviour, the more I became liberated by it. I was on a roll and confidence couldn't be higher. There was no stopping me or Saiorse now.

The girl in reception looked taken aback. Nonplussed even. Yes, definitely nonplussed, and she did it rather well. Mind you, she had good reason for such a complex expression, for what I had asked her almost certainly didn't form part of her normal daily routine.

'Would it be possible to see the Mother Superior?' I had said. 'I want to get her to bless my fridge.'

'I'll get Sister Magdalena,' had been her reply.

That's right young lady, just pass the buck to Sister Magdalena as soon as things get a little tricky, why don't you?

Sister Magdalena looked long and hard at the fridge.

'And you're walking round Ireland with it?'

'Hitching.'

'Hitching. Oh I see.'

'And what are you raising money for?'

'I'm not. I'm doing it to win a bet.'

'I see.'

No she didn't. She didn't see at all. She went on, 'Well, Mother Clare is busy at the minute, but she may be able to see you before prayers.'

'Oh, that would be terrific.'

It would also give her something to pray about.

I took a stroll in the abbey's grounds, along the lakeside where I was surrounded by fuchsias and rhododendrons. I arrived at a small chapel, which I later discovered was built by the abbey's original owner, Mitchell Henry, a Manchester tycoon, landlord and member of parliament for Galway. He must have had some affection for Norwich Cathedral because he had instructed this Neo-Gothic chapel to be built as an exact replica in miniature of that church. Thankfully, the architects had the wisdom not to scale everything down, meaning that the chapel could be entered without going down on one's hands and knees and crawling through the door.

Mother Clare was a delightful woman with a gentle open expression. When Sister Magdalena announced to her what I was doing, her face lit up and she exclaimed, 'Good heavens! What have you got in the fridge? Is it any harm to ask?'

'I'm afraid it's got my dirty clothes at the moment.'

'Well, at least they'll stay cool. And you're taking the fridge all around the country?'

'I am.'

'Well, congratulations to you on your energy and enthusiasm.'

'I was wondering if you could bless the fridge and then sign it.'

'Of course.'

Naturally. It was all in the day's work of a Benedictine nun.

They must have taken a shine to me, these nuns, because I was invited to stay for an evening meal, but was then disappointed to find that this involved sitting on my own in a special visitors' dining room. I had hoped to sit with the nuns and quiz them about their lives, perhaps even ask one of them out. I like a challenge. After dinner I was asked if I would like to come and watch their choir practice. I did so, but soon regretted having said yes. They practised for a long time, and to be fair they needed to, but for me the novelty wore off after the first hour and a half.

Still shaken by the ordeal of choir practice, I was driven into Letterfrack, the nearest village, by Sister Magdalena. This was very pleasing, for when I had begun my journey I hadn't expected to get a lift from a nun. On the way, I sneezed quite loudly.

'Bless you,' she said.

How nice to hear this from someone with the appropriate qualifications.

15
The Longest Night

Some sort of music festival in the area meant that there were no vacancies in any of the bed and breakfasts in Letterfrack. Sister Magdalena left me outside a building which bore absolutely no resemblance to an old monastery, which was called The Old Monastery Hostel. A hostel, eh? I wasn't without misgivings, but at least its name maintained the ecclesiastical flavour to the day's proceedings. I went in and found nobody about. A message, chalked up on a blackboard, greeted travellers on arrival. 'Welcome. Please make yourselves comfortable by the fire. Someone will be with you shortly. Everything you need is on this floor; kitchen, living room, bathrooms and toilets. Breakfast is served at 9 am downstairs in the café. Breakfast is free and includes hot organic scones, hot cereal and organic coffee and tea. Relax, be happy and enjoy your stay.'

Too many things were organic for my liking. Without a pair of sandals, a musty aroma of henna about me, or my hair in a ponytail, I felt that I wouldn't be welcome here. I turned to my left and found myself in a large dormitory. Bunk beds seemed to be everywhere. For the first time on the trip since day one, I began to feel that I had bitten off more than I could chew. I selected a top bunk and marked out my territory by dumping my rucksack on it. I wheeled the fridge over to the window and left it there. I had made it into the dorm without anyone seeing that it was mine, and here was the opportunity to have a night off from the attention that went with being its owner. Besides, I thought it would be quite fun to let everyone in the hostel view each other with an element of suspicion, trying to establish which one of them was the idiot travelling around with a fridge. It might be the source of some healthy uneasiness.

A Chinese-looking fellow came in. I said 'hello' but he didn't respond. Either his knowledge of English didn't stretch as far as 'hello', or he was a git. Looking around the vast dormitory I could see the evidence, in the form of rucksacks dumped on bunks, of about fifteen other potential gits. Two nights ago, when I had lain in bed and wondered when I would next find myself 'not sleeping alone', this wasn't what I had in mind.

A young American couple came in, and I realised that the dormitory was mixed. The couple were followed by a big lady who I took to be Dutch. I was working from size alone, so this was a long shot. Whatever nationality she was, she had a greater grasp of English than the Chinese chap, because when I said 'hello', she said 'hello' back. I smiled politely at her and then turned to him and gave a look which was designed to say 'See, did that hurt?' He didn't see though, he was busy laying socks out on his bunk. It looked like he had embarked on some kind of ancient ritual in which the future could be read in the socks.

I caused at least three disapproving sharp intakes of breath from the room when I plugged my mobile phone into one of the power points to recharge it.

'Sorry,' I announced, realising that this sort of behaviour was about as incompatible with organic scones as you could get.

It had to be done though, because I knew that *The Gerry Ryan Show* would want to talk to me in the morning, and besides, enough ground had been covered now to warrant a call to Kevin in England in order to let him know that his hundred pounds was in some jeopardy.

'Hello, Kevin?' I said, sitting on top of a stile halfway up a mountain in the Connemara National Park.

I don't have many good things to say about mobile phones but one plus point is the freedom they offer you to choose exciting mountainous landscapes for your office space. A short walk from the hostel had brought me to a spot where, to the north, I could see moorland dominated by the Twelve Bens mountain range, and to the west, the deeply indented Atlantic coastline with its many inlets and creeks. I was looking forward to Kevin's next question,

'Whereabouts are you?' he obliged.

I told him, at some length.

'And what about the fridge? I suppose you dumped that days ago?'

'No. I've still got it with me, well, not exactly at this moment, it's back at the hostel.'

'Hostel? So you're living like a King then?'

'Most of the time I am actually.'

Unfortunately like the King of Tory.

'Yeah, yeah, I bet.'

'I'm just warning you that it looks like I'm going to *do* this. I am going to hitch-hike round Ireland with a fridge. So you'd better start talking to your bank manager about arranging a one-hundred-pound overdraft.'

'Look, you're not even halfway round yet. Things will go wrong. I'm not going to start to worry until you're a couple of miles outside Dublin. The thing you forget is–'

The line went dead as the signal disappeared.

At least that's what he thought. The fact is that I had pressed the button which cut him off. Another plus point to the mobile phone. I didn't need a dose of cynicism just now. I shouldn't have called. Showing off. I just hadn't been able to resist it.

As I walked down the hill back to the hostel, for some reason I began singing the Johnny Nash song, 'I can see clearly now the rain has gone, I can see all obstacles in my way.'

I stopped and said to myself, 'No, I can't. That's the beauty of this. I can't see any obstacles at all.'

I had cut off the conversation with Kevin just at the moment when he had been about to point out what some of the obstacles might be. I figured that the person who didn't know that there were any obstacles, was always going to be ahead of the person who had to go around them because he or she knew where they were. This philosophy could either get me to where I wanted to be, or land me in hospital as a result of having run headlong into something which had very little give in it.

It was a straight choice. A walk down to the local pub, or an evening in the sitting room with the hardy backpacking community. For health reasons I chose the latter.

The sitting room was a large room with a dining table at one end and a great open fire dominating the other. The dining table was full of people with dyed hair and pierced noses, with their heads buried in thick paperbacks. By the fire, there were some chairs where a less formidable looking group were seated. The most comfortable looking armchair was occupied by the hostel dog, and moving him would clearly be considered sacrilege and wouldn't win me any friends. However, there was one tatty looking chair free, so I sat down in it. Immediately I felt conspicuous. It had been a bad mistake not bringing a book in with me. Everyone else appeared to be reading, and it looked as if I was there purely to keep the others from this laudable activity. Seeing that the kitchen was within easy reach through an archway, I stood up, clasped my hands and rubbed them together.

'Right,' I said, like an embarrassing teacher who was trying too hard to be liked by his pupils, 'does anyone want a cup of tea?'

Most ignored me completely, but some managed to look up from their reading and shake a head. The class of 4b were a tough lot. Wholesale rejection. Not a good start.

Moments later, and for the second time in a day, I found myself in somebody else's kitchen. Naturally enough, I couldn't find the tea bags anywhere. After some banging about and cursing under the breath which must have aggravated the readers in the sitting room, I was forced into popping my head round the door with the humiliating question, 'Does anyone know where the tea bags are?'

There was at least one tut, and two sighs. An American guy, who was nearest to the fire, looked up at me, 'Do you not have your own?'

'What?'

'You're supposed to bring your own.'

'Oh, yes, of course.'

I sat down, thinking that someone would find it in their hearts to offer me one of their tea bags. Initially no one did, but when I concentrated on looking really forlorn, the American girl on my right capitulated, 'You can have one of my tea bags if you want. But they're lemon and ginger. Do you like lemon and ginger?'

I had no idea. Independently of each other, I had no aversion to either, but I had never experienced the two together before. Why should I have done? I didn't experiment with drugs.

'Lemon and ginger? Yes, I think so, thanks, that's very kind of you,' I replied, taking the tea bag and disappearing back into the kitchen to cover it with boiling water.

On my return, the American girl watched with interest as I took my first sip. As the tea collided with my taste buds, I immediately came to the conclusion that ginger was as beneficial a partner to lemon, as mittens were to concert pianists.

'Mmm, interesting flavour,' I coughed, only just refraining from my initial instinct to spit it straight back out again. 'Interesting'. What a splendidly ambiguous adjective. It was my favourite euphemism for food that I didn't like at dinner parties.

'Interesting recipe . . . interesting flavour'. Interesting that you contrived to create such a hideous, foul tasting dish.

I began to chat with the two Americans, and couldn't work out whether they were just good friends travelling together or whether their relationship went beyond that. I certainly didn't want to be kept awake tonight by any noises which might clear the matter up. There were two others sat by the fireside. One was a Swedish girl, who joined in my chat with the Americans, and who had a large and fresh-looking love bite on her neck, which I hoped hadn't been the product of a night spent in this hostel. The other member of the fireside team was a girl who I found rather pretty, and whom I would have sat next to if the hostel dog hadn't got in there first. She said nothing, but read constantly. However, at faintly amusing moments in our conversation, she smiled, which made me suspect that she wasn't really reading but eavesdropping on a conversation to which she wasn't prepared to contribute.

'So what are you doing here in Ireland?' I was eventually asked by the American guy.

I attempted to give as little away as possible but my caginess only served to make him more inquisitive, and as the questions continued, I eventually made the mistake of revealing that I was in Ireland because of a bet.

Naturally enough, he wanted to know what the bet was. I lowered my voice and told him about the fridge business. Suddenly, the pretty girl who was reading, looked up from her book.

'Are you the guy with the fridge?' she asked.

'I am.'

'You stole my lift.'

'What?'

'Yesterday. You stole my lift.'

Up until this moment, the coincidences in my life hadn't been that impressive. The best I had managed involved bumping into people I knew at airports. Sleeping in the same dormitory as the girl who I had pushed in front of when hitching, was probably going to edge into the lead. I owed her an apology.

'I'm so, so sorry,' I said.

'It's all right.'

'I would have asked the driver to stop for you too, but there simply wasn't room.'

'Because of the fridge, right?'

'Er, yes.'

'I waited two and a half hours there, you know.'

All right, don't make things worse. I felt bad enough as it was.

Tina was hitching around Ireland before returning to her native Denmark to study psychology. Like so many from her part of the world, she had that disarming ability to fully participate in an English conversation without anyone else needing to make the slightest compensation for the fact that it wasn't her native tongue. She was extremely pleasant and I began to feel very bad about the hitching business. Had we been in a hotel, I could have got to my feet and said that the least I could do was buy her a drink, perhaps even order a bottle of champagne, but in present circumstances my hands were tied rather. All I could do was offer her a cup of lemon and ginger tea, provided my American supplier didn't let me down. In the event, I took her address in Denmark and promised to send her an atonement present. She smiled courteously and went off to bed. As she reached the door I had this terrible urge to call out after her, 'I'll be up in a minute, darling', but I realised there was no audience for such a remark, and restrained myself.

When the conversation started to dry up, I said my goodnights and made my way into the dormitory. It was dark, and I was unsure of which bunk was mine. I became conscious of the immense embarrassment I would feel were I to crawl into the wrong bunk. The big Dutch woman, Tina, and the unfriendly Chinese man were all potential victims of my disorientation and their reactions to a visitor climbing in to join them could range from a welcoming embrace to a kung fu kick to the groin or screams that this was the wrong kind of atonement present. However, I could just make out the faint outline of the fridge, which was by the window, and knew if I got to that, I could take my bearings from it and work my way back to my bunk. This was yet another first, a fridge used for navigational purposes.

I tried to undress as quietly as I could, but the more I tried, the more clumsy I became. I knocked belongings off my bunk and on to the floor, and very nearly toppled over whilst attempting to remove my jeans, getting my foot stuck in one of the legs. Each sound I was making seemed deafening. I was developing a heightened awareness of sound which wasn't going to be my ally when I shortly took on the formidable task of falling asleep.

It began well enough though, as I got comfortable rather quickly. But it soon became apparent that I was making the same mistake I make when I try to get to sleep on planes. I think too much about the whole process. As I wriggle into a newly coiled position in the inadequately proportioned airline seat, I think to myself, 'Yes, that should do it . . . that's a comfortable position . . . five minutes of that and I should be right off.'

Of course it is only a matter of seconds before a slight ache develops somewhere in the body and you realise that this posture isn't the gateway to uninterrupted slumber that you had hoped.

I'm not a light sleeper and have no problems in this department normally. In fact I'm good at sleeping. I sleep well. I make hardly any mistakes. If there was an Olympic event called 'sleeping', I would have a good chance of being selected for the British team. Actually, I think they should introduce 'sleeping' to the Olympics. It would be an excellent field event, in which the 'athletes' (for want of a better word) all lay down in beds, just beyond where the javelins land, and the first one to fall asleep and not wake up for three hours would win gold. I, for one, would be interested in seeing what kind of personality would be suited to sleeping in a competitive environment. And what a prospect – a commentator becoming excited at a competitor 'nearly nodding off', or expressing disappointment at the young British lad tragically being woken by a starter's pistol, when only another five minutes in the land of nod would have won him a bronze. (And who would want to miss the slow-motion action replays?)

I looked at my watch. It was 1.30. It wasn't as if I hadn't been close to falling asleep. It had nearly happened twice. On each occasion my drift towards this peaceful state had been disturbed by a small explosion. This was the hostel's central heating system which had been spitefully designed to fire up every forty minutes. The intervals between explosions afforded enough time for one to get extremely sleepy, but not sufficiently so to avoid an abrupt awakening at the next outburst from the hostel's boilers.

At 2.00 am, most of those who had been lucky enough to relinquish consciousness had it restored by the noisy return of the occupant of the bunk below me. Telltale signs such as belching and singing, suggested that this man, when faced with a straight choice of what to do with his evening, hadn't gone for the healthy option. It wasn't escaping my noticed that this man had made the correct decision for this situation, for as soon as he had completed a blundering and noisy shedding of his clothes, his head hit the pillow and he began snoring. Well, not quite. He was *almost* snoring. The deep breaths were there, and the accompanying snorting sounds were there too, but only at a faint volume. It was clear this man had the potential to snore very loudly, but that this was something he preferred to warm up to. It was vital to fall asleep *before* he reached his full volume.

I failed in this regard, and one hour later he had worked his way up to a level of snoring which would have won him medals in the European Championships. All the evidence was there to suggest that in another quarter of an hour he would reach his peak, and produce snores which would rival some of the best in the world. I was alone in my concern because I could tell from the clearly audible breathing patterns of the others in the dormitory, that everyone had managed to fall asleep except me.

Being on the receiving end of snoring wasn't a new experience for me, but I had never experienced the sound coming from directly beneath me before. Somehow this made it considerably more disconcerting, and gave the distinct impression that some kind of geological upheaval was imminent. In the dead of night rational thinking vanishes, and although Ireland wasn't renowned for its earthquakes and volcanoes, at least two clamorous rumbles from beneath my bunk made me sit bolt upright in fear.

I'm against the death penalty. I believe that it is a mistake to show that killing people is wrong, by killing people. However I'm not against the random killing of people who snore. Okay, I accept that it is harsh, barbaric and against every decent human value, but the simple fact is that there is no other cure for snoring. People have tried myriad remedies, and none of them work. All right, you can wake them, but they're only going to fall back to sleep again and begin all over again. The only truly effective way to stop someone snoring is to kill them.

I lay in my bunk considering my options. Suffocation seemed the most appropriate, but strangling I liked also. My feeling was that there wasn't a court of justice anywhere which would not be sympathetic to the mitigating circumstances of my present plight. But then, quite suddenly, he stopped. He just stopped snoring as if he had received news from a politician that a ceasefire had been agreed. The silence was no comfort. I knew that this was only a temporary cessation of hostilities and that he would begin snoring again soon, so I was aware that this next period was crucial if I was going to fall asleep. I had to act now. I rolled on to my side, closed my eyes and offered up my consciousness.

There were no takers. Evidently, mine wasn't a personality suited to sleeping under this kind of pressure. I had no place in the British Olympic sleeping team after all. It was one thing falling asleep in training, and another when you were up against the clock.

The night dragged on.

Here, in brief, are the other major events of the night:

3.30 am. Drunk recommences snoring.

3.45 am. Sympathy snorer on other side of dormitory starts up. (Stereo effect created.)

4.30 am. Get up and go to toilet. Stub toe on corner of bunk.

4.33 am. Return from toilet and stub same toe on different corner of bunk.

4.55 am. Give serious consideration to shouting at the top of my voice, 'LOOK EVERYONE, GET OUT OF MY ROOM!!'

5.05 am. Consider suicide as an option.

5.07 am. Reject suicide as an option on the grounds that it would be too noisy, and wake people up.

5.15 am. Decide this night is penance for stealing Tina's lift. Give up, and resign myself to a night of no sleep.

5.16 am. Fall asleep.

6.30 am. Woken by Chinese-looking man's alarm clock going off.

6.31 am. Decide killing is too good for Chinese-looking man. Will take contracts out on his loved ones.

8.00 am. Decide to get up.

8.01 am. Discover that I have an unnecessary and unwarranted erection.

8.01–8.30 am. Wait for dormitory to empty.

8.32 am. Dormitory almost empty. Risk getting up. Big Dutch lady sees unusual bulge in my boxers. She smiles.

8.40–9.10 am. Breakfast, spent avoiding eye contact with big Dutch lady.

9.30 am. Leave the premises, swearing never to stay in a hostel again, as long as I live.

The longest night was behind me.

16

Down And Out In Galway

The nation needed an update on my recent adventures. On air, Gerry Ryan astutely picked up on one common thread which ran through them all.

'Tony, you seem to be spending most of your time in pubs, I think it's important to point that out at this stage.'

'Well, the trouble is, Gerry, I can't get out of them. I go in and I've got a fridge in tow, and it isn't long before the exit door is barred and that's it, I'm stuck there.'

'I must use that as an excuse myself one day.'

He was right, of course; I had been spending most of my time in pubs. The irony is that the one night when I didn't go anywhere near one, I ended up with less than two hours' sleep.

'Watch out folks,' said Gerry, winding up our interview, 'he's in Letterfrack, and he's heading for Galway today, so if you see a gentleman looking reasonably benign with a fridge by his side, please do stop and say hello and if he doesn't seem threatening, well then, please give him a lift. Bon voyage once again Tony, we'll keep in touch.'

I pulled the fridge down to the roadside, tired, but knowing that these conversations that I had on national radio were the equivalent of filling a vehicle's tank full of petrol. I was fresh in the minds of the nation's drivers and once they set eyes on the fridge, they were only too happy to throw open that passenger door.

Then a problem. There was only one spot suitable for hitching, and someone was already hitching in it. I wasn't prepared for this. I ought to have been. Eighteen years of Tory government back home should have left me comfortable enough with the concept of competition.

'Oh hi,' I said to my peer, nervously, 'I'll just move on twenty yards or so shall I?'

'No, no. You're all right here. I'm in no hurry.'

'What?'

'I don't mind at all, off you go.'

And with his hand, the young lad offered me the roadside before him.

'But you were here first.'

'I know, but I'm not the man with the fridge, am I? Honestly, I'm in no hurry, off you go. Best of luck to you. Where are you headed?'

'Clifden, then Galway, I think.'

'Ah, you'll have no problems. Not with that thing in front of you.'

Padrig, a student at the woodwork school which was directly behind us, sat on a nearby wall and chatted to me whilst I hitched away. A number of cars came by and indicated to me that they were shortly turning off, by pointing to the left.

'I hate it when they do that,' said Padrig, 'because there *are* no left turns on the stretch of road between here and Clifden.'

I had to admire his pedantry.

A young van driver pulled up who knew Padrig quite well, but he only had room for one person and a fridge in his van, so it was a case of 'second come, first served' and Padrig stayed where he was. He didn't mind one bit, and he waved enthusiastically as Brian drove me off towards Clifden. Brian shared what was becoming a universal approval of my quest, and made a stop to show me off at the hand-weavers craft store where he worked, where I was given a cup of tea and a sandwich, and encouraged to sign the visitors book.

By one o'clock I had walked through quaint Clifden, the town which passes for the capital of Connemara, and set myself up on the solitary main road out of town. Fatigue was setting in, and I was barely able to keep my eyes open as I slumped down on my fridge and stuck my thumb out once again. A driver in a lorry from the building site opposite saw me and called out, 'Is that a washing machine?'

How nice, a variation on a theme.

'No, a fridge,' I replied.

'Oh right. I hope you do okay where you are. I've seen hitchers there for a very long time.'

Ah, but they probably didn't have fridges, I thought.

Half an hour later, with my continued presence by the roadside bearing out his words, the builder returned with his load, and on seeing me, shrugged sympathetically. I shrugged back. It had been a meaningless exchange, but oddly, it had lifted my spirits ever so slightly, just at a point when they needed it. Shrugging, I decided, was good. More people should shrug. You never see a politician shrug (they see it as a sign of weakness), but surely one of the reasons the problems in Northern Ireland have been so prolonged is because the politicians on either side never shrug. There is no other physical gesture which comes as close to an embodiment of the fridge philosophy – a quiet acceptance of what has gone, and a healthy lack of concern about what is to come.

Two Spanish-looking types cycled by on bikes, catching sight of the fridge and nearly falling off. When they had gone past, one of them turned and yelled back.

'Hey, good luck, man!'

That was nice of him. It made me feel good, a Spanish cyclist responding positively to a fridge. Perhaps I'd do this in Spain next year.

The cyclist's wish was fulfilled and good luck arrived in the form of Matt, whose job was driving around Mayo and Galway repairing any tills, slicers and scales which went on the blink. I suppose that just as things needed delivering, they needed repairing too. Matt was getting married in three months.

'It's embarrassing though,' he said, 'because if you're getting married in a church, you have to go on a pre-marital course.'

'Run by who?'

'The Catholic Church, the priests.'

'And how long is this course?'

'Two days.'

Terrific idea. Two days of advice on how to cope with married life, from a body of people who have never been married, and don't indulge in any sexual activity. (Now don't scoff, it's true – they don't.)

'And what happens at the end of the course?'

'They give you a certificate. You can't get married in a church without it.'

'So it's compulsory?'

'No, it's not compulsory, but you have to do it.'

Matt dropped me in the car park of a big shopping centre on the outskirts of Galway, having driven about forty miles out of his way to do so, and after thanking him profusely I began pulling my belongings into the town centre. The trolley, which up to now had performed way beyond my expectations, for some reason or other insisted on shedding its load every thirty yards or so. A less tired man would have coped with it better than I did. It was a long way into the town centre, and I passed no hotels or B&Bs on the way in. Had it not been for the occasional supportive toot of a car horn, or shout of encouragement from a friendly Galway shopper, I might have lifted the fridge on to the nearest skip and called the whole thing off.

I had decided to reward myself with a nice hotel tonight, regardless of cost, but was dismayed to find them all full. Or maybe that was just what they told me. I must have looked a bedraggled figure, struggling into reception carrying a rucksack and pulling a fridge behind me on a distinctly wobbly trolley, so I probably didn't represent the select clientele they actively sought. The last receptionist to reject me produced a list of bed and breakfast phone numbers.

From the street, I put the mobile into action. A woman answered.

'Hello, Stella speaking.'

'Hello Stella, my name is Tony, do you have any vacancies?'

'I do Tony, for how many is it?'

'One.'

She gave me the address and started to give directions. I stopped her, 'No, it's all right, I'll get a taxi.'

'Where are you?'

'Quay Street.'

'Oh, you don't need to get a taxi, you're very near.'

'Are you sure? It's just that I've walked a long way already, and I've got a fridge with me.'

There had been no need to mention it, but experience so far had shown me that if people had heard about my adventure, their attitude changed dramatically towards me. Stella was definitely not in the know.

'A *what*?'

'A fridge. I'm travelling with a fridge.'

'I see. Well either way you'll not want to be bothering with a taxi, it's not far.'

It *was* far. It was very far, and what's more Stella's directions made no sense. Half an hour and three mobile phone calls later, I finally reached the guest house, in the heart of the Galway suburbs, and Stella, a smiling middle-aged woman with suspiciously black hair, answered the door.

She clocked the fridge, 'Oh, so you weren't joking then. You should have got a taxi with that thing.'

Over a cup of tea I learned two important pieces of information. That *Pet Rescue* was Stella's favourite television programme, and that her memory for names was on a par with her ability to issue accurate directions.

'Whereabouts in England are you from, Chris?' she asked.

'London.'

I was about to tell her that Chris wasn't my name, but I checked myself, finding that being called Chris made a pleasant change.

'Ooh London, that's a coincidence, Chris, because I've just had another lad from London arrive, a quarter of an hour ago. He's upstairs, you might meet him later.'

I never did, but Stella explained that when he had arrived, because of his English accent, she had assumed that he was me, and had asked him where his fridge was. She didn't tell me what his reply was, and we can only hazard a guess, but I was impressed that he had been prepared to stay the night. It is surely a brave man who goes ahead and checks into an establishment where the first question is 'Where's your fridge?' Especially if, as he had done, you had arrived by motorcycle.

Stella cooked a homely evening meal for myself and Owen, the student lodger from Kildare, to whom I had carelessly introduced myself as Tony.

'Do you want more dessert, Chris?' Stella asked me.

Owen looked around the room for a Chris.

'Yes please,' I replied, with the only sensible answer to that question.

Owen shrugged. Good lad. Correct response.

Gerry Ryan had spoken highly of Galway;

'You'll be much welcomed in Galway I can tell you, there are some fine hostelries, and indeed a very learned and cultured people they are too,' he had said.

But exhaustion meant that my experience of Galway was limited to an evening with Owen, in front of the TV in Stella's living room, watching Ireland play Liechtenstein at football. And I had to call on all my reserves of energy even to manage that much. I quite enjoyed the game, but mainly because the positioning of the microphones at the ground were such that the comments of some of the crowd were clearly audible: 'Come on Kennedy! Move your arse on you!' offered an old man supportively.

It worked, Kenny did move his arse on him, and Ireland won 5-0. Owen was happy enough, and as I said goodnight, I congratulated him on his team's performance. It would have been churlish to have pointed out that Liechtenstein were hardly giants in the world of football.

I was woken in the morning by my mobile phone ringing. It was Galway Bay FM wanting to do an interview. My number was evidently doing the rounds. They said they would call back in twenty minutes, and as I waited, I tuned into their frequency to get a flavour of what they were all about. I heard the adverts. One stood out above all the others. An excitable voice announced with gusto: 'Come to Ballingary, County Tipperary, this Saturday May 24 from 10 am to 6 pm, for the event of a lifetime – SHEEP '97!'

I liked it already. The overly excited man continued, 'Events include the RDS National pedigree sheep championships, plus competitions for lambs, wool and sheep shearing. There'll be a display by David Fagan, the current world shearing champion, and many information and trade exhibits, assessments and repair of silage pits, machinery displays, *and* a major high-speed wilting demonstration! So call 067 21282 for further information, and remember, if you're in the business of sheep rearing, then get along to SHEEP '97!!'

Never mind whether you're in the business of sheep rearing or not, SHEEP '97 has got to be a must for the entire family hasn't it? Is there a healthy ten-year-old anywhere who wouldn't be chomping at the bit to get to an 'assessment or repair of a silage pit'? And only a fool would miss a 'major high-speed wilting demonstration'. Most of us don't get to see any wilting, but those of us who do, only see it taking place at a snail's pace. At last! An opportunity to see wilting not only done well, but at high speeds. The mind boggled. If fate delivered me anywhere near Ballingary on Saturday, then SHEEP '97 could count on my presence. I could take Roisin. If she phoned. That was a point – why hadn't she phoned? Ah well, patience Tony, patience. To my delight, just before Keith Finnegan began his interview, the SHEEP '97 ad came on again, and this time I noticed that the accent of the voiceover artist was such that the word 'shearer' sounded like 'sharer'. So, for some, this advert included the sentence, '. . . plus competitions for lambs, wool, and sheep sharing.'

That should guarantee a few pervy-looking types turning up for entirely the wrong reasons, and with their own very personalised definitions of 'high speed wilting'.

Keith Finnegan, understandably enough, covered much of the same ground as Gerry Ryan and *Live At Three* had done. 'Why?' being the most important and natural question to ask. Once I had explained my case, and told him I was headed south, Keith happily signed up to the merry band of those who wanted to help me, and put out an appeal for a taxi driver to take me to the main road out of town. Within seconds, a driver from Ocean Hackneys responded, and said he was on his way to pick me up. I thanked Keith, hung up, smiled, looked in the mirror, and pinched myself. No, I was awake all right, this was really happening.

I took out my map and scanned the area south of Galway for a suitable destination. I saw a place called Ennistymon and recognised it as being the town on the piece of paper handed to me in Westport by Tony, the man who had offered to take the fridge scuba diving.

Ennistymon it was then, unless fate intervened.

Rescued

I asked Noel, the taxi driver, why he had responded to the radio station's call.

'Because you've got guts and a sense of humour.'

I suppose both were prerequisites for what I was doing.

Noel signed the fridge with a flourishing hand and left me standing with my thumb out just the other side of a roundabout at the edge of a busy dual carriageway. The mobile phone rang again. I heard a cockney voice, "Ello, is that Tony?'

'Yes, is that Andy?' I thought it was Andy from Bunbeg, ringing to see how I was getting on.

'No, it's Tony. From Swan Rescue.'

'What?'

'If you tell me whereabouts you are, I'll come and pick you up.'

What on earth was going on? An Englishman called Tony appeared to have taken me for a swan and was on his way to rescue me.

'I 'eard you on the radio this mornin',' explained Tony, 'and I thought I'd come and give you a lift, so tell me exactly where you are.'

I did precisely that, to which he responded, 'Stay there, and I'll be with you in ten minutes. Look out for a small white van with Swan Rescue written on the side.'

It was difficult to imagine a more peculiar set of circumstances. I now found myself by a roadside hitching but not actually wanting a lift, and, to be sure of not getting one, I had to hide my fridge, fearing that its fame would cause someone to stop, regardless of whether I was hitching or not. I propped my rucksack up against it and draped my jacket over the top. I had broken new ground in the world of hitch-hiking. I was taking bookings.

Twenty minutes later I was beginning to think I had been the victim of the world's oddest hoax call, but sure enough the Swan Rescue van appeared, and I was rescued. It didn't seem to matter that I wasn't a swan. The net had been thrown wide enough that day to encompass wayward hitch-hikers.

'How far are you going?' I asked Tony.

'I'm not *going* anywhere, but I'll take you as far as Gort.'

'What do you mean you're not going anywhere?'

'I'm not going anywhere. I came out specially to give you a lift – you know – to lend an 'elpin' 'and. I'll take you as far as Gort, that's about an hour from here.'

The behaviour of the English people I had run into was making it very difficult to nail down a theory that the reason my trip so far had been such a bizarre success, was that Irish people were crazy. One Englishman had spent a morning on the telephone trying to organise a helicopter to take me out to an island, when a boat was leaving only a few yards away, and here was another, making a two-hour round trip for no reason other than to lend a helping hand. Two of the more eccentric pieces of behaviour hadn't been performed by the Irish, but by my fellow countrymen. However, both Andy and Tony had embraced wholeheartedly a love of the Irish way of living life.

'I spent most of my life in Hampton Court,' explained Tony, 'but I love it 'ere. You *live* life 'ere. In England you exist.'

I think it was fair to say that Tony wasn't exactly rushed off his feet over here either. The fact that he could afford to make this purely philanthropic journey suggested to me that there simply weren't enough swans in the Galway area that needed rescuing. It seemed an odd life sitting by the phone waiting for an emergency call of a swan in distress. Would he be busier if he didn't limit himself totally to swans? I was intrigued as to what his response would be if he received a call with reference to an injured duck. 'Oh, I'm sorry, you've got the wrong number – we're *swan* rescue. You want *duck* rescue; if you hold on I'll get you the number'.

Tony dropped me in a driveway at the end of the dreary and sparse Gort main street. Most of the traffic passing appeared to be local, and I began to feel like a swan which hadn't so much been rescued as picked up and moved on to another less salubrious pond. There wasn't an awful lot to Gort, and what there was of it, didn't exactly inspire. Gort. It looked like it sounded. I settled down to what I believed would be a long wait.

I hadn't been there long when I was approached by a smiling drunk with no teeth.

'Oi, you're the man with the fridge!' he shouted.

It was yet another English accent. He took a swig from a can of cider and pointed to another one he had in a string bag. 'Do you wanna drink?'

'No thanks, I'm trying to avoid drinking at lunchtime.'

'Me too, but I've got a broken jaw.'

I recalled Gerry Ryan's words: 'I must use that as an excuse myself one day.'

'My name's Ian, what's yours?' he offered in tribute to playground talk.

'Tony.'

'Where are you headed?' he slurred.

'Ennistymon.'

He pointed meaningfully just beyond me and pronounced, 'Give me five minutes.'

Was this another booking? If it was, and if this man was the driver just off to pick up his car, I would have to find a polite way of turning it down. It mightn't be easy, but it would have to be done.

Five minutes later a decrepit looking vehicle emerged from a narrow lane behind me. Inside it I could see four bodies, one of which was my toothless chum, who was beaming away in the back. He wound down the window and shouted out, 'Jump in! We can take you as far as Ennis.'

I needed to think long and hard about this, but there wasn't time, so I thought short and hard and decided to risk it. In the end, I was swayed by the fact that the driver had no can of drink in his hand, and considerably more teeth than Ian. I know that a glimpse of a full set of teeth isn't necessarily a tried and tested method of verifying someone's driving skills, but I believe it's generally used in an emergency.

I was bundled into the back with Ian and a small child, and the fridge was unceremoniously dumped in the boot. We were in an old Toyota Carina which was the vehicular equivalent of Ian's face: gnarled, toothless, but still running. It made Antoinette's car seem shiny and new.

I was in the company of travellers. Ian was a veteran of twenty years on the road, whilst Neil, Vicky and their small son were relative newcomers to this community existence. They liked it though, preferring a caravan to a semi-detached in Sheffield. We talked about their lifestyle, which seemed agreeable enough, although it was based on a fundamental belief that the rest of society should be prepared to subsidise it.

'How do you manage for money?' I asked.

I was given two simultaneous replies of 'We get by' from Ian and 'Don't ask' from Neil. I favoured Ian's reply because it had less-sinister connotations. 'Don't ask' left open the possibility that they raised funds by selling hitch-hikers into slavery. I changed the subject.

'Where is your base at the moment?' I asked, incompetently addressing them as if they were in the RAF.

'Right slap in the middle of the Burren,' replied Ian.

The Burren – that rang a bell. I'd read about that. One hundred square miles of sculpted grey limestone formed by glaciation and wind and rain erosion. A surveyor for Cromwell in the 1640s had described it as 'a savage land, yielding neither water enough to drown a man, nor tree to hang him, nor soil enough to bury'. A summary which rather gave away the principle objective of Cromwell's excursions in Ireland.

'Are we near the Burren here then?' I enquired ignorantly.

'It's just east of where we are now,' said Vicky. 'You came from Galway and you're headed for Ennistymon, aren't you?'

'Yes.'

'Well, you would have driven right through the middle of it if you'd followed the coast instead of coming through Gort.'

Good old Swan Rescue. I had been rescued from experiencing one of the geological wonders of the world, said to remind some visitors of the surface of the moon. Instead I had seen Gort. Still, something to tell the grandchildren.

Paddy, a green keeper at the local golf course, was my final ride. When he stopped, he had thought that I had bought the fridge in town and was bringing it home. It was reassuring to get lifts from people who weren't aware of what I was doing as a result of hearing it on the radio. It proved that the task in hand could be achieved without media assistance, though it was questionable whether it would be so much fun. From the car I called Tony and Nora's and arranged to meet Tony at a pub called Daly's in Ennistymon's main street.

In Ennistymon I felt like I was in the unspoiled heart of rural Ireland. It was a pretty place with colourful shop fronts and an abundance of small bars, but there was no sense of all this being there for the benefit of tourists. I looked up and down the main street and counted more than twenty bars. Presently I learned that at one time there had been forty-two, all there largely to serve the customers for the cattle market which used to swell the town's population many times over.

I located Daly's, a tiny bar directly next to two others – Davoren's and P. Begley's. I noted that P. Begley's was closed and assumed it had fallen victim to the intense competition. I walked into Daly's and was greeted by the usual turning of surprised heads. One head wasn't so surprised. Tony's.

'Ah look! The eejit has landed!' he announced.

A pint was poured and the fridge was lifted to a place of honour on a bar stool alongside us, and to any pub newcomer it would have appeared like just another regular drinker. Tony told me that he had to go and pick up his daughter from school and that when he got back he'd take me on a sightseeing tour of the area.

I noticed that a man with a healthy head of white hair and matching beard had been surveying the fridge with interest as he slowly supped on his pint. After a few minutes we made eye contact, and he nodded to me, pointing at the fridge on its bar stool, 'Ah sure, it's nice enough to see it out of context.'

I was delighted by the measured delicacy of his remark, which was in stark contrast to the usual uproarious reaction which the fridge would elicit. I went and joined him.

His name was Willy Daly, and he was the owner having a quiet drink in his own pub. A few minutes into our conversation I discovered that he had probably earned a sit down, since he ran a farm, a pony-trekking business, a pub, a restaurant and he had seven children.

As if that wasn't enough to keep a man busy, in the month of September he was the chief matchmaker in the Lisdoonvarna match-making festival. He told me that this festival had been going since before the turn of the century and had started when affluent farmers from neighbouring counties converged on the town to 'take the healing waters' of a health spa. They would get talking about their eligible sons and daughters back on their respective farms, and soon a tradition of bringing people together developed. Years ago in rural Ireland, meeting others further than a few miles away wasn't easy, and close inter-marrying had begun to produce offspring whose only real skill was waving at planes. So any device which would facilitate breeding with someone who didn't have the same surname and a similar shaped nose, was more than welcome. These days the festival has an international element. A lot of men and women travel from as far as America and the Philippines in the search for a suitable mate or life partner. According to Willy, many middle-aged American women who had maybe been married a few times and were financially solvent, would come looking to fall in love with an Irish character with scruffy clothes and bad teeth, who could play a few tunes on the tin whistle and drink a lot.

'They're not seriously looking for a man with bad teeth?'

'They are too. The biggest attribute for an Irishman from an American point of view is if your teeth aren't good. In America, the men get to sixty, seventy, or eighty, and their teeth are too good for the rest of their body. I once put a woman together with a man who only had one tooth, and she was delighted. "At least it's his own," she said.'

I knew where Ian the traveller ought to spend his Septembers.

'A lot of these women are successful,' Willy continued. 'They'll maybe find a man who hasn't had any contact with a woman for many many years. They'll maybe have twenty or thirty years of unused love to offer.'

Should make for an interesting wedding night.

'You couldn't match my fridge with another one could you?' I politely enquired.

He laughed. 'Ah, now that is beyond my area of expertise.'

Honestly. And he called himself a matchmaker.

As Tony and I drove off on his sightseeing tour, I learned that there were two alternative spellings for Ennistymon, and that the local authorities had failed to make any decision on the matter. How you spelled it, depended on whether you were coming in or going out of town. As you arrived, you were greeted with the sign 'ENNISTYMON', but on your departure, it was a sign with a line through 'ENNISTIMON' which had the last word. A totally pointless compromise and fudge.

The tour included the dramatic Cliffs of Moher, the village of Doolin, Lisdoonvarna itself, and the Burren Smoke House, where Tony's sister-in-law worked. She was a bubbly woman who insisted on showing me a video usually shown to tourists of how a salmon is smoked. I patiently sat through it despite a spectacular lack of interest (I had never considered being au fait with the procedure involved in smoking a salmon a social advantage), and afterwards I was rewarded with a good-sized portion of the final product to take away. The irony was that I had no way of keeping it fresh even though I was touring the country with a fridge.

Apart from the woman who was serving behind the bar, the evening clientele of Cooley's were entirely male, and I was the youngest by some margin. There was a chap playing the banjo rather well up at the far end of the bar, and a less competent guitarist attempting to accompany him. As Tony and I walked in, the resident drunk called out, 'Hey Tony, go and get your box.'

At first I thought it was someone calling for me to go and get my fridge, but the other Tony disappeared outside and made for his car. I smiled to those present, keen to give the impression that I knew what a 'box' was, and why one might be needed on a social occasion like this.

The drunk, doing his utmost to focus his bloodshot eyes on me, put his hand on my shoulder in a gesture of friendship which serendipitously also prevented him from falling over. He explained needlessly, 'He's gone to get his box.'

Yes, I thought, and there was a good chance we would be putting this fellow in it at the end of the evening.

Tony returned with an accordion, and musicians and instruments materialised from nowhere. The resident drunk suddenly produced a pair of spoons from his pocket, and proceeded to play them with great skill and dexterity. After the ability to order a drink, this must have been the last of his faculties to go. I had always thought of the spoons as being played as a novelty purely to get laughs, but in the correct hands it made an authentic percussive instrument. The four-piece band became a five-piece when Willy Daly entered carrying a bodhran (the tambouriney thing hit with a stick) and joined the merry band of players. He must have had a device within him which could instinctively sound out a session when it was beginning.

What followed was a great treat for me. This was Irish traditional music as I had hoped to see and hear it, spontaneous and from the heart, and not produced for the sake of the tourist industry. As I sat there with my pint in my hand, enjoying the jigs and the reels, I watched the joy in the player's faces and in those around them who tapped their feet and applauded enthusiastically. Music the joybringer. No question of being paid, or any requirement to perform for a certain amount of time. Just play for as long as it makes you feel good. This was self expression, not performance. Someone would begin playing a tune and the fellow musicians would listen to it once through, hear how it went and join in when they felt comfortable, until, on its last run through, it was being played with gusto by the entire ensemble. This process provided each piece with the dynamic of a natural crescendo which could almost have been orchestrated.

The banjo player was from out of town, but his playing assured him the hospitality that might be showered on a long-lost son. He had an extremely large belly hanging over his trousers, which were held up by a belt which looked incapable of withstanding the strain. Were it to break, then his weight would be re-distributed to such a degree that he would surely topple over forwards. It was too much responsibility for a belt which was showing signs of fraying.

He bonded with Tony, recognising him for the accomplished accordion player that he was, and they smiled at each other in mutual admiration. The less talented guitarist continued to play, providing the right and wrong chords in equal measure. Though at times he spoiled the sound that the combo were producing, he received no admonishment or looks of censure, and was made as welcome as the most able musician.

After an hour or so, the unaccompanied singing began. For this, each singer would close their eyes and present their party piece to a reverent audience who would offer their comments on the lyrics at the end of each song. Songs were sung in turn, much in the same way that drinkers in an English pub might exchange jokes. Some patiently waited, anxious to display their talents, and others had to have a song coaxed out of them. Significantly, the ones who had to be encouraged gave the best performances, but there was no competitive element and each singer, good or bad, was given commensurate respect. I racked my brains for a song I could sing should I be asked, but happily the honour wasn't bestowed upon me. I made a mental note to come up with something for these occasions, because I liked this approach to singing – closing your eyes and belting it out from the heart. It seemed like a style tailor-made for the drunk, but Tony proved that intoxication wasn't essential, as his contribution, which was the product of four soft drinks, was one of the more heartfelt and soulful renditions of the evening.

Tony was still singing in the car as he drove us home. The song included the line 'I picked up a hitch-hiker who was handsome and tall', and for a moment I thought it was going to be about me, but I listened intently and there was no mention of a fridge anywhere. So I wasn't a folk legend just yet.

The next morning I just had to mention it. I had been surprised that Tony hadn't, and I couldn't leave without raising the subject.

'Have you given any more thought to taking the fridge scuba diving?'

'I have, and I've realised that we won't be able to lift the thing once it's filled up with water. We need air bags, and I don't have any.'

Damn, neither did I.

'Never mind, no one would believe that we'd done it anyway,' I said.

'I'm sorry. We can put the fridge on one of Willy Daly's ponies and take it trekking if you like.'

Honestly, for an inanimate object, it received more offers than I did.

'I think that might frighten the pony. Maybe we'll just leave it to hitch today.'

When Nora dropped me outside an ugly development of holiday bungalows on the road from Lahinch to Kilrush, I had absolutely no idea where I was going. Up until that moment I always had at least a destination in mind, even if the reason for it had been as flimsy as someone having mentioned a pleasant pub in the area. But this time I had nothing, I was simply going to wait and see.

No one could have foreseen the night that was ahead.

18

Bachelor Boy

Cars were scarce and the sky was as unpredictable as my mood. I had slept well, but for some reason I felt irritable. It began to rain, gently at first, but then quite steadily to the point where I needed to get the wind-cheater from my rucksack. Naturally, it wasn't sitting welcomingly at the top of the rucksack, but nestling somewhere in the depths of the bag. I began delving. Three delves later I was starting to become angry. Try as I might, I couldn't locate that waterproof. The rain was now coming down harder and I was beginning to get quite wet. There was nothing for it but to shout at the rucksack. This I did. It made me feel better but offered no protection against the rain. I delved again, this time with a violence not normally associated with such a task. God increased the rain output. I wanted to kick the rucksack and shake my fist at the sky but realised that to do so would mean I was turning into Basil Fawlty.

I was in a no-win situation. Clearly the only way to find what I sought was to empty all the garments in my rucksack one by one on to the road-side, but then the rain would give them a good soaking and they would fester in the confines of the bag for the remainder of the day. However, to remain where I was with no protection, was an invitation to head colds, influenza and pneumonia to 'Come on in!' Had I been thirty years younger I would have known exactly what to do. Burst into tears. Cry my little heart out. But I was older now, and social programming meant that was no longer an option. With age comes wisdom, circumspection, maturity and resourcefulness. I had an idea. I knew exactly what to do. I took three steps back from the rucksack, ran at it and gave it an almighty kick. Then I looked up to the heavens and waved my fist angrily.

'Look rain, just piss off!' I cried.

It worked. The rain eased off. Fifty yards away, a young woman crossed over on to the other side of the road. No doubt she still remembered her mother's warnings not to get too close to people who shout at the sky.

I didn't need the windcheater any more, this was just fine drizzle. But fine drizzle is deceptive. Twenty-five minutes of it can get you extremely wet, but drivers don't consider it to be serious enough to make them sympathetic to a hitch-hiker's cause. I sat down on my fridge in resignation. I had forgotten that it was wet and that well-wishers had signed it. Now I would have the inverse of 'Best Wishes' written all over my arse. To most it would look like gobbledegook, but it would read correctly to those drivers viewing me in their rear mirror after having driven past, and it would appear that I wasn't in the least bitter at their failure to stop.

'Darling, that was unbelievable. That guy was hitching with a fridge, and he had "Best Wishes" written on his bottom.'

'How quaint.'

It was another excited lorry driver, Tom, who saved the day.

'Where are you headed?' he asked.

'I don't really know.'

'Well, isn't that true of all of us?'

Tom delivered building supplies and pearls of wisdom.

'I could drop you at Killimer where you can get the ferry across the River Shannon to Kerry,' he advised me.

The ferry to Kerry. It had a nice ring about it. I got out my map.

'Yes, and then I could head down to Tralee.'

'Exactly,' said Tom, 'find yourself a rose in Tralee.'

'Yup, sounds good to me.'

It was late in the day but I finally had a rough game plan. Tom dropped me at the ferry terminal where he posed for pictures with me, the fridge, and some girls from the café who had seen the fridge and come rushing out to greet it. I was becoming slightly miffed that this fridge was getting more attention than I was. There was an hour's wait for the ferry, which was enough time for the café girls to prove once again that there *is* such a thing as a free lunch.

Once on board I realised that I was the only passenger on foot, and since the weather was still inclement, most of the drivers remained inside their vehicles. It occurred to me that all the cars would drive off before I had time to set myself up on the road, so my only real way of securing a lift the other side was to wander round asking. This was a particularly undignified practice since it involved tapping on people's windows and begging. I didn't feel comfortable with it but it had to be done, because it would be another hour before the ferry dumped its next load, and even then it would be difficult to find a spot where drivers would stop as they drove off the ferry.

Either I was being particularly unlucky or I wasn't very good at it, but with the southern bank of the Shannon estuary drawing ever closer I was still without an offer. Perhaps the fact that I was separated from my fridge, which was out of sight over by the side of the ferry, was having an adverse effect on my confidence. A coach driver turned me down because he wasn't insured to take me, a Range Rover full of American golfers simply didn't have room, and everyone else I asked said they were heading in a different direction.

Finally, I approached a tatty car which I had been leaving until the cause was desperate. The two dishevelled looking men within it looked up at me as I tapped on their window.

'Excuse me, but you're not going anywhere near Tralee are you?'

'We're going to Listowel,' replied the driver, without warmth.

'That's on the way, isn't it?' My earlier glance at the map was proving invaluable.

'I suppose so.'

'You couldn't give me a lift there could you? It's just that no one seems to be going that way and I'm a bit stuck.'

The two fellows, who I took to be builders such was the distribution of sand, cement and dust throughout their hair and clothes, looked at each other and the older one, the passenger, nodded.

'Yes, all right. We'll take you to Listowel.'

They had been rather reluctant, but at least I wasn't stranded.

I introduced myself, and as I walked down the boat to get my stuff, I realised that these guys, Pat and Michael, knew nothing about the fridge. Everyone who had stopped for me up to now had at least seen that I had a cumbersome piece of luggage with me. I wondered what the response would be. I didn't have to wait long.

'Now what in God's name is that?' asked Pat.

'It's a fridge.'

'I thought so.'

They both viewed it in disbelief.

'Is there enough room in the car for it?' I checked politely, knowing that there was.

'Oh yeah. We'll stick it in the back,' said Michael, scratching his head. 'Excuse my French, but what the fuck are you doing with a fridge?'

I explained, and Pat and Michael shared a look which appeared to mean 'well, at least there's two of us'.

Pat, who was the driver and the younger of the two, began to relax and chat freely with me after about twenty minutes. Michael, however, sat frozen in the front seat convinced that they had foolishly allowed a dangerous psychopath within easy stabbing range. He shuffled uneasily when I spoke, and flinched every time I made a sudden movement. I got the impression that he hadn't believed a word I'd said, and was convinced that the fridge contained the vital organs of my victims.

As they dropped me in Listowel, Pat got out and signed the fridge whilst Michael remained glued to the passenger seat, checking my movements in the rear mirror, in case I made a last minute attempt to overpower Pat, grab the keys and drive him to my hideout and begin the torture process.

'Well, good luck,' said Pat, shaking my hand.

'Thanks.'

And from the front of the car I just made out a mumble from Michael, 'Yeah, good luck to ya.'

This was one very relieved man.

A quick pint was in order, to celebrate the successful negotiation of a tricky part of my journey. Pat had recommended a bar called John B Keane's, belonging to the author of *The Field*, which had been made into a film starring John Hurt and Richard Harris. As I walked down the bustling main street towards it, I passed a sign with an arrow pointing to a CASUAL TRADING AREA. What was this? A place specifically for the buying and selling of casual clothes? Would I turn the corner and see stall upon stall packed with slacks, corduroys and Hushpuppies? Or was it a place where the *approach* to trading was casual? Stallholders lolling about in reclining chairs, reading books and only occasionally giving attention to customers between chapters. John B Keane's was quite busy for five o'clock in the afternoon. My first impression as I looked around was there were so many contenders for Resident Drunk here that I must have walked into a Resident Drunks' convention. Spirits were high, and the introduction of a stranger with a rucksack and a fridge caused an increase in volume, excitement and laughter.

Val, a thin fellow in his fifties with glasses, moustache and with a peaked blue cap on, was the most vociferous. He announced that he was a plain-clothes policeman and required some questions to be answered.

'What's in the fridge?'

'A couple of pairs of shoes.'

It was true. That morning I had struggled to get my shoes stuffed into the top of the rucksack, so what better place to put them?

'No one keeps shoes in a fridge,' said Val, logically enough.

'I do.'

'Let me see. I'm a policeman.' Then he announced to the room, 'I have to see what is in that fridge, there may be a bomb.'

His authority was strongly questioned by those who knew him, and he was lambasted with remarks like 'Leave the poor fella alone' and 'If Val's a policeman, then my arse is president'.

'No, it's all right,' I declared, 'I have nothing to hide. I respect that the police are simply doing their job.'

Big laughs. Val got down on to his hands and knees and prepared to open the fridge door.

'There's no way anyone would keep shoes in a feckin' fridge!'

As he opened the door an expectant crowd gathered round. To Val's dismay, a pair of brown shoes fell out on to the carpet. Huge cheers. Val turned to me, 'Where are you from?'

'London.'

'Where in London?'

'Wimbledon.'

'Ah Wimbledon. So you're the Wimbledon Wanderer. What's your name?'

'Tony.'

'Tony who?'

'Tony Hawks.'

'Hawks. Hawks. Like the hawk in the sky. Hawkeye. You're a good man. Anyone who keeps shoes in a fridge is a good man.' He turned to the barmaid, 'Elsie, get this man a pint.'

I will never again in my life earn a pint in such a way.

The fridge sat centre-stage on the carpet in the middle of the saloon bar's floor, and drinkers filed past paying homage to it like it was some kind of holy relic. Two old women called Finola and Maureen were fascinated by the whole business of the bet, and fired off question after question. Laughs greeted each reply, and the questions became more outlandish.

'Do you sleep in it as well?'

'Of course I do. It's like the Tardis in there. Open up that door and you go into a two-bedroom flat. Two bathrooms, one en suite from the main bedroom.'

Maureen, who was waving a large whiskey around in front of her like a lantern, started to tell me something about this being writers' week in

Listowel and that she was on the committee, and then she started to ramble on about her son in New Zealand, but a combination of her accent, slurring, and Val intermittently shouting at her to shut up, made her difficult to follow.

'Shut up Maureen! Leave Hawkeye alone,' Val would cry.

I had only been in the pub half an hour and already I had a nickname. At last I had discovered one area where the Irish move quickly.

'Where are you staying, Hawkeye?'

'I don't know, Val. I haven't even decided if I'm going to stay here in Listowel.'

'Well, if you do, you can stay at my place. It's a big house on the hill – very quiet and peaceful. You will be in the bed of tranquillity.'

I appreciated his attempt at lyricism, but he made the proposed place of slumber sound too much like a final resting place for me to jump at the offer.

'That's very kind of you. If it's all right, I'll see how things pan out.'

'Pan away. Pan away. Hawkeye. Hawkeye, the Wimbledon Wanderer.'

A very old man at the bar who sounded like a male equivalent of my first landlady in Donegal Town, only with an even slower delivery, announced that he was eighty-four. Sometimes that is enough for an old person conversationally, but he had more to add. He looked down at the fridge and said, 'That fridge has the spirit of the nomadic urge in it.'

There was clearly no generation gap involved in embracing the concept of a travelling fridge.

Maureen insisted I sat down next to her whilst she wrote out the address of her son in New Zealand. She handed me a piece of paper on which I could just make out the number 7, but not one word was legible. I promised to look him up if I was ever in New Zealand, although I anticipated that 7 Gty$a RelT Broi/9unter, GoptS-yyi, might be a difficult address to locate.

On the other side of me two ill-groomed ne'er-do-wells were sat with their feet up, enjoying the show that everyone else had been putting on for them.

One of them, the one with a moustache and marginally less grime all over his clothes, leant towards me and asked, 'Are you a bachelor?'

This was not a question I had expected.

'Yes I am,' I replied, a little suspiciously.

'Course he is,' said the other, 'you don't think a wife would let him take off round Ireland with a feckin' fridge in tow would you?'

An aspect of married life that I had never considered.

'Why do you want to know?' I asked, defensively.

'Well, there's a bachelor festival in Ballyduff tonight, and we were just talking and saying how it might be a laugh if you entered. You could enter the fridge too, unless the feckin' thing is married.'

I had no idea really. I assumed that when you buy a fridge brand new, it's single. That's the danger of buying a re-conditioned number. You've no idea how many acrimonious divorces it may have been through.

'Maybe it's married to him,' said the one with the moustache. 'They're travelling together aren't they? Maybe they're on their honeymoon.'

The pub clientele were in fits of laughter. It was time to set the record straight.

'The fridge and I aren't married. We are just good friends and there is nothing going on between us.'

As a witness to this, I wouldn't be calling Ann-Marie, the landlady who had seen me drag it from my bedroom dressed in a wetsuit.

These two jokers were Brian and Joe, who laid hardwood floors for a living, and appeared to get most of the glue involved in the process over themselves rather than the floors. Both were married and so weren't eligible to enter the bachelor festival themselves, but they knew the owner of Low's Bar where the event was taking place and were sure they could get me in as a late entrant. The general consensus in the pub was that I should go with them and try my luck, and even though I had no idea what a bachelor festival was, or what might be required of me, it sounded more appealing than a night at Val's.

Driving off with two slightly dodgy-looking characters who I had known for fifteen minutes was the biggest risk I had taken so far. Were I never to be seen again, then justifiable questions would be asked about the wisdom and judgement I had shown in those last hours.

The fridge was deposited in the back of the van and I climbed into the cabin and put my seatbelt on, knowing that it might mean the difference between survival and a bed of tranquillity. We sped off towards Ballyduff.

My mobile phone rang. Extraordinarily, it was my agent calling from London.

'Hi Tony, it's Mandy. Whereabouts are you?'

Honestly of all the unnecessary questions! Isn't it obvious? I'm speeding down the road in a Transit van on my way to the Ballyduff bachelor festival with two hardwood flooring guys, where do you think?

'Oh hi Mandy, it's a little difficult to explain exactly where I am. I'm in transit.'

'But you're in safe hands?'

Huh.

'Sort of.'

'Radio Four have phoned and asked if you can do *I'm Sorry I Haven't A Clue* next Thursday. Will you be back in time?'

'I don't think so, and even if I am, I doubt my brain will be in any condition for the delivery of ready wit and repartee.'

'What shall I tell them then?'

'I'm sorry, I haven't a clue.'

Brian and Joe called out 'Hi Mandy! How ya doing?' and the phone's signal disappeared as we bumped our way round another bend somewhere in the heart of County Kerry. Poor Mandy, she must despair of me at times.

Career successfully on hold, it was time to get on with the more important business in hand.

'So, what exactly will I have to do at this bachelor festival?'

'Oh, a bit of an interview, maybe a party piece.'

'And what happens if I win?'

There I was deluding myself again.

'You win a week at the Ballybunion bachelor festival.'

And I suppose if you won that, they packed you off to another one somewhere else. No wonder they marry young in Ireland – purely to avoid this endless circuit of bachelor festivals.

I'm not sure whether Ballyduff is a town which figures greatly on any tourist map, and there was unlikely to be a wide range of choice in the field of accommodation. In fact, a field might be the best it had to offer. I had no worries though because Brian's wife and kids were up visiting relatives in Northern Ireland, and he said it wouldn't be a problem to stay at his place.

It was quite a plush residence built on one storey, which suggested to me that smearing glue over his clothes all day provided him with a very reasonable income.

Perhaps it had been the conversation with Willy Daly about the history of the matchmaking festival which led me to believe that this also might be a time-honoured event, steeped in convention and revered by single women from miles around who came to peruse the eligible with a view to pouncing. (Unlike Lisdoonvarna, I reckoned that it probably didn't have a reputation to attract Americans yet, so saw no reason to black out any teeth.)

When we arrived at Low's Bar at around nine, it was too early, and the only evidence that there was going to be a bachelor festival in the pub was a small sign saying 'BACHELOR FESTIVAL TONIGHT'. The pub itself wasn't the old, traditional hostelry I was expecting, but a large newly refurbished establishment with TV screens everywhere, a dancefloor with a DJ, and staff in matching uniform. This pub belonged in the town centre of Swindon, not in a tiny rural outpost in the west of Ireland. It had another thing in common with a pub in the town centre of Swindon – it was virtually empty. We were told things wouldn't get going till around midnight, and withdrew to the small pub over the road where the music wasn't blaring and we could converse without doing lasting damage to our vocal chords.

Several pints and an unstimulating game of darts later, we returned to find Low's Bar heaving with young people. The DJ was announcing the imminent commencement of the bachelor festival. Festival? I looked around me and saw nothing to justify the use of the word festival. The atmosphere was exactly that of a nightclub where audience interest in the stage was fuelled by a desire to watch a few drunken friends and acquaintances humiliate themselves. The men outnumbered the women, which suggested that the women folk of Ballyduff were either already sorted or knew of better ways to go about getting so. The imbalance in the sexes certainly wasn't the result of a huge entry for the bachelor festival.

There were six of us.

The DJ kicked off proceedings with a booming announcement through the PA in an Irish version of the mid-Atlantic accent all disc jockeys use. The first two young men he invited on stage were fat and drunk. They mumbled incomprehensibly into the microphone and sang like pining dogs. The audience shouted encouragement at them which sounded like general abuse.

In one sense I was heartened – the competition so far wasn't up to much, but on the down side, the audience weren't the most sophisticated I had ever witnessed. I still had absolutely no idea what I was going to do when I was called up there. I turned to Joe who was stood alongside me like a supportive personal manager. 'What shall I do?'

'Oh, just tell a couple of jokes.'

This, given my profession, ought to have been an area in which I could excel. I felt pretty confident that none of the other bachelors had the experience of a Royal Gala under their belt (unless the King of Tory held one), and I knew that this should give me the edge over them, but hard as I tried, I couldn't recall any section of my act which I felt would satiate the baying rabble who made up the audience.

A guy called John was before me. He was a considerable improvement on the previous two entrants. He wasn't drunk and he sang rather well. For the first time I began to feel some nerves. Finally it was my turn, and the DJ began his intro.

'And now we have a late entry, he's a young man who is travelling round the country with a fridge. You may have heard him on *The Gerry Ryan Show*, ladies and gentlemen – Tony Hawks!'

Cheers and whistles as I made my way to the stage. I still had absolutely no idea what I was going to do or say. The microphone was handed to me by an unusually slim assistant who fixed me with a demented smile.

'Good evening ladies and gentlemen,' I began cleverly, drawing on all my experience, 'I am delighted to be here. I *am* a bachelor, not surprisingly I suppose, as a man who has chosen to travel around the country with a fridge, but I have always harboured a deep desire to marry a woman from Ballyduff.'

So far so good. This remark was cheered by the females in the audience, one girl somewhere out in the darkness urgently shouting 'COME ON!!' almost as if I'd done enough already, and that we could both disappear off now to finalise the wedding details with the priest. A general hubbub continued for what seemed a very long time but was only a matter of seconds, with diverse views on the merits of my marrying a local girl being offered at volume by most in attendance. I stood there, temporarily mesmerised by the yells of a frenzied and expectant crowd. I almost had an out of body experience in which I hovered above myself, had a bit of a look, and said, 'How the hell did you get yourself into that?' A particularly piercing female voice brought me round to reality. Implausible reality.

'HAS THE FRIDGE GOT A FREEZER COMPARTMENT!?' she demanded at the top of her voice.

A sudden hush descended. It was almost as if she had touched on a point on which everyone needed clarification.

'I'm not taking questions yet,' I replied.

I got a laugh. Thirty seconds in, I was going quite well.

Things deteriorated from here. By a minute I was sweating and at a minute thirty I was in some trouble. Somehow I managed to come up with a section of my material which might save the day, and performed it with as much confidence as I could muster. It didn't save the day. What it did, was win me a few more seconds struggling in front of a crowd who were now vaguely supportive but who were never going to fully appreciate the only things I was capable of doing for them.

'I'm not sure what I should do now,' I admitted to them honestly.

'Do Tony Blair – things can only get better!' shouted a male voice unhelpfully.

'Do the Stutter Rap!' called another, revealing a tragic past.

Joe, who was stood behind me, whispered keenly, 'Do some more of the jokes. More of the funny stuff.'

I would have done if I could have remembered any of it. The excesses of the past few weeks had temporarily erased it from my memory. Then I had an idea.

'I know what I'll do, I'll sing a song,' I announced, to sceptical cheers. 'I've learnt what you have to do over here – you close your eyes and sing from the heart. This isn't an Irish song, because I don't know any – but it's a song I wrote myself a few years back. So here goes.'

Already this had created as much hush as the enquiry about the freezer compartment had done. I took a deep breath, closed my eyes and sang from the heart.

> If I had a dollar for each lonely night
> That I had spent longing for you
> I wouldn't be drifting or travelling light
> For there have been more than a few
> Cos I've been a drifter, and whilst I've been drifting
> The real world has broken me in two
> And if I had a dollar for each lonely night,
> I'd be rich, blue and lonely
> Instead of just lonely and blue

Singing has a special place in the hearts of the Irish. The respectful quiet I was afforded for this performance and the rapturous applause it received proved that. I had won them over.

'Goodnight!' I announced with a rock and roll wave.

Surely that had assured my place in Ballybunion. As I proudly walked from the stage with the cheers still ringing in my ears, I noticed that the DJ wasn't there to introduce the next bachelor. I was intercepted by the unusually slim assistant, whose demented smile had now become a demented grimace. He waved me back on.

'You'll have to do some more, Callum's in the toilet,' he said.

'What?'

'You've got to keep going till Callum the DJ gets back from the toilet. He heard that you were a bit of a comedian and he thought you were going to do about twenty minutes up there, so he thought there'd be time to go to the bog.'

'Can't I introduce the next bachelor?'

'No, cos Callum's got the running order with him.'

What did he need the bloody running order with him for? Wasn't there any toilet paper? The assistant pushed me back out to the microphone. What followed undid all the good work that the song had done because I couldn't think of anything further to offer. The chorus of unhelpful suggestions began again, and all the time I could hear Joe persistently whispering behind me – 'Do some more of the jokey stuff.'

Callum was taking his time. For the first time in my career, my success on stage was entirely dependent on a disc jockey's bowel movements. I floundered. If you had wanted to demonstrate to someone the meaning of the word 'floundering' you simply could have led them there and pointed at me. 'There, see that bloke there – now that's "floundering".' The day needed saving and Brian provided the requisite initiative. Recognising that I wasn't in the midst of one of show business's most outstanding performances he had nipped outside to the van to fetch something he felt might help. Just as the audience contributions had reached a level where an outsider walking in would have believed there was a riot about to happen, Brian marched up the middle of the dance floor pulling my fridge behind him.

'The fridge! It's the fridge!!!' cried excited voices.

Brian drew it up alongside me and laid it to rest by my side. He withdrew and left the two of us, an Englishman and his fridge posing like oddities before Ballyduff's revellers. We must have looked quite a pair because someone called out, 'Hey, look how good they are together! I reckon he's not a bachelor after all!'

'I am,' I replied. 'But we're part of a team. There's room for another, but it's a case of "Love me, love my fridge".'

The audience liked this and rewarded it with a polite round of applause. The sound of a polite round of applause must have been so unusual as to cause Callum the DJ to curtail his bathroom activities and to reappear looking mildly panic stricken. He looked at me and shrugged, as if to say 'How did you get a polite round of applause out of that lot?' I shrugged back. By the end of this trip I would certainly be all shrugged out. I wanted to lean into the microphone and say, 'I have to go now, my work here is done.'

Perhaps a little too grand.

'I'm going to hand you back to your DJ now,' I said with immense relief. 'Goodnight, you've been great!'

Ugh! *'Goodnight, you've been great!'* Well, I had certainly drawn on all my show business experience there to leave the audience with one of the all time offerings of trite insincerity. No one minded though and for the second time in the night, I left the stage to rousing cheers. One familiar female voice cut through the rest, 'HAS THE FRIDGE GOT A FREEZER COMPARTMENT!?'

She would make someone an interesting wife.

Half an hour later the winner was announced. Brian, who knew the organisers, had already informed me of it.

'Well the good news is Tony, that you won. The bad news is they can't give it to you, because you've got to give it to a local.'

This wasn't such bad news. I wasn't sure if I really wanted an entire week of nights like this in Ballybunion. Besides justice was being done. The main reason for my gaining favour had been that I was travelling with a fridge, and that is by no means sure fire evidence of one man being any better a bachelor than the next.

I sat down and watched the fridge at the end of the dancefloor completely surrounded by young people anxious to sign it with pens, crayons, and whatever else they could lay their hands on. Beside it stood Paddy, the winner of the 1997 Ballyduff bachelor festival. No one was paying a blind bit of attention to him. A similar fate befell the rest of the bachelors, including myself. It seemed that the few females of Ballyduff who had turned out to this special night preferred the company of a small appliance to a man. For some, it would be a preference which would continue well into their married lives.

As the DJ wound up the night I wrested my fridge from its deranged inscribers who were continuing to cover it with names, messages and jokes. For a moment, I felt strangely protective of it. I realised that in the interests of sanity, these weren't feelings I should look to encourage.

Eye make-up pencils, felt pens, and a ubiquitous maroon crayon had all been used to transform the fridge into a modernistic *objet d'art*. A closer study revealed that the Mother Superior's message had been almost obliterated. Her words 'God bless you Tony and Saiorse' were barely visible beneath the profane scrawlings of Ballyduff's youth. Almost a metaphor for the Church's present standing in society.

Apart from a particularly crude joke which now adorned the fridge door, one other message caught my eye. On the back, just below 'Stay Cool!! Luv Chris and Jean', it read, 'Life is a mystery to be lived, not a problem to be solved.'

There you go. Even amidst the most disorderly inebriated rabble, wisdom is to be found. Brian, Joe and I drew on some of ours, and called it a night.

19

I Did It Dunmanway

I had been lucky with the changeable weather. Up until now, when it had been raining I had been fortunate enough either to have been inside a vehicle or a pub. I had been granted periods of precious sunshine but clouds had always been hovering impatiently, threatening a return to the climate for which Ireland had made something of a name. Today was different. Clear blue sky without a hint of cumulonimbus or stratus to stop the radiant sunshine from prevailing. The refreshing unpolluted Kerry air was up for grabs and the door needed only to be thrown open for a glimpse of a lush green landscape basking in the healthy rays of an inviting sun. A beautiful morning awaited.

Unfortunately we spent it in the dark, dingy windowless back room of a pub in Tralee.

'You can't lay a hardwood floor without wood,' Brian had said.

He knew his stuff. His mobile phone was turned on, and as soon as news of the required delivery of wood reached him, we would proceed to Killarney, but until then, what better way to while away a morning like this, than by playing countless games of darts.

Darts. Dart players. Unlikely to conjure up the same levels of excitement in females as, say, your average surfer might. For some reason, the fit, muscular, tanned and scantily clad brute gliding across the waves will always edge it over the pasty fat bloke drinking beer and aiming his diminutive projectile at a small target. I longed to be outside in the sun, and the longing affected my darts. Whatever variation of the rules was adopted, I consistently claimed third place for my own, whilst Brian and Joe traded victories in a titanic struggle for outright supremacy. It was almost enthralling.

'How far is it to Killarney from here?' I asked, having just scored sixteen with three darts.

'Oh, about another hour,' said Joe, doing some mental arithmetic. 'Sixteen eh? Not bad. Better than your last two goes.'

Once we had word of this eagerly awaited delivery, darts would be abandoned for the day and Brian and Joe would have to begin smothering themselves in glue and seeing to it that a floor would get laid. Lucky old floor.

By lunchtime, there was still no word of the delivery, but we headed off to Killarney anyway. I didn't understand the thinking behind this, but I didn't question it since Killarney was where I had set my sights on being by the end of the day. When we arrived there, Brian and Joe took me on a tour of the town which involved showing me the interiors of three pubs. Thankfully, all were without windows and offered a dimness which was a welcome contrast to the resplendent sunshine which those who had been foolish enough to venture outside had to suffer. In one of the bars a gaunt old man who looked like he was stony broke, on learning that I was the fellow who was travelling with a fridge, leant over to me proffering a pound coin

'Here, take this and God bless ya,' he commanded.

'What's that for?'

'For whatever charity your collecting for.'

'I'm not doing it for charity.'

'Yes, you are now. C'mon, now take the pound.'

'Honestly, I'm not doing it for charity.'

'C'mon now, why else would anyone bring a fridge round the country with him? Take the pound now, c'mon.'

It was a full five minutes before I could convince him that I wasn't a registered charity and was by no means worthy of his pound.

'Ah well, please yourself,' he said eventually, and promptly spent double the amount by buying me a pint when I wasn't looking.

Brian and Joe's delivery of wood never came. It was close to five o'clock when we said our goodbyes after a meal in a basement Chinese restaurant swathed in artificial light. Brian and Joe dropped me at a bed and breakfast on the outskirts of town and headed back for Ballyduff. It was all in a day's work for your average hardwood-flooring boys.

I took a shower and made the two-mile walk down to Ross Castle on the shores of Lough Leane. As I walked, the tourists rode by on their pony and traps. A pony and trap idea if there ever was one*. Killarney appeared to be the tourist capital of the west of Ireland, no doubt because it is the gateway to some of the most breathtaking scenery in the country.

Ross Castle was the last stronghold under Irish control to be taken by

---

*Please check your cockney rhyming slang dictionaries.

Cromwellian forces in 1653. I arrived there at 18.53, which was perfect timing since it closed at 18.00. The final tourist dregs were returning to their lodgings to clean themselves up for dinner, and I was left to enjoy the beauty of this spot in relative solitude. I struggled along the shore of the lough, climbing over rowing boats and through bushes until I had found the ideal location for enjoying the sunshine for the first time in the day. It was a totally secluded and magical spot, perfect for viewing the sun setting over the lough and the distant mountains, Macgillycuddy's Reeks, which were reflected in the waters. Nature's way of recognising that they were worth seeing twice.

As I sat looking over the reflective waters with their stunning back-drop, I too became reflective. I began to wonder whether my 'fridge journey' could be considered an allegory for life. I decided that there was some persuasive evidence. Each day I was faced with a number of choices, some were easy and others were harder. The same was true of life.

I had learned not to worry; to make my choice and allow things to happen. For the most part they turned out to be good, and when they weren't – like the night from hell in a hostel – then they were character building. There weren't any wrong or right paths to choose, just different ones, and where they led was governed by the attitude adopted towards them. It seemed to me that was true of life also.

So what else? Well, I couldn't manage alone. The nature of hitching, especially when encumbered by a kitchen appliance, is such that you are reliant on others. We mayn't expect it, but there may come a time in all of our lives when we have to hitch, either physically or figuratively. It doesn't matter how important, wealthy or talented you are, if your car breaks down somewhere and you are forced to stick out your thumb and hitch, then your fallibility and the fact that you are no *better* than the next person will become abundantly clear to you. You *need* someone else's kindness to take you to safety. What I was beginning to discover was that signing up to this Trust was as liberating as it was fun.

Fun. That brought me to the final thrust of my lakeside dialectic – my purposeless journey was, like life itself, cyclical. My starting point, Dublin, represented the beginning of life, and throughout my journey, it was destined to be my eventual 'resting place'. Since my fridge had cost more than the £100 bet itself, I had no valid economic motivation for the trip, and in terms of great human achievement it would go down in the annals of history alongside Timothy 'Bud' Budyana and his backwards marathon. Given this 'purposelessness', the only justification for my exploits was that I ensured they were *fun*. It was apt that the Irish themselves had invented the only word that really embraced the spirit of it all. The 'craic'. Once the people in this country realised that what I was doing I was doing purely 'for the craic', they understood fully what I was about, and took me to their hearts. Here, dangling my feet in the waters of this splendid lough, I resolved to take the same approach to life itself.

The 'fridge philosophy' was taking shape. One thing was sure though. It would need another name before it went on general release.

I took it easy that night, leaving the fridge holed up in my room and keeping out of pubs. I walked around the busy Killarney streets in search of a suitable restaurant for an unkempt individual, dining alone. I considered treating myself to lobster in an expensive-looking fish restaurant, but the sight of the lobsters displayed in a tank, struggling around with their claws taped up, put me off the idea. On the menu in the window it said,

YOU PICK YOUR OWN LOBSTER FROM OUR TANK.

I didn't like the sound of that either. This would change my status entirely from diner to God-like figure. Instead of 'innocently' ordering something off the menu, suddenly I was being asked to exercise an executive decision over which creature should actually die that night, in the interests of my palate.

I dined in a quaint, homely little restaurant where no demands were made upon me to select any animals for slaughter, and I ate an Irish stew which reassuringly felt like someone's Mum had cooked it. I walked home debating whether I should continue hitching in the morning, even though it was a Sunday when there would be none of the commercial traffic which had been my bread and butter. By the time I reached the guest house I had decided that the following morning I would give it two hours by the roadside and if that brought no reward then I would abort and return to the lakeside for more amateur philosophy.

I sat on my bed and surveyed the map. I felt immensely proud when I saw what ground I had covered. I had broken the back of the journey. My next goal was to get out to Cape Clear Island, and once that had been achieved I was surely in the home straight. I gave myself the mental equivalent of a pat on the back. Then I realised. Bad news. Today was May 24th!

Bugger. I had missed 'SHEEP '97'.

*

We all make mistakes. All are forgivable in the end. But after five hours standing by the side of a deserted road in the wilds of West Cork, I was finding it very difficult indeed to grant myself absolution just yet.

It had been going so well. At breakfast in the guesthouse I had made the acquaintance of two Australian tourists, Chris and Jan, and talked them into making their journey to Cork with an Englishman and a fridge for company.

It hadn't been easy at first, since Chris and Jan hadn't been in the best of moods, as our opening exchange had proved.

'Good morning,' said I. 'Beautiful day isn't it?' And it most certainly was. The good weather seemed to have broken out and looked set to stay.

'About time,' countered Jan. 'We've had nine days of rain in Scotland.'

Chris and Jan were *doing* Europe. Much of it was leaving them unimpressed. They weren't easy to please. An interesting yardstick was Chris's opinion on Venice.

'Venice? That's over-rated isn't it? We thought it was just a grotty old place with a load of water running through it.'

I seemed to remember it having one or two other redeeming features.

Once again, it was the fridge to the rescue. Mention of it, and its role in my travels lightened their mood considerably and resulted in smiles and the offer of the lift which I had been angling for all the time. I even persuaded them to go to Cork via a place called Skibbereen which meant I could alight there and continue hitching down to Baltimore where the ferry left for Cape Clear Island.

We set off, and I was entrusted with the map reading, Chris and Jan maintaining that they 'didn't have a clue' in that department. It was a measure of the beautiful views of Killarney's lakeland scenery that my Australian friends enthused about them and even stopped the car to shoot video footage. One bonus of travelling through this region with tourists was that I got to stop and see the panoramic views and places of interest. Bantry House, a magnificent stately home with spectacular views overlooking the bay, received meagre praise from Chris.

'The toilets are free, and that's an improvement on a lot of the places we've been.'

We didn't go inside the house, because the £5.50 entrance fee was deemed to be too expensive.

'We saw a load of these old places in Vienna,' said Jan, 'and there's only so much old furniture you can look at.'

Fair enough. I wasn't really bothered about going in either. The architecture, grounds and its overall setting were of more interest to me than the roped-off rooms and endless portraits of ancestors. Unlike Chris, I wasn't entirely satisfied with the toilet arrangements. Free they may have been, but one cubicle serving both sexes meant standing in an extended queue when one could have been exploring the Italianate gardens. In a rejection of my British heritage, I shunned the queuing option and slipped between two hedges into a secluded area where I disgracefully gave the plants a generous watering. I then heard a voice and saw a woman leaning out of a top window in what were obviously the private living quarters of Bantry House.

'Do you mind?' said an aristocratic English voice. 'That is our private garden!'

'Sorry,' I whimpered, like a naughty child who was secretly feeling rather pleased with himself.

'Honestly!' said the woman, and slammed the window closed.

The 'honestly' had a ring about it which suggested that this incident was the last straw and that she would storm down to her husband and say, 'Right, that's it! No more tourists! I simply cannot abide these awful people coming on to our land one moment more.'

I walked back to the car with mixed feelings. I was glad I had urinated where I had, but was disappointed that all I'd managed by way of a riposte when challenged, was a feeble apology. Where was the feisty 'If you don't like it, get yourself more lavs, you posh old cow!'? Childish, yes, and possibly unjustified but I was feeling some degree of anger that the British still lived in some of these magnificent and ancestral homes. Change obviously doesn't come about overnight.

When I told Chris and Jan the toilet story, they warmed to me enormously. I was almost an honorary Australian now, having metaphorically at least, pissed all over the British. We began discussing life in Australia and paid little attention to the road signs and our general route. When I saw a sign saying that Skibbereen was sixteen miles in the direction we had just come from, I began to become suspicious that all wasn't right here. We pulled over, collectively studied the map and concluded that somehow we had overshot Skibbereen. It wasn't clever of me to have secured a lift to go exactly where I wanted it to and then to have allowed it to go sixteen miles too far. It was too much to expect Chris and Jan to double back on themselves, and I was left by the roadside to face the consequences of my mistake.

And boy, did I pay the price. Dunmanway on a Sunday afternoon. A ghost town where the phantoms had moved out because it was too quiet. Not a soul to be seen and one vehicle about every ten minutes on one of the bleakest stretches of road I had ever laid a fridge on.

Five miserable hours in Dunmanway. It was so, so boring. No one was going anywhere. Fast. I searched for the good things about my predicament. The sun was out, and that was it. To try and liven things up I played games with myself, awarding myself points if I correctly guessed the colour of the next car, but the fact that I was alone made it difficult to introduce any real competitive edge. I even tried to write a parody of the Frank Sinatra hit 'My Way', in tribute to this particular leg of my journey. From time to time I sang its last few lines at the top of my voice, to prove to myself that I was still alive.

> I've hitched around this land,
> Me and my fridge, in a crazy plan way
> But more, much more than this
> I did it Dunmanway

Okay, I admit I didn't spend all of the five hours by that barren track of road. At one point I walked into the assortment of buildings which masqueraded as a town and found a bar where I drank two pints of Murphys. I then walked into the main square and fell asleep on a bench. Boy, I knew how to live life. When I awoke, a confounded woman was nervously surveying me and my baggage, and when I smiled and hauled myself and my fridge to the roadside and began hitching, she rushed into the church behind her. If nothing else, this ghastly experience I was having had brought someone closer to God.

She must have said a prayer for me, that lady, because a mere two and a half hours later a young lad called Kieran pulled up and drove me ten minutes up the road to Drimoleague. Drimoleague was much like Dunmanway, only less frenetic.

An hour and a half after that I finally arrived in Baltimore thanks to Barry and Moira, a lovely couple from Bandon who supplied the last leg in this marathon journey. Passing through the town of Skibbereen was particularly galling, since it was taking place almost seven hours later than it would have done had I not been such an arse with the map earlier in the day.

In Baltimore, an enchanting little fishing port, I checked into a guesthouse with views over the pretty harbour and sat down outside the pub next door with Barry and Moira. I bought them both a drink by way of thanking them for driving well out of their way to bring me here. As the sun set, and the beer hit its mark, the horrors of the day evaporated and my placid mood returned. When Barry and Moira left, I fell in with an English crowd from the Tunbridge Wells diving club. For a while I was confused as to what sort of diving they could do since I had always believed that Tunbridge Wells, like Switzerland, was landlocked. Anyway, once this lot had heard of my adventures, they declared that they had airbags and an underwater camera and would dearly love to take the fridge scuba diving. I thanked them, but declined the offer. Maybe I needed to slow up a little now.

And Cape Clear Island seemed just the place to do it.

20

In Search Of A Haven

When the ferry docked at the jetty which the locals laughingly called the harbour I seemed to be the only passenger who was seeking accommodation for an overnight stop. Cape Clear Island was going to be my retreat from the mayhem of the last two and a half weeks. It had all the qualifications for the job, being a kind of Tory Island of the south, with trees instead of a King, and a more hospitable climate. Today it was swathed in warm sunshine. As we had arranged after my phonecall from the mainland, I was met by Eleanor, one of the few islanders who rented out rooms, and whose car even nudged ahead of the one belonging to Toothless Ian and the Travellers for decrepit dilapidation. She made no comment as I lifted the fridge on to her back seat, and the car struggled up and down the island's single-track roads until we reached her house at the top of a hill.

I intended to remain here for three or four days, to dry out, rest up and generally prepare myself for the final week soldiering on towards Dublin. However at four o'clock, the ferry took all the day trippers back to the mainland and the island completely emptied of all its walkers, sightseers and birdwatchers. I felt isolated and alone. In a moment, the plan to stay three or four days turned into one night at Eleanor's.

I was back in one of those areas where they don't pry. Throughout my brief stay in the house of Eleanor and her family, the fridge sat in the hallway, but not a single remark was made about it. It *must* have been a talking point, a fridge sitting in their hallway absolutely covered in signatures and good will messages, but there was only one brief exchange on the subject. That night I ate with Eleanor, her family and the two lodgers. As we tucked into our apple crumble, Eleanor's husband Crohuir leant towards me surreptitiously.

'Is that your fridge in the hall?' he asked timidly.

'It is.'

He took a moment to gather himself for his next assault.

'It's very small, isn't it?'

'Yes.'

Subject closed.

After dinner, I walked back to the harbour, described to me by one islander, without irony, as the hub of the island. On the way I passed a tennis court which had been built in the most dramatic of locations, almost on a cliff edge, overlooking the Atlantic. That would be some place to play, I thought.

When I arrived at the 'hub', someone must have dismantled the neon lights and advertising hoardings and sent the hordes of partying jetsetters home, because all was quiet. There were two pubs and absolutely nothing else. Both of them were empty. I took a drink in one and was eventually joined by an Englishman who told me that he brought his family to the island every year for the walks and the birdwatching. Tonight he'd left them indoors so that he could taste some of the crazy nightlife alone.

'Have you played tennis on that tennis court?' I asked.

'Oh, don't talk to me about tennis,' he complained, 'my kids have been dying to have a game ever since we got here, but they can't.'

'Why not?'

'There aren't any tennis balls on the island.'

'You're joking.'

'I'm not. Not one. The shop's run out and the guy who was supposed to bring some out from the mainland forgot.'

Island life encapsulated.

On the walk home the sky was clearer than any sky I had ever seen before. The stars twinkled like teeth in a glitzy TV toothpaste ad, and the Fastnet lighthouse lit up the island every six seconds almost as if it was strobe lighting slowed down to match the pace of life here. On reaching Eleanor's, I looked out to the horizon and conceded to myself that this was a unique place indeed. It wasn't for me though, and I would be leaving on the nine o'clock boat in the morning. For some, this isolated tranquillity would be a boon but I had learned that although I enjoyed peace and quiet, I liked to have access to an alternative. Call me whacky, but I needed to be someplace where you could get tennis balls when you wanted them.

Unexpectedly, I travelled to Cork by taxi. I met an English couple who had been on the island to attend the first protestant wedding there for over one hundred years. They had viewed me with some amusement as I had lifted my fridge on to the ferry, and after some initial English reticence they informed me that they had booked a taxi to take them and their elderly aunt to Cork airport, and if I wanted to squeeze in I was more than welcome. It was a tight fit and the taxi driver was a mite unsure of what to make of a man who had taken a fridge to a wedding. He said nothing, partly because his hands were more than full with the slightly eccentric aunt who kept him busy chatting in the front.

'This road is very tidy,' she said pointing ahead of her.

The taxi driver nodded non committally, a response he was to rely on more and more as the journey progressed.

'Did you enjoy the wedding?' the aunt asked me.

'I didn't go, I wasn't a guest, I'm just travelling around the country.'

'Oh. How lovely. What you should do is go to Seattle, and then head up the coast from there.'

She appeared to think we were on the west coast of America. I thanked her and said that I'd give it some thought after I'd reached Dublin.

After I'd spilled out of the taxi in front of the City Hall in Cork and waved it goodbye, I looked with some satisfaction at the considerable traffic and substantial buildings around me. It had been some time since I had been anywhere with this much vitality. Although it didn't strike me as being a particularly beautiful city, nonetheless I had a good feeling about it. I was just considering my next course of action when I was approached by a middle-aged Scot.

'You must be Tony, and that must be your fridge,' he said forthrightly.

'It is and I am. I mean, I am and it is.'

I was making no sense, but he didn't mind. He had been following my progress on the radio and kept insisting how wonderful an idea it had been to travel with a fridge. Then, two minutes into our acquaintance, came the offer.

'If you've no sorted anywhere to stay, ye can come and stop with me and me wife Sheila. We'll sort ye out, give ye a chance to clean up, do your washing and all the rest of it.'

'That's very kind . . . er–'

'Dave. The name's Dave Stewart.'

'Thanks, Dave. It's just that I haven't made any plans just yet. I thought I might head to a pub called Westimers.'

'Oh aye. Do you know someone there?'

'Not really, it's just that on the first morning I spoke to Gerry Ryan, they called in and said if I ever came to Cork, they'd throw a fridge party for me.'

'Oh aye. I heard that. Good idea.'

Dave gave me directions to Westimers and wrote out his address and phone number should I want to take him up on his kind offer. I crossed the road and a student came rushing out from inside a pub demanding to sign the fridge. I had re-entered the world of the 'splendidly off kilter', and I liked it.

At Westimers there was much surprise that I had responded to an offer which had been made nearly three weeks previously.

'Eric will be sick that he's missed you,' said Alan the barman.

Eric, the boss and original instigator of the offer, was away on a fishing trip in County Mayo and couldn't be contacted. Still no matter, that was no reason for the rest of the staff not to make a fuss of me, and I was given drinks and the now standard free lunch. The decor of the pub explained its rather odd name, Westimers. The Wild West was its theme and the walls were adorned with saddles, stetsons and gun wielding cowboys. Perhaps it was his love of the American West that had originally caused Eric to take *my* pioneering quest to heart.

I had just begun talking with a lunching businessman at the bar about how I was considering making a trip down to Kinsale, when Alan interrupted, 'Tony, there's a phonecall for you.'

This was weird. No one knew I was here. Correction, one person did.

'Hello Tony, it's Dave here. You know, Dave you just met on the pavement. Now stay where you are, I've been on to my mate who is the features editor at the *Evening Echo*. Don't go anywhere because they're sending a reporter down to meet you.' Things moved fast in Cork.

One newspaper interview later, I returned to my pint and was soon approached by a young man who told me he could take me to Kinsale in quarter of an hour. Things moved fast in Cork.

Everyone in Westimers thought it was a good idea if I used Cork as a base for a few days' sightseeing, not least because that meant if Eric phoned they could tell him of my arrival and see if he wanted to go ahead with the fridge party. There was much amusement amongst the staff as they watched me pack my fridge as an overnight bag, a role that hadn't been asked of it since my jaunt to Tory Island.

Okay, the quarter of an hour was closer to an hour, but just as he had said he would, Barry was soon transporting me to my next destination. It was somehow in keeping with the vein of my trip that he should turn out to be a sales rep for Caffreys, and that his first call at the Hole In The Wall pub in Kinsale necessitated my drinking complimentary pints whilst he went about his business. The fridge and beer had developed a truly symbiotic relationship, and together they were unstoppable. Things happened.

A canvassing Labour politician marched past the pub garden with his entourage, and spotted me and the fridge holding court with a number of intrigued fellow drinkers. He obviously felt the notoriety that this fridge had gained in his country meant that being photographed alongside it could genuinely enhance his chances of election. His aides hastily organised a photoshoot, and suddenly there was Michael Calnan with his arm around me, beaming unnaturally and toasting the fridge with a pint of Caffreys, supplied by the equally opportunistic Barry. Kieran, the owner of the pub, was just attempting to usher all of us round to the left so that the name of his pub formed the backdrop, when Barry noticed that a traffic warden was putting a parking ticket on his car. There then followed an extraordinary scene in which Barry attempted to get the ticket rescinded, for which he produced in his defence, a Labour politician and a man pulling a fridge behind him. Against such formidable opposition, the meter maid put up a sterling effort at insisting that the ticket should stand, but when the chorus of drinkers in the pub garden chimed in with a chant of 'Let him off, let him off, he's driving the man with the fridge!' she finally capitulated. There was no doubting that the politician had borne little influence, and that it had been the fridge which had swayed things. You've heard of 'People Power', well now please welcome 'Fridge Power'. Already it had got someone off a parking ticket – there was no knowing what meritorious cause of downtrodden citizen against oppressive State it would embrace next.

When the fridge and I returned from our political struggle, we learned that Kieran hadn't been idle. He had organised a boat trip for the next morning around Kinsale's harbour, and complimentary accommodation at the White House Hotel opposite. Barry then went about arranging me a free bar meal with another Caffrey's customer, a restaurant just around the corner called the Blue Haven.

Honestly, what a day! I hadn't been able to put a foot wrong since I had stepped on the ferry at Cape Clear Island. It was as if a spell had been cast in which I could have anything I wanted. It was just a shame the magic had worn off by the time I made my clumsy and slurred advances towards Brenda, the Blue Haven's waitress. Her haven, whatever colour it was, remained firmly off limits.

21

Fridge Party

Pat Collins' little fishing boat did us proud. I wondered what instructions Kieran had given to Pat the previous night because he quite happily gave up an hour and a half of his morning, and entirely without motive he was taking a man and his fridge on a tour of the harbour, indicating any points of interest. He helped me on and off the boat with the fridge, and even posed for a photograph with his arm round it, but saw no reason in wasting any time enquiring as to what the hell as I was doing with the bloody thing. I suppose he felt that those were questions for a younger man to ask.

As we headed out to sea along the estuary of the Bandon River we passed Charles Fort on our port side. This star-shaped bastion fort was built by the British in the seventeenth century to protect Kinsale harbour from naval attack. However, William of Orange had the bright idea of attacking it by land and took it rather easily, with all its defenders looking out to sea. The Japanese had done something similar to the British at Singapore in the second world war. Simply not cricket. At the mouth of the estuary, Pat pointed out the spot where a German submarine torpedoed and sank *The Lusitania*. Also not cricket. History seemed to demonstrate a tremendous unwillingness by people to play by the rules. Still, as long as the great Umpire in the sky was taking note . . .

The sea out here was decidedly more choppy, and our small vessel began rocking and rolling like someone's Dad at a wedding. From the helm Pat turned around and gestured behind us,

'You want to watch that fridge,' he said.

I smiled, delighted by Pat's concern, and the gentle absurdity of his words. *'You want to watch that fridge.'* It was almost as if the fridge had a reputation for profligacy and philandering. God forbid. It hadn't even been plugged in.

Kieran was a thick-set man in his thirties with an admirable desire to help me out. When I got back from the harbour tour he had organised for me, he said he'd drive me back to Cork. On the way, we called at the

194 *Round Ireland with a fridge*

'Moving Statue of Ballinspittle', a grotto with a large statue of the Virgin Mary, so called because thousands of people claimed to have seen it move. But hang on a minute, Kieran knew exactly where the statue was, and without hesitation drove us straight there. Surely if the Moving Statue lived up to its name, no one would be entirely sure where it was going to be. Wouldn't enquiries have to be made? Didn't the local radio station have the latest 'Moving Statue news'?

'The Statue was last seen outside a supermarket in Bandon and was rumoured to be heading towards Clonakilty. We'll be bringing you more Moving Statue news later – now, on with the Death Notices – Rory O'Brien was tragically taken from us when a statue moved in front of his motorcycle on the R600 . . .'

Back in Cork I bought a newspaper and discovered that I had made the front page of *The Cork Evening Echo*, just alongside a Welsh groom who had finished his stag night in hospital after falling through the glass in a greenhouse. Evidently yesterday hadn't been a particularly newsworthy day. Never mind, I was the beneficiary, because there it was – a full-page picture of me and Saiorse, just beneath the headline,

HERE'S A COOL IDEA!

There followed a pun-packed article which continued on page three, where there were a further two photographs. Evidently yesterday had been a spectacularly un-newsworthy day. In Cork I was big news. I had made the front page of the *Evening Echo*, without evening having to fall through any greenhouses.

I checked into a hotel which Westimers had booked for me. Apart from the lift being out of action, the bathroom door having no handle, the shower curtain falling down, the window not opening, and the phone providing no outside line, it was just fine. Eric had authorised its booking, having phoned in from his fishing trip and learned that I was in town. He was cutting his fishing trip short especially so that the Fridge Party could be scheduled for the following night. I still had no idea what this party would involve. Whenever I broached the subject, those that I asked shrugged stylishly.

Eric and his wife Caroline were unable to throw any light on the matter when I met them for a drink that evening.

'We'll just see what happens,' said Eric.

Eric explained that he had called into *The Gerry Ryan Show* on that first day as something of a joke because he had been having some prob-

lems with the guys who did the refrigeration in his pub and the suggestion of a fridge party was a way of winding them up.

'So the joke's backfired on you now I'm here,' I said.

'Not at all. We'll have a great night.'

It was decided that I should make tomorrow a tourist day, and Eric
promised to take me and the fridge to kiss the Blarney Stone. This, as
legend would have it, would confer on us a magical eloquence, an area
in which for at least one of us there was room for improvement. Most of
the Irish I had met needed little assistance in this regard. For myself, I
was looking forward to being asked how I had found the whole Blarney
Stone experience: 'It was so moving, I was lost for words,' was going to
be my witty reply.

Not for the first time on my trip I began the day on national radio speaking to Gerry Ryan. He was intrigued by the notion of a Fridge Party.

'So what exactly do you intend to *do* at this thing?'

'We don't really know.'

'What about getting people to turn up with the bits and pieces from
their fridges, the ice tray or the egg tray or anything else that identifies
them as a fridge groupie.'

'Sounds good to me, although quite where it goes from there I have
no idea.'

It didn't matter. According to the fridge philosophy, we would wait
and see.

I got up, made use of the few facilities in the bathroom which were
operational and made my way over to Westimers to meet Eric. Outside
the pub was a huge blackboard with a misspelled chalk message
inscribed upon it,

FRIDGE PARTY TONNIGHT

I felt a tingle of butterflies.

It was the maritime port of Cobh which became my sightseeing venue
for the day, Eric having phoned to explain that he had forgotten about
his involvement in a charity golf event, and therefore couldn't make the
Blarney Stone outing after all. My winning line about being 'lost for
words' would have to be put on hold.

From behind the bar, Alan and Noelle were insistent that I should
take the fridge on the day trip.

'It'll be lonely if you leave it all on its own all day.'

Tough. I needed to conserve energy for tonight and I knew that if I took the fridge with me, some kind of adventure would befall us, and no doubt we would end up getting hopelessly delayed in a watering hole somewhere or other.

Getting to Cobh involved my first train journey in Ireland. It was marred by my having made the mistake of sitting opposite a man whose hair looked as if it hadn't been washed since 1967. It smelled like it hadn't been washed since 1952. It looked extremely heavy, the equivalent of having three damp cloths placed on his head. The pungent aroma of his hair easily justified a move up the train, but I didn't do so, partly out of a cowardly wish not to cause offence, and partly because I believed he and his hair would soon get off at one of the many stops which the sluggish train was making.

Cobh is a wonderful example of a Victorian port, commanding one of the world's largest natural harbours. The only negative thing I can say about it is that the man with the smelly hair lived there, and as a result I was absolutely gasping for fresh air on arrival. I climbed the hill to take a closer look at its magnificent cathedral. With a population of only eight thousand, Cobh didn't seem to deserve such a sizeable edifice, and the burden on its congregation for its refurbishment was equally disproportionate: £3,700,000. What is it with churches? Without exception *all* churches in Europe need money for refurbishment, yet in the mid west of America you'll very rarely see a church appeal for restoration. Which is odd, because they were the ones which were built by cowboys.

On the train home I saw someone reading the *Evening Echo* with my picture on the front, and I pondered the concept of fame. This was an area where I had found myself in the unique position of having complete control over my status. If I wanted to get recognised and be the centre of attention then I took the fridge out with me. If I wanted to have some time to myself and revert to some semblance of normality, then I left it indoors. It was beautiful in its simplicity. How Michael Jackson and Madonna must long for such an arrangement. Still, they should have thought of that before they sold million upon million of albums and plastered their faces on posters all over the world. I mayn't have had their wealth, but I had certainly outwitted them on the fame thing, and that was satisfying.

That night in my hotel room, I paced anxiously, rehearsing the speech I was going to make at the party. I had no desire to find myself floundering as I had done at the Bachelor Festival. This time I was subscribing to Baden Powell's motto for the scout movement – 'Be Prepared'.

I set off for the pub. Things began well. As I crossed the footbridge dragging my fridge behind me, I bumped into a group of about half a dozen girls from Cork school of art who were on their way to the party. If they were a sample of the kind of audience the fridge was going to attract, then things boded well for the evening.

'Look, it's the Fridge Man!' said a pretty girl with a cheeky little face, who I immediately identified as being the one I fancied most. There followed a constant stream of questions, all of which I was able to provide answers for, except one. 'So what exactly *is* a fridge party?'

'I really don't know. We're just going to have to wait and see. I think it's up to us.'

These were unchartered waters and there was no previous experience to draw on to ascertain what environment might be the most appropriate for the holding of a Fridge Party. However, there was to be no such difficulty in identifying the wrong environment for such an event, because it awaited us as we entered Westimers. The whole ambience of the place had changed. The lights were dimmed and loud music was blaring out from the stage where a young male duo surrounded by synthesizers and drum machines were performing.

'What's going on?' I shouted to Alan who was behind the bar.

'They're a band called "Pisces Squared". Unfortunately two months ago they were booked to play tonight, and we couldn't get hold of them to cancel.'

Right. So that meant that the background noise for the Fridge Party was cover versions of the hits of Erasure and Soft Cell, all stamped with the duo's trademark of excessive volume. I shouted hellos to some familiar faces – Dave, my Scottish PR man who had brought his wife to meet me, and Barry the Caffreys salesman who had arrived with his girlfriend and chums. However communication was limited to rudimentary greetings, such was the noise from 'Pisces Squared'. Now I'm no expert on astrology but here were two Pisceans with whom I was definitely not compatible.

The boys' manager hovered proudly by the stage, offering them encouragement and completely failing to notice that their techno pop message was falling on deaf ears. It became clear through the body language of the boys and their manager that this gig was something of a showbiz break and a milestone in their career to date. And so, a wholly unsatisfactory situation existed. An ambitious band, with eager manager in tow, were playing to an audience of the kind of eccentrics and quirky misfits who had been attracted by the concept of a Fridge Party, some carrying items which they had brought from their home refrigerator. The lead singer of the band looked visibly shaken.

Then there was the other side of the equation. A young Englishman, for whom tonight was to be a celebration of his extraordinary travels with a refrigerator across the length and breadth of Ireland, was unable to understand a bloody word anyone said to him because of the cacophonous din being created by a band sounding like they were in the death throes of their career.

'They're good, aren't they?' shouted Eric, the architect of this farrago, pointing to the band. He motioned to me and my harem of art students. 'Sit down over there and we'll bring you over some beer. Fosters gave us a case of beer by way of sponsoring the evening, so you may as well have it.'

The Fridge Party was sponsored? It was hard to imagine the phone conversation which might have brought that about.

There was one unexpected bonus resulting from this evening's spectacular shambles, and that was that I could devote my attentions to Mary, my favourite art student. I sat next to her and from close range we shouted intimately, occasionally making ourselves heard over the monotonous strains of the house band. From time to time a fridge devotee would come over to pay homage and sign the fridge, but Piscean decibel levels prevented any lasting exchanges. I didn't mind. It meant I could carry on my flirtatious bellowing with Mary.

'SO HOW MUCH LONGER HAVE YOU GOT TO GO ON YOUR DEGREE COURSE?'

'NOT REALLY, MAYBE LATER. I DON'T THINK YOU CAN DANCE TO THIS, CAN YOU?'

The development of our relationship was temporarily interrupted when I was asked to go outside and give an interview to a media studies student laden with recording equipment. When I returned some ten minutes later, the art students were looking a little sheepish.

'What is it?' I asked, but no one could hear me over the music.

Then I saw my jacket.

There cannot be many generic groups who include fabric paint in the list of items which they take with them on a night out, but art students are evidently one. During my absence they had made good use of this fabric paint, and there on the back of my denim jacket was a drawing of the fridge, and above it emblazoned in big bold red letters were the words,

FRIDGE MAN

Nervously, the girls watched me to gauge my reaction. After all, they *had* breached generally accepted social etiquette by painting all over someone's jacket whilst it had been left unattended. I, however, was delighted with their naughtiness.

'It's brilliant!' I announced, but they couldn't hear me over the music. Never mind, they could tell from my beaming smile that I approved.

Although the girls were by now quite drunk (substantial inroads had been made into the case of beer that Eric had carried over to us) their artistic ability was apparently not impaired in any way. I was genuinely pleased with their work. What's more, I became aware of the greater significance of their actions. As I pulled the jacket over my shoulders and stood proudly before them, I realised that I had *become* the 'Fridge Man'. The title, which I had jokingly bestowed upon the solitary figure I had seen by the roadside all those years ago, now belonged to me. I was now the embodiment of my own obsession.

Understandably enough, the band cut short their set.

'Goodnight Cork!' shouted the lead singer with a wave, and in a triumphant manner which had to be admired.

The audience, or 'Cork', managed a pitiful smattering of applause and the manager gave the boys a shake of the head which must have meant 'skip the encore'.

I was caught rather by surprise by all this. I had just managed to establish that Mary wasn't on a degree course at Cork School of Art but was the best friend of one of the others, when I heard a voice over the PA calling me to the stage.

'Ladies and Gentlemen, please welcome the Fridge Man.'

I felt like a ludicrous third-rate novelty act, only with less to offer. I was cheered to the stage by drunken whoops and hollers which were ominously reminiscent of Ballyduff. I quickly rifled through my pockets to find the notes for the speech which was going to set this performance apart from that fiasco. I had followed Baden Powell's advice and this time I was prepared.

'Good evening,' I began solidly. 'How many people have heard about me and the fridge?'

Cheers from the art students and hardly anyone else. Oh dear. Whilst

I had been holed up in a corner devoting my time to Mary, the pub had filled up with an entirely different crowd who were waiting for the club out the back to open in half an hour. All the fridge devotees had apparently buggered off, presumably having grown tired of both the venue and the lack of interest that I was showing in them.

On an echoey microphone I explained the concept of fridge travel to an audience whose attention span had already expired. Many had given up on me and had begun talking. All the preparation I had made was entirely useless. Naively, I had based it on the assumption that I would be faced with an audience who would be faintly appreciative. The piece of paper I was holding was as much use to me as a handkerchief to a sky diver whose parachute hadn't opened. For all the advice of Baden Powell – I still found myself going down as well as one of his scouts giving a short talk about reef knots. I abandoned my plans of performing a passionate discourse on how others should set their fridges free, and quickly switched to the much easier option of holding a second-rate competition. It was either that or die on my arse, and dying on my arse might make me less attractive to Mary.

'Okay, it's competition time, and the chance to win a two-week holiday in Barbados!' I announced.

A lot more people started listening now.

'As you may or may not know, on *The Gerry Ryan Show* this morning we asked you to bring in various pieces of fridge paraphernalia. The best one will win the holiday. So who's brought something from their fridge?'

A lady immediately appeared in front of me and handed me an ice cube.

'Aha! We have our first entry. Frankly it smacks of blatant opportunism but this lady has entered an ice cube. Quite whether she brought it from home or simply plucked it from her drink is a moot point, but nevertheless it's entry number one. What else have you got out there?'

No response.

'Okay, let's throw the net a little wider. I'll accept any item from the domestic world,' I said, desperately trying to prolong my time on stage and salvage some credibility. 'Come on, you can't let a lady win a two-week holiday in Barbados on the strength of having lifted an ice cube out of her drink.'

One of the art students rushed up and handed me a pair of scissors. The concept of participation began to catch on. A spoon followed, and then a tape measure.

'Come on, keep those entries coming. In a minute we'll have a vote and let you, the audience, decide on the winner.'

A plastic fork was next, then a comb, and quite magnificently, a drawing of a toaster. I could never have expected the standard of entries to be so high. I gave one last call for last-minute efforts. There was a sudden rush, including quite a bulky item, a dishwasher tray which I assumed someone had stolen from the kitchens. It proved very hand as a receptacle for all the other entries, which I now announced.

'So here is the final list of entries for the 1997 Fridge Party domestic item of the year. Please cheer to indicate your approval, and the one with the loudest cheer will win.' I cleared my throat. I now had the full attention of the room.

Boy, I was some performer. 'Okay, we start off with some scissors!'

A cheer from the girls who had entered the scissors.

'An ice cube!'

A cheer from the gang who had entered the ice cube. A pattern was emerging here. It continued, with each one being cheered by its own self-interest group.

'. . . a comb! A small plastic fork! A battery! A paintbrush! A drawing of a toaster! . . .'

I waited for a cheer here because this was my favourite entry, but sadly the response didn't do it justice.

'. . . A tape measure! A spoon! A sewing kit! A lighter! And an empty glass!'

The empty glass was surely the least impressive of all these entries, and yet received the largest cheer, purely on the strength of having been entered by the largest gathering.

'I don't believe this! You're a partisan lot, aren't you? Surely we can't let the prize go to someone who has simply handed in an empty glass?'

'You haven't announced the dishwasher tray!' shouted the man who had entered the dishwasher tray.

'Oh yes – I forgot that. Okay, who thinks the dishwasher tray should win?'

A huge cheer went up and victory was duly claimed. I invited the entrant on stage and sought confirmation from him that he hadn't simply nicked it from the pub's kitchens.

'No, I brought it from home myself,' he assured me and the audience.

'I see. You've got an industrial-sized dishwasher at home, have you?'

'I have.'

He deserved the non-existent prize alone for his willingness to lie.

'Are you sure you're not lying?'

'Yes, I'm sure.'

'Well, in that case you have just won two weeks in Barbados.' Huge cheers.

'But unfortunately for you, *I'm* lying.' Even bigger cheers. And some laughs too. I had begun to forget what it felt like to get those.

'Would you like to dance?' I shouted to Mary from the fringes of the dancefloor.

We were in the club at the back of Westimers which was absolutely packed. Any vestiges of a Fridge Party had been comprehensively washed away by this deluge of revellers.

'Yes I would,' came Mary's reply.

I think I might have gulped. I hadn't expected her to say yes. I now had to grapple with the possibility that she might fancy me. I certainly fancied her. She had very sexy lips.

We danced like no one was watching, and an hour later, not far from the pub, we sat on a wall by the canal and kissed in exactly the same manner. We were so drunk that we had lost all touch with the fact that we were in a public place and were quite oblivious to the presence of a young guy who was stood over us. When I eventually noticed him, he made no remark about our disgustingly passionate kiss which had presumably resembled two people attempting to eat a meal out of each other's mouths. Instead he said, 'Have you got a marker?'

'What?'

'Have you got a marker? I want to sign your fridge.'

I had forgotten we had Saiorse with us. How embarrassing, carrying on like that in front of a fridge.

'Yeah sure,' I said, and fumbled around in my pocket until I found a marker pen for him.

'Thanks,' he said on completing his signature, and off he went into the night.

Mary laughed.

'Have you ever had a kiss interrupted for that before?' she asked.

'Oh God yes. It happens to me all the time.'

Although we were disgustingly, hideously, and embarrassingly drunk, we kissed inspirationally. On each break for air, both of us felt moved to say things like 'That was nice' or 'That was lovely', and the thing was, we both meant it. Mary's kiss was extraordinary. As far as I could tell she had been chainsmoking all evening but yet her mouth and breath bore no trace of cigarette's stale taste. You could keep your Moving Statue of Ballinspittle, this was what I called a miracle.

'I feel really close to you now,' I whispered, kissing her gently on the neck.

'And me to you,' she replied, hugging me with a surprising intensity. Then I fell off the wall.

'Do you want to come back to my hotel?' I asked buoyantly, after we had established that the grazes weren't too serious.

'I don't think that would be a good idea, would it?' came the sinking reply.

Why do girls do that? Say the 'I don't think it would be a good idea' bit, but then add 'would it' on the end. Like they want confirmation from you. And like you're going to give it.

'I don't think that would be a good idea, would it?'

'Well, of course you're absolutely right. It was probably the worst idea I have ever had, and I've had some crap ones in my time. Your coming back to the hotel with me was a rubbish idea, forget I ever mentioned it.'

The fact is though, I knew that it probably wasn't a good idea. We needed to pass out in our own spaces.

'I'll get you a taxi.'

We kissed again. Kissing her really was terribly good fun.

'Come with me,' I said, as we separated ourselves.

'What? I thought you were going to get me a taxi?'

'Not, come with me *now*, come with me *tomorrow*. Come with me to Dublin. Let's finish my journey together.'

Mary looked at me like she hadn't had a drink all night. Shock can have a very sobering effect.

'Come on,' I continue bravely, 'just you and me . . . well, and a fridge.'

It couldn't have been more romantic. Remarkably, she was starting to look tempted. I persisted.

'Mary, do it! Take a chance in life. Come with me. It feels right – we feel so close.'

'I can't, I've got work tomorrow.'

'Oh. What exactly is it you do?'

Maybe we weren't as close as I had thought.

22

In The Doghouse

I felt battered and war torn as I made the short walk to Westimers to say my goodbyes. As I trundled along, I couldn't understand why my elbow was aching, but on raising my shirt sleeve I saw that it was grazed, and then remembered the heroic way in which the injury had been sustained. Just like Sir Ranulph Fiennes, who returned from his expedition to the South Pole with frostbite so serious that three of his toes only just escaped amputation, I too had paid a price for my valiant exploration. I studied my wounds and decided that severe though they were, the need for amputation would be unlikely, at least until my return to the UK. I rolled my shirt sleeve back down and resolved to get on with the day without giving it another moment's thought. I couldn't complain. I had known the dangers of both sitting on a wall, and kissing, and had chosen to do both at the same time. I was in pain, but the hurt wasn't so bad that I couldn't carry on. Heck, you get used to it when you're a risk taker.

A guy in a car which had just passed leant out of his window and shouted, 'Hey, Fridge Man! How ya doing?'

I assumed that he must have been at the party last night, because I had left the fridge back at the hotel and was therefore in 'anonymous' mode. But when the same thing happened again, moments later, the truth dawned on me. Of course. I had 'Fridge Man' written on my back.

I had surrendered my advantage over Madonna and Michael Jackson.

'Hello there, Tony, how are ya?' called another driver, who stopped this time.

That was odd. How did he know my name? I didn't have Tony written on my back as well, did I?

'How have you enjoyed your stay in Cork?' he said, getting out of his car. He was the taxi driver who had driven me and the wedding party from Baltimore to Cork. When he heard I was about to set off on the road again, he said that he'd be back to Westimers in ten minutes to take me out to the main road.

Things happened fast in Cork.

'Where are you headed then?' asked Alan as he and the rest of the staff stood outside the bar to see me off.

'As far as I can get. Waterford would be good. Wexford would be even better.'

Today was going to be my last day's hitching for a while because I had learned that this weekend was a big bank holiday weekend in Ireland, and holiday traffic was useless to me. I wasn't going to 'do it Dunmanway' again. I was going to hole up someplace and enjoy the holiday weekend in the same spirit as the rest of the country, before the final leg to Dublin.

From the taxi, I called Mary at work to say goodbye. It felt odd. In a matter of a few hours she had turned from soul mate back into relative stranger. The feeling was compounded when the girl on the switchboard said 'Mary who?' and I didn't know.

'Well, what does she do?'

'I don't know.'

'We've got three Marys here.'

'Oh. Well, all I've just got is a number written on a piece of paper.'

'We've got one Mary in accounts, one in admin, and a newish girl – I'm not sure what she does – but she's just gone home feeling sick.'

'That'll be her. Definitely.'

'Hold on, I'll just see if I can get her.'

Before I could point out the lack of wisdom of this course of action, my line was hijacked by some irritating jangly synthesizer music which someone somewhere perceives may make people more relaxed whilst they are waiting on the phone. My views are quite forthright on this one – I think it's an affront to one's personal dignity. Before I could become truly exasperated, the jangly sounds were interrupted by the voice of 'Oh Bright One'.

'I'm afraid that Mary isn't here today, she's just gone home feeling sick.'

'Oh right,' I said, pretending to be surprised. 'Never mind, thanks anyway. And hey, you hang on for that promotion.'

'What?'

'Nothing.'

I knew I wouldn't have to wait long for my first lift. Almost everyone in Cork must have known that the eejit with the fridge was in town. I'd been on national radio advertising the world's first Fridge Party (and probably the last), and my picture had been plastered all over the *Evening Echo*.

'Oh, I recognised your fridge straight away,' said Liam, my first lift of the day, a policeman who had just come off duty.

He took me twenty minutes or so down the road to a place called Middleton, where he signed the fridge and posed for a picture in his uniform, pretending to bust me for having a fridge trolley with bald tyres. A good sport.

At Middleton I had a few problems. The particular stretch of road on which I found myself was extremely popular with hitchers and I found myself at the end of a queue of three. Slowly but surely I worked my way up to pole position and other hitchers arrived to take up the vacant number two and three slots. I was immensely irritated when these two newcomers got lifts *before* me. What was going on? I wanted to call out, 'DO YOU KNOW WHO I AM?'

I assumed that the drivers must have known the hitchers, for I could see no other reason for the flouting of the 'first come, first served' convention, unless 'fridge fatigue' had set in. Maybe I had become over-exposed. It was over an hour before I was invited to hop into the car of Tomas, a fisherman who had been to Cork to see a chiropractor.

'I'm in my fifties now, and things are beginning to pack up,' he said. 'You're a young man, you won't get the aches and pains yet.'

That depended on how many walls I fell off.

'What are you doing over here in Ireland?' he asked.

'Oh, I'm just travelling around having a look at the place.'

I could have said more, but I was intrigued by the fact that Tomas had watched me lift the fridge on to the back seat but had said nothing about it. Secretly I was hoping that he mightn't ask.

His knowledge of European history and politics was extensive. Much of the journey was spent discussing Tito's achievements in unifying Yugoslavia, and a savage recent past which had see his work undone. He was a bright man with an active interest in the world. But, brilliantly, he had no interest at all in why his passenger had apparently chosen to travel Ireland with a fridge for company. As he dropped me just outside Dungarvan and drove away, the subject had never been raised, and I punched the air.

'Yes!'

I had wanted that to happen.

Five minutes later a police car did a U-turn and drew up beside me. Two policemen got out. For the first time I began to wonder if what I was doing might transgress some ancient Irish law. Perhaps hitching with a domestic appliance on a public highway carried a maximum sentence of five years.

'Look, he's even got "Fridge Man" written on his back,' said one to the other as they giggled their way towards me.

It was clear that I wasn't in trouble.

'We've heard you and seen you on TV. Some weather, isn't it? My, but you've got a colour on you. We were driving by and I said to John, "Jesus Christ – that's the man with the fridge!"'

He continued to effuse for some time. I fended off questions about my trip for the next ten minutes, missing the opportunity of countless lifts as they sped past a scene which to them must have looked like two cops booking a fridge for speeding.

'Have you had any bad experiences?'

'Not one.'

'Ah well, when we get good weather in this country everyone is on good form.'

And the weather was good, and a long way from the driving rain normally associated with bank holiday weekends. It was hot. Really hot. Almost as if someone up there had got Ireland mixed up with the south of France. It was glorious.

'Can you give me a lift then?' I asked the two officers, cheekily.

'Oh jeez, we'd love to, but I don't think we're allowed to. You wouldn't be insured.'

'Well, what about if you arrested me?'

'Ah now that's a good idea. We could arrest you, and then release you saying that we had decided to prosecute you by summons.'

A discussion then followed in which we attempted to decide upon the exact crime I could have committed. Murder was considered too harsh, drunk and disorderly not serious enough, and loitering with a fridge apparently wasn't an offence. I wanted them to charge me with ram raiding. A special kind of ram raiding in which the offender hurls a fridge through a shop window, arranges it nicely, prices it up and pops back the next day to see if it's been sold.

Unfortunately, one of the policemen finally decided that he was too close to promotion to risk this kind of bogus arrest, and that they couldn't be sure that their superior officer would see the funny side.

'Of course, I could just smash one of you in the face and then you'd have to arrest me,' I observed, prompting hysterical laughter.

I wish I could be more menacing at times.

The two uniformed men got back in their car and called out, 'Well, goodbye and good luck.'

And with those gentle words my brush with the law was over. I had never had such a relaxed and pleasant conversation with two policemen before and I doubted whether I ever would again.

It isn't often as a hitch-hiker that you get on so well with the person that stops for you that you go back to their house for tea, get driven on a further twenty-five miles so that you can reach your intended destination, go out drinking with them, on to a nightclub, and then finally stay over at their parents' house.

Such was the way with Tom. He was in his thirties, single, and clearly had something of the charming rascal about him. We had such a lot in common (apart from the rascal bit, obviously), including both having taken part in a bachelor festival. Tom had won his and had gone on to compete at the international festival in Ballybunion.

'What actually happens at that?' I asked.

'You just drink for ten days. Literally,' he replied.

'What? Just lots of bachelors together?'

'God no, there are loads of girls.'

'Right. And they go there looking for husbands?'

'I suppose so.'

'But you can make the interviewing process as rigorous as you want it to be.'

'Exactly.'

It was an odd concept, and somehow typically Irish. A festival with the express goal of turning bachelors into husbands, places them in an arena where they are surrounded by booze and birds for ten days. Hardly an environment likely to cause a major rethink, and rejection of their bachelor status – 'God, I can't stand this hellish life anymore, I must chuck it all in and settle down.'

'Did any of the bachelors go on to get married to anyone they met there?' I asked.

'Not that I know of.'

Now there's a surprise.

Tom lived in Waterford, and that is where we took tea. His parents lived in Wexford and that was where we spent the night. We didn't get there until three in the morning, having spent all night in a pub called the Centenary Stores which, just like Westimers, happened to have a club as an annexe out the back. When his parents awoke to a note from Tom saying that he had brought a houseguest home with him, and then they had seen a rucksack and fridge at the foot of the stairs, they must have begun to worry about the kind of circles their son was now moving in.

Tom was in the doghouse in the morning, having overslept by an hour and a half for the game of golf we had arranged to play with two of his friends, Baxter and Jeff. When we got to the course we were lucky enough to be granted a later tee time by the stern-looking club professional, and we proceeded to play eighteen holes of pretty dire golf. Hey, but it didn't matter that the golf was bad, this was a holiday for me. Time off from the fridge.

However, as I loaded my hired golfclubs on to their trolley, it did seem to me absurd to have spent nigh on a month pulling a fridge along behind me, only to choose as my first leisure activity a game in which you pulled gear behind you on a trolley for hours on end.

When the golf was over, Tom was in the doghouse again, this time for not having phoned his girlfriend last night or this morning. We discussed excuses he might adopt for extrication from this tight spot. The truth, which I had advocated, was deemed by Tom simply not to be an option.

'Oh yeah, I'll just say, "Sorry dear, I forgot to call you because I was busy looking after the hitch-hiker who is travelling the country with his fridge." She'll just turn to her friend and say, "Ah, Tom's on to the more elaborate excuses now."'

His girlfriend was in Galway where he was about to drive and join her for the rest of the weekend. He reckoned that bringing her flowers was the only answer. Maybe he was right. 'Say it with flowers' because nine times out of ten trying to say it with words will only land you in it even further. There isn't a 'Sorry' big enough to match a good old-fashioned bouquet, and most men know it.

Before he left, Tom drove me round Wexford in search of a place for me to stay. Everywhere was booked up. Evidently a large proportion of Dublin's population descended on this part of the world for the holiday weekend. Tom had a solution, though.

'You could stay at Butch's,' he said.

'Could I?'

'Yeah, he's just opened a hostel.'

Ugh. That word. Hostel.

'Err . . . it's just that–'

'It's really cool. Much nicer than most hostels. It's only been open a couple of months.'

I didn't have a choice. I was disappointed though. I had promised myself that I would never stay in a hostel again as long as I lived. That was ten days ago. Just ten days. I owed myself a huge bouquet of flowers.

I was greeted by Butch and Karen, who were young and normal looking. Somehow I had expected everyone involved with hostels to look like extras out of the movie *Hair*. They both got the giggles when I put them in the picture about me and the fridge, but eventually calmed down enough for me to explain my reservations about hostel life.

'I just can't sleep if there are loads of other people in the room.'

'It's all right,' said Butch, 'I'll put you in a room with only one other guy. He's from England, like you.'

It sounded bearable, although I was fully aware that his being 'from England, like me' was no guarantee that he didn't snore.

Tom had been right though, this was a cool hostel. Over a cup of tea, which was reassuringly unherbal, Butch told me how he and his girl-friend had bought up the derelict property and converted it into the hostel. It bore no sign of the starkness and deference to self reliance of the one in Letterfrack, and appeared to be closer to a kind of hostel for the less hardy, who drank Coca Cola, ate meat and popped things in the microwave to save time.

'She's gone, though,' Butch added, a touch ruefully.

'Who has?'

'The girlfriend. We split up just before the place opened.'

'Oh. Well, who's Karen then?'

'Ah, she's not my girlfriend,' he laughed, 'she's from New Zealand. She stayed here for a few days and then asked if she could work here for a while to get some money together. She's a good worker.'

She came in carrying a dustpan and brush, as if to illustrate Butch's point, but then she sat down and joined us for tea, throwing it into some doubt again.

'I've finished for the day. Thank goodness for that,' she said.

The subject turned inevitably to fridge travel and I found that now I could almost answer every question by rote. I got off the subject by firing questions at Karen about her travels which she must have been equally familiar with answering.

'Do people just assume you're Australian at first?' I asked.

'Yeah. But the accent is different, you know.'

'Yes. Don't you say "sex" instead of "six"?'

'Apparently. Australians are always trying to get us to say it, so they ask questions like "What's eight minus two?" But we're wise to it and we just answer "half a dozen".'

I looked at her and decided that she was rather attractive in her own way. I found myself contemplating what 'half a dozen' with her might be like.

'I like your red shorts,' said Karen. 'They're cool.'

'Thanks.'

I was unable to return the compliment with a flattering remark about what I had just been admiring about her. It wouldn't have been considered good manners.

A balding man in his forties came in and broached a familiar subject. 'So you're the guy travelling with the fridge then?'

This was Dave, my roommate. He proceeded to ask the entire set of questions that I'd just been asked, only in a Yorkshire accent. This was a pain, but provided he didn't snore, I could forgive him anything.

The plan for the night was simple enough. Sit like a couch potato alongside Butch and Dave and watch the Poland versus England World Cup qualifier on the TV in the hostel's pleasant little lounge, and then grab some rejuvenating and much needed sleep in the form of a very early night. But something happened which changed all that.

The hostel filled up.

Wexford is a vibrant but compact little town, and it was evidently brimming over with holidaying Dubliners. Butch had even checked in two married couples and their kids, such was the extent to which the town's boarding facilities had been stretched. Butch was delighted actually, announcing that this was the first night the hostel had been full since it had opened. I found it difficult to share his enthusiasm. It now meant that there were six people in my room instead of just me and Dave, and one of them was bound to be an inveterate snorer.

So, instead of the quiet night, I went to a barbecue with Butch, wandered into town and drank steadily in one of Wexford's many splendid pubs. I ended up at the Junction, the kind of club where everyone leaves saying 'Right, I swear that's the last time I go to that cattlemarket', honouring the oath until the next time they've had a skinful, and someone says 'Ah come on, it's not that bad.'

When I woke at 9.30, the mission had been successfully accomplished. Six hours of undisturbed sleep; okay, not sleep, unconsciousness. The room smelt as if experiments in germ warfare had been taking place in it during the night. I soon found out why.

'It's the four teenage lads down from Dublin – they've been farting non-stop since they got in,' said Dave, as I joined him, Karen and Butch for breakfast in the hostel's small rear garden.

'And what time did they get in?'

'Eight o'clock.'

'Blimey, that's impressive.'

'They made a hell of a racket when they came in,' Dave went on, 'I'm surprised they didn't wake you.'

'They would have done if I hadn't drunk myself into a sufficiently comatose state, but I can't do that again tonight, my body simply won't take it.'

'I think you're going to have to,' said Karen, 'because everywhere in Wexford is full for the next two nights, and you'll find it the same all the way up the coast between here and Dublin.'

'Well, I'm not going back in that room except to get my stuff out,' I protested. 'That room is the smelliest room on earth. It's frightening to think that only four arses could produce such a putrefying stench.'

'Just another one of the many miracles of the human body,' said Butch flippantly, who proceeded to point to the corner of the garden. 'You could always sleep in the doghouse.'

Everyone laughed. Except me. I looked. The doghouse. The doghouse, eh? I immediately got to my feet and wandered over to have a closer look at it. It was a small wooden structure about six feet long, and four feet high at the apex of its pitched roof. I looked inside and saw that it was full of junk.

'Where's the dog?' I enquired.

'That went with the girlfriend, but the doghouse stayed. It's a kind of shrine to the failure of our relationship.'

Never mind shrine, it was an oasis. In present circumstances, a very appealing piece of real estate. I got down on my hands and knees and crawled in a little way. It was dark and had a musty smell, but compared to my room, which was presently occupied by a quartet of farters, this was a relative herb garden.

'Tony, get out of there, it's full of bricks and building shite,' said Butch.

'Yes, but I could clear that out.'

'Don't be stupid man, it's a doghouse. You're not seriously thinking of sleeping in it?'

'I am. It's got everything. A secluded location, privacy, and an en suite toilet,' I said, pointing to the garden.

My earnestness was greeted with incredulity. Butch, Karen and Dave couldn't see what I could clearly see – that sleeping in the doghouse was by far and away preferable to what was on offer in my present room. Above all it meant I could get an early night and allow sleep the healer to repair some of the mental and physical damage of the past three weeks. Without it I could collapse.

'I bet you wouldn't sleep in there,' said Karen.

'Careful,' said Dave. 'He's a dangerous man to bet with. I mean look what he's doing with that fridge.'

'He's too tall to fit in it. He won't do it,' reiterated Karen.

'I bet I do. I bet you a hundred pounds I do.'

'I haven't got a hundred pounds.'

'You will have in the morning,' interjected a very amused Butch.

'All right then, 16p. I bet you 16p that I sleep in this doghouse tonight,' I said, proffering my hand for the sealing handshake.

'Okay. 16p it is.'

Karen took my hand in hers and we shook. It was a long, lingering handshake, in fact it just seemed to keep going. Karen made no attempt to release my hand, and for some reason I felt that the onus was on her to do the releasing. As we shook, we looked into each other's eyes, a moment which was almost embarrassing in its intimacy. In the corner of my eye, I was aware of Butch and Dave shuffling in their seats nervously. I gulped. I must learn to stop doing that. I don't think it's particularly cool.

It was I who released the handshake. I had become unnerved by the eye thing. Some different form of communication had just gone on, and although the meaning seemed clear enough, history had shown that this was a language I was well capable of misinterpreting. Karen, I suspected, spoke the language fluently. Most girls do. Boys don't speak it at all, but just understand a smattering of key words. Their job is not to make a pig's ear of the translation. They normally fail quite spectacularly.

It took an hour and a half to clear out the 'building shite', as Butch had so eloquently described it. On completion I surveyed the new sleeping quarters. Spartan, yes, a little bleak maybe, but they were dry, and the weather looked set on remaining glorious so the suspect roof was an irrelevance. All in all it was accommodation fit for a King of Tory.

Most of that day was spent like Sundays should be, sitting around and doing not very much in particular.

'Dave, Karen and Butch, do you want another cup of tea?' I said. It sounded like I was addressing a 1960s folk band.

They said 'yes', of course. They liked their tea, did Dave, Karen and Butch. Dave, like Karen, was living in the hostel until a boat on which he was planning to take tourists on fishing trips had been repaired. He was a nice chap, but he let himself down by being a little too eager to talk about boats.

'She was a forty-five-footer,' he would say, 'with a fibre-glass hull, and running rigging on an aluminium mast. My last boat had standing rigging, but also on an aluminium mast. I swear by them, aluminium masts.'

He was at his most dull when he was in the act of rolling his own cigarettes, something which Karen also did. For some reason, people who roll their own cigarettes always become mind numbingly boring whilst occupied in that act itself. It is almost as if the intricate detail of the rolling causes the brain to lock in with it somehow, resulting in slow and longwinded sentences. Because they are concentrating on the job, the 'rollers' make no eye contact with those on the receiving end of their drivel and therefore fail to notice the extent to which their listener has ceased to be transfixed. There was one occasion when Dave and Karen each simultaneously rolled themselves a cigarette, with excruciating results.

'You know the modern marine diesel,' droned Dave, 'is an astonishingly durable piece of kit. The main problem is that it's underused compared to versions of the same basic engine which more often than not will run for thousands of hours performing their shore-bound tasks in buses, taxis and the like.'

'You're right, Dave. My Dad had a boat with a diesel auxiliary and he only used it at weekends,' replied Karen, head bowed over the sacred Rizlas, 'and he always said that diesels die of neglect – not over-work.'

Not until the construction of the limp cigarettes was completed, and they were popped into mouths and puffed at, did the conversation stop sounding like a cassette tape for an insomnia cure.

The subsequent simultaneous rolling of a tenth cigarette drove me to do something with my day, and I borrowed Butch's bike and cycled to Curracloe, a six-mile stretch of sandy beach just north of the town, where I got my first glimpse of an Irish traffic jam, as hordes of holiday-makers clogged up roads designed to take a tractor or two and not anything like this wholesale invasion.

I'm sure that Curracloe beach is stunning on any other weekend of the year, but for this one the tourists had taken it over and done a pretty good job of masking its beauty. Ghettoblasters, litter, ice-cream vans, screaming kids, and snogging couples were distributed along the beach and amongst the dunes. Most people were sunburnt. The Irish sing, talk and drink well, but when it comes to tanning, they perform abysmally. I winced as I watched them parading their grossly uncovered bodies before the sun's powerful rays – shoulders, thighs and bald patches already a bright rose colour, soon prompting a remark from an equally crimson relative – 'I think you may have overdone it a bit.'

On the way home I noticed the registration number of the car in front of me:

HIV 966

Not personalised I hoped.

As I cycled along I imagined one possible exchange the owner of this vehicle might have with a policeman.

'Is this your vehicle, sir?'

'Yes, it is.'

'What's your registration?'

'I think it's HIV but I'm not positive.'

I took Karen to the pub that night. It was like having a date. I had specifically made the invitation to her and not extended it to Dave, who was sat alongside us watching some disappointing television. Two motives had been behind his exclusion: one was a desire to have an evening without any mention of the durability of aluminium, and the other, well – the other was probably to do with 'the other'. It was foolish, and I knew it, not least because I had only slept a few hours in the last seventy-two, but it was probably the corollary of this that I was too tired to make the sensible decision.

When we got back to the hostel, I threw in a corker of a line, 'Would you like to come back to my place for a coffee?'

Karen laughed.

'Are you *really* going to sleep in there?'

'16p is 16p. I'd be a fool not to. Why don't you join me in there for a nightcap?'

'Okay,' she giggled.

I was in new territory. I had never invited a girl back to a doghouse before.

We made two coffees in the kitchen, carried them out to the garden, and climbed into my lodgings.

'Hey, it's surprisingly cosy,' said Karen.

And it was too. Before leaving the pub, I had filled it with cushions taken from the living room, and unzipped my expensive sleeping bag and laid it out like a bed cover. I was glad it was getting some use at last, even if it wasn't quite fulfilling the lifesaving role I had envisaged for it.

'What you need in here are some candles,' remarked Karen.

'Yes, I haven't got the lighting quite right.'

It was almost pitch darkness.

'I'll go and get some,' she said keenly.

For someone with 16p at stake, she was almost acting irresponsibly.

The candles almost completed the transition of doghouse to love nest. The rest was up to me. Karen was showing all the signs of someone who wasn't going to slap my face if I leant over to kiss her. I decided to have a go. I took a deep breath and attempted to swivel round so I was facing her, but cracked my head on the low part of the pitched roof. Not unnaturally, it hurt quite a lot, but I made a snap decision to try and complete the kiss regardless. It was made difficult by the fact that Karen had begun laughing uncontrollably. I stopped short of her mouth, and suddenly saw the funny side myself, breaking into fits of giggles. The moment of passion had been hijacked by hilarity. I hoped that this wasn't going to be a feature of all my future lovemaking.

The laughter subsided. There we were, inches apart, directly under the apex of the roof, so with ample headroom. Surely now the kiss was inevitable. Slowly I moved my mouth towards hers. She closed her eyes, I closed mine and we waited for my gentle forward momentum to bring us together. Until a voice outside halted it.

'I THOUGHT I HEARD SOME VOICES OUT HERE – SO HE'S REALLY GOING TO DO IT THEN?'

Dave had arrived.

He got down on to his haunches and peered inside whilst I hurriedly threw myself back into a non-kissing position, catching my head on the same bit of roof as I did so.

'I've got the kettle on. Do you want a cup of tea?' Dave asked.

'Yeah, okay,' said Karen.

'Yeah, okay'? What did she mean 'Yeah okay'? The answer was surely an unequivocal 'NO'. 'NO, DAVE LEAVE US ALONE, WE DON'T WANT TEA, WE WANT TO KISS EACH OTHER, NOW GO AWAY.' Not, 'Yeah, okay.'

'How about you, Tone?' he added.

'Yeah, okay.'

He was a difficult man to say no to.

Dave wasn't an insensitive man. After only forty minutes squashed up in one end of an already crowded doghouse advocating the advantages of a steel hull over a wooden one, he realised that there might be something marginally more exciting going on between Karen and I, and made a remark which I might have welcomed a little earlier. 'I'll go in a minute and stop cramping your style.'

Neither Karen or I made any protest. There were no entreaties of, 'No, please Dave, you hang on here for another hour or so, it would be interesting to find out more about how seriously rotting wood can lead to a cracked bilge stringer.' We were unambiguously in favour of him going away.

Our silence ought to have been a cue for Dave to leave immediately, but he just hung on and hung on. He kept looking like he was going to leave, even teasing us with the actual words 'I'll go now' from time to time, but the problem was, he didn't correctly understand the meaning of 'now'. Half an hour later I was on the very brink of saying, 'Dave, will you please, please piss off', when, for some inexplicable reason, he pissed off of his own accord. Perhaps he was getting tired, and had finally begun to pick up on telltale signs that he wasn't that welcome – little things like Karen and I no longer responding to a word he said.

I moved closer to Karen, taking care not to bang my head this time.

'I thought he was never going to go.'

'Me too.'

And we kissed. Almost in celebration.

It lacked passion. The past hour had taken its toll. We continued kissing though, initially through a lack of anything else to do, but as the minutes passed the desire began to return. Hands started to make their first exploratory moves. Tentative forays were made beneath garments and it soon became apparent that the need to be tentative could soon be abandoned.

Things were hotting up.

Until a voice outside cooled them down.

'ARE YOU GUYS REALLY IN THERE?'

Butch had arrived.

'DAVE SAID YOU WERE IN HERE.'

Cheers Dave.

'MAKE WAY FOR ME, I'M COMING IN,' he shouted.

I hoped the neighbours weren't hearing all this.

Butch was impressively drunk. He treated his reluctant audience to an embittered diatribe, the main theme of which was the present unsatisfactory state of his love life. It was very funny, and even in these circumstances, he had us both laughing. But funny or not, we still wanted him to go. He seemed blissfully unaware that his tirade about unsatisfactory sexual liaisons was preventing the initiation of a new one.

'Oscar Wilde summed it all up,' he railed, '"What is love? It is when two fools misunderstand each other."'

I thought yes, and will you please bugger off and give the two of us a chance to misunderstand each other. We've been dying to misunderstand each other for the past hour and a half. In fact the only thing we have been able to understand about each other is that we're desperate to do a bit of misunderstanding. *Understand?*

Eventually he left, but not before wheeling the fridge up to the door, saying, 'I've brought the fridge along to keep an eye on you both.'

Yes, yes. Very funny. Now GO!

There is a reason why people don't make love in doghouses more often. Dogs don't even do it. They would rather suffer the indignity of doing it outside with people watching than do it in a doghouse. To our credit though, Karen and I had a go, and under the circumstances I think we did pretty well. One of the main problems was that the doghouse was too short for my body, and my feet had to stick out of the door. With this particular evening being a clear and chilly one, this meant that I had cold feet throughout the entire proceedings, in more ways than one. Because of this need for exterior feet dangling, the doghouse had to be left open, and this allowed occasional gusts of cool breeze to penetrate areas where one wouldn't normally welcome a rush of cold air. The lack of headroom also proved problematical on occasions, and if either of us lost concentration or momentarily forgot where we were (difficult, but hey, I like to think it could happen), then we were all too quickly reminded of our immediate vicinity with a blow to the head. (It is with some regret that in presenting an accurate depiction of the night's events, I have been unable to use the words 'blow' and 'head' in anything other than their purest sense.)

All in all, the artificial obstacles which we had to overcome made the whole encounter feel like an event in *It's A Knockout*. (The mini marathon, I like to think.) We had represented Banbury as best we could, but it was unlikely that our performance had been enough to nudge us ahead of Kettering and on to further competition in Europe.

I woke in the morning and looked outside. There was the fridge looking back at me. It was jealous, no doubt about it, but that was understandable enough. After all, it had never been plugged in, and now I had.

And I had a splinter to prove it.

23
Triumphal Entry
(A title I had considered for the previous chapter)

Today was a bank holiday Monday. If it had been a Sunday I might have gone to confession. After all, I had something to confess now, praise the Lord.

'Father forgive me, but last night I slept with a girl in a doghouse, in full view of a fridge.'

I wonder how many Hail Marys you'd get for that. It probably wasn't on their Sin-Penance guideline chart.

As a matter of fact, any confession I might make would have to begin with the words, 'Forgive me father, for I'm not actually a Catholic.'

That was definitely not on the Sin-Penance chart.

After the emotional highs of a short ceremony overseen by Dave and Butch, in which Karen coughed up her 16p and we all taped the coins to the side of the fridge, I began to feel exceptionally tired. My dwindling energy levels needed to be replenished by the calories which a cooked breakfast could provide, so I walked down to a café on the Quays which Butch had recommended. As I tucked into my scrambled egg, the truth dawned on me that my journey was almost over, and that Dublin was only a few hours' drive away. Feelings of both relief and sadness were overtaken by concern. I might only be a day away from a huge anti-climax.

Up until now, the policy of 'just seeing what happens' had served me well, but now there was a definite case for forward planning. I felt strongly that the finale to such an epic journey required some ceremonial commemoration, and by the time I had finished my breakfast I knew what had to be done.

I ordered a second pot of tea and called the office of *The Gerry Ryan Show* from the mobile, and outlined my idea. They loved it.

'We'll call you back in ten minutes, Tony,' said Willy, one of the show's producers, 'this is worth interrupting our bank holiday special for. We'll work out exactly how you should do it and then get you to talk about it to Gerry on air. We'll have you on as the first item tomorrow morning too, just to give the thing a big build-up.'

Just the response I was looking for.

Gerry waxed lyrical, as ever.

'I have on the line, Tony Hawks, the Fridge Man, who on his journey round this fair isle has been taken into the hearts of the Irish people, and he has been showered with the kind of hospitality normally saved for a national hero, and he's sunk a bevy or two along the way too. How are you this morning, Tony?'

'Oh, I'm fine, Gerry.'

'I believe that you are about to complete your epic journey, well done. Congratulations to you. Now how do you intend to round off a trip like this?'

'Well, I want to march into Dublin with my fridge and I want people to join me as I go.'

'Good idea, a kind of triumphal entry.'

'Exactly.'

'Well, you know Caesar never brought his legions into Rome, but I think on this occasion we can make an exception – you can bring the fridge into Dublin.'

'And I thought it would be a good idea if people joined me on this march with a domestic appliance of their choice.'

'Even better idea. Some friends for the fridge.'

'Exactly, because it's not just about fridges this, so bring a kettle, a toaster or whatever, because there are all kinds of appliances which need liberating from the confines of the kitchen.'

'You heard him, folks. The man is talking sense, so unplug your kitchen or domestic appliances and join Tony on the march tomorrow, be it with a kettle, a toaster, an iron – or even a cooker, a fridge freezer or microwave.'

A microwave. I should have done my journey with a microwave, I could have done it in a third of the time.

'Now Tony, listen closely,' continued Gary, 'whilst I outline the planned route for this march. We want people to join you with a kitchen appliance of their choice at Connolly Station at 11 am, and having gathered there with food mixers, spatulas or whatever, the procession will then move, in triumph, up Talbot Street, up Henry Street, and then into the ILAC Centre in May Street where we will have an extravaganza beyond imagination awaiting you there, for you finally to lay this whole trip to rest. So come on everyone – we want to make Tony's entrance into the capital city a spectacular Disneyesque-style Roman entrance, we want him to be borne, if not on a real chariot then at least on one in the imaginations of the Irish people. Tony, you rest up now and I'll talk to you tomorrow.'

Good. That was a bit of a result. One phonecall over breakfast and the country was being mobilised in my support. It was going to be difficult to re-adjust to life back in London.

I was rather pleased with the plan, and another pot of tea was in order. I had just begun a daydream in which I was picturing myself being cheered along Dublin's thronging streets, when a vaguely familiar voice hauled me back to reality.

'So Tony, how's the form?'

It was Jim, one of Tom's mates who I had met in town on Friday night. I told him how the form was, and exactly how exhausted I was becoming.

'Why don't you stay at ours tonight? Jennifer won't mind,' he said generously.

It was an offer I couldn't refuse, although I suspected that failure to do so, mightn't meet with universal approval.

I needn't have worried. I had been flattering myself to think that Karen would be remotely bothered one way or the other.

'God, I wouldn't want another night in there,' she said, after I had explained my intentions, 'besides, I really need to get some sleep tonight too.'

I decided that Karen was a cool girl. That's not to say that my pride hadn't taken a slight knock. A part of me had clearly hoped to find myself in the doghouse, for not being in the doghouse.

It was time for me to present her with her gift.

'Here, these are for you,' I said with a smile.

'Wow, fantastic. Are you sure?'

I nodded.

'Thanks a lot, Tony, I really appreciate that.'

They were too big for her, but the red shorts would give her something to remember me by.

The next morning Jim very kindly got up early and dropped me by the Dublin road at 7 am. This gave me four hours to complete the distance which I had been assured was little more than a two-hour drive.

'You'll be absolutely fine,' Niall had said at a quiet dinner party Jim and his wife Jennifer had rather sweetly thrown in my honour, 'there'll be loads of cars heading back up to Dublin after the bank holiday weekend.'

It had all seemed plausible enough, but the experience on the ground was offering up another story entirely. Not many cars, and an overwhelming lack of interest in the hitch-hiker with the fridge.

By 8 am I had made it about ten miles, courtesy of a lift from Cyril, a white-haired but healthy-looking man in his sixties. He said that he had thought the fridge was 'a big white box', which was accurate enough, and in essence all it had been to me for the past month. I had made no effort to take advantage of its abilities to keep things cool. At this point I was unaware that as the morning's events unfolded, anything which could keep *me* cool would be a distinct asset.

I shouldn't have accepted the lift from Cyril. Evidently when it came to hitch-hiking I had learned no lessons in the last month, because I made exactly the same mistake that I made with my first lift of the journey. In my desire to get the day's travels kick-started, I had accepted a lift from someone who was only going a few miles, and in so doing I had relinquished a favourable spot for hitch-hiking, only to find it superseded some minutes later by an extremely poor one.

I was attempting another first. As far as I knew no one had ever hitch-hiked to a live nationwide broadcast before. Chauffeur-driven cars are more the norm. I had been arrogant enough to assume that the reputation that went before me meant that I could do it with no difficulties, but I hadn't reckoned on Cyril dropping me at this particular location, the hitch-hiking equivalent of a barren desert with vultures circling overhead.

I was standing beside the R741 at the junction of the turn off to Castleellis. The junction was in the middle of a long stretch of straight road where the cars were getting up far too much speed to consider stopping for any hitch-hiker. The only ones going slow enough to stop for me without causing a major accident were ones who were turning off, and were therefore no use to me anyway. It was a hopeless situation. By 9.00 I was getting desperate. I tried waving at cars, but this made me appear like a crazed convict on the run, and consequently reaped no reward. My growing concern edged towards mild panic when I got a call on my mobile phone from *The Gerry Ryan Show* asking me to talk to Gerry after the next record finished. I was just preparing myself for the interview when the signal disappeared and the line went dead. Not only was this an appalling stretch of road for hitching, it was in an area where the phone signals came and went with the same regularity as my breaths.

For the first time in three and a half weeks I was distinctly *un*calm. I *had* to be in Dublin by 11 am, and yet I was going nowhere with little prospect of change in that position. I had to try something different.

I left my fridge and rucksack by the roadside and began to walk down the narrow lane towards Castleellis. I had no idea what I was going to do, but all I knew was that I couldn't afford to stay where I was. After a hundred yards I passed a driveway and saw three men struggling with the task of loading a mare and foal into the back of a horsebox. I waited until the job was done and then called out to them.

'Excuse me, but you don't happen to know if there's a callbox around here do you?'

'Well, there is,' one of them replied, 'but that would be in the village, and that's some walk now.'

'It's just that I'm supposed to do an interview on the radio, and I can't get a signal on my mobile phone.'

'Well,' said another, 'we'd give you a lift, but the Range Rover's full of gear and there's barely room for the three of us.'

They seemed friendly, and circumstances required a degree of pushiness. So I pushed it.

'I couldn't squeeze in with the horses could I?' I said, desperately attempting to disguise my desperation. 'It's a matter of some urgency.'

I was a desperate man.

'Well . . . it's just that the foal's not used to travelling in the horsebox.'

'Maybe I could calm it down. You know, soothe its nerves with some gentle words.'

I was a very desperate man.

'Well . . .'

'I promise not to sue you if I get kicked or anything.'

I was heading off the desperation scale.

Time was an issue now. No lift here and a long walk into the village would mean I'd need Damon Hill for my next lift. It was a possibility because he had a house in Ireland, but even so we were looking at very long odds.

The tallest of the three looked at me, shrugged, and then pointed to the horsebox.

'Oh, all right then, in you get.'

Yes! Boy, was I grateful.

'Oh thank you so so much, that's such a help,' I said, possibly over-doing the gratitude. 'I've got some luggage I'm afraid.'

'That's not a problem.'

They hadn't seen it yet.

I walked back and waited for them at the crossroads and as the Range Rover pulled up, the driver caught a glimpse of the fridge. His jaw visibly dropped.

'I don't feckin' believe it!' he said. 'I've been listening to this fella for the past two weeks!'

'What do you mean?' said the one in the back seat.

'I've been listening to him. He's been all round the country with his fridge.'

'With his *what*?' gasped the passenger.

'With his fridge. His fridge – this is the fella with the fridge.'

The passenger leaned out of the window.

'Jesus Christ, you're right – he's got a feckin' fridge!'

'Never!' said the one in the back, whose view was obscured by a pile of saddles.

'He has! Get out and look.'

He got out and looked.

'Fuck me, it's a fridge.'

'I told you.'

'This is the fella off the radio. The fella with the fridge.'

'What in feck's name do you mean, Des, fella off the radio?'

'I told you, he's been travelling round the country – I think it's for a bet.'

'A *bet*? A *fridge*?'

Lucky I wasn't in a hurry.

It was a further ten minutes before who I was and what I was doing had been sufficiently discussed for us to consider going anywhere. One of the three fellas simply couldn't believe what I was doing.

'But a feckin' *fridge*! Why a feckin' *fridge*?' he kept saying.

It didn't matter how many times I told him why, he still shook his head in disbelief.

I climbed in the back with the horses and did my best to be a calming influence on the foal. The reality was though that it was much calmer than I.

Time was ticking by.

This was one of the most bizarre journeys I had made in my life. In less than two hours' time, the last hour of *The Gerry Ryan Show* was being given over to a celebration of my journey around Ireland. Yet here I was, the lead player in that event, stuck in the back of a horsebox with a mare, a foal and a fridge, being towed through the country roads of County Wexford by three hysterical horse trainers.

I slumped down on to the hay floor of the horsebox and considered my position. To be precise, it was below a horse's arse somewhere in southern Ireland. But it had a greater significance, and there was a profound parallel to be drawn, at least for someone with a mind as confused as mine. Three Wise Men. A stable full of hay. A Triumphal Entry into a nation's capital city. Wasn't it obvious? I was the new Messiah.

Maybe my journey wasn't over, but was just beginning. Perhaps the lessons I had learned and the wisdom I had attained in the past month heralded an era of pre-eminence for the fridge philosophy. The future was pre-ordained. I had to take the message of the fridge out to the people, I had to spread the word.

'I am the Lord!' I exclaimed. 'Don't you see, horses, I am the Lord!'

And with those words, the mare raised its tail and ceremoniously dropped three large dollops of quality manure into my lap. It was too well timed not to be a reaction to my risible claim. Had I made it to another human they might have turned to me and said 'Horseshit!' but the mare was unable to offer a more practical demonstration of the same sentiment.

Apart from the unholy response of a horse, there was another reason to doubt my Messianic credentials. According to the New Testament, Jesus actually managed to turn up to his Triumphal Entry. It was looking increasingly more likely that I would have to rely on second- and third-hand accounts to find out exactly how mine had gone.

The Three Wise Men dropped me by a callbox in Ballycanew, just outside Jericho.

'Good luck,' said Des. 'We were just saying that we haven't named the foal yet, so we've decided we're going to call it "Fridgy".'

Fridgy. New life, in the form of a young horse, had been named after the fridge. I was quite touched. The fridge had become part of a family when it had been christened Saiorse Molloy, but now in its own peculiar way, it had started an adopted equine family of its own. I thanked my three friends and told them that if in years to come I saw a horse called 'Fridgy' win the Grand National, then it would be the happiest day of my life.

'How is it going, Tony?' said Gerry, as he kicked off the interview.

'Not that well, so far. I've had a slightly dodgy morning's hitching, and I've only got as far as Ballycanew.'

'Goodness, if you don't hurry it up, you won't make it. Well if there's anyone in a car, bus or van anywhere in the vicinity of Ballycanew, then do look out for Tony and his fridge and speed him on his way to Dublin, it is after all a matter of national importance. We've got to get him to Connolly Station for eleven o'clock so you can join him with your chosen domestic appliance, in the triumphal procession to the ILAC Centre. Obviously Tony, people will be turning up in their droves, but have you got any last words which may encourage the undecided to get down there and show their support?'

'Well, all I can say Gerry is that some marches are *for* things and some are *against* things, but never has there been a march for *absolutely nothing*. Now is our chance to put that right. Grab your toaster and kettle and discover like me, how great it feels to devote yourself to something truly purposeless. By doing something with absolutely no point to it, we eliminate the possibility of failure, because in a sense the worse it may go then the more it can be considered a success.'

'Absolutely. Very rousingly put Tony, and not at all confusing. Well, there you have it good people of Ireland, now is your chance to join a march which will liberate the nothingness and pointlessness in all of us.'

'That's right. Of course we're using the word "nothingness" in its most positive sense here.'

'Naturally. Now Tony, good luck on the rest of your hitch this morning, and we look forward to talking to you later on. Both our crack reporters Brenda Donohue and John Farrell will be giving us a detailed word picture of exactly what's happening during the triumphant march and the ensuing celebration in the ILAC Centre. It's going to be quite an event, and remember to get yourselves down there because this is the time to make your domestic appliance count. Tony, good morning.'

'Good morning Gerry.'

When I emerged from the callbox, a lorry immediately drew up alongside me, and the driver wound down his window.

'I just heard you on the radio there, if you wait here for twenty minutes, I'll be back and I'll take you as far as Arklow.'

And he was gone.

I had no reason to doubt that he would be back, but I couldn't afford the luxury of twenty minutes, and if I could get a lift before, then I would have to take it.

Whilst hitching, I tried to think of chants which I and my fellow marchers could shout as we strode proudly through Dublin. I came up with a few, but my favourite was one I would have to teach the crowd on my arrival.

TONY: 'WHAT DO WE WANT?'
CROWD: 'WE DON'T KNOW!'
TONY: 'WHEN DO WE WANT IT?'
CROWD: 'NOW!'

It seemed to strike the right chord.

Kevin and Elaine beat the lorry driver to me. They had heard the interview and had made a small detour especially, and since they too were going as far as Arklow, I jumped into their small van and we sped northwards. They were a young couple, both about twenty and probably the youngest of all those who had stopped for me.

'If I phone ahead, Elaine's mother will cook us all breakfast in Courtown Harbour,' said Kevin.

'I'd love to really, but I'm running really late.'

'That's a shame, because she does a fine breakfast.'

Just beyond Arklow I was back hitching again. I looked at my watch and saw that it was 9.45 am. Meeting my deadline was still possible, but a long wait here and *The Gerry Ryan Show* would need to hastily rethink its last hour.

A red car pulled up, and I ran forward to address the driver.

'Where are you headed?' I asked.

'Dublin,' came the magical reply.

I was cutting it fine, but it was all still on.

Peter was unemployed at the moment and on his way to visit friends in Dublin. Not long since a student, he still seemed comfortable with a way of life which was extremely relaxed and laid back. Unfortunately one area where this manifested itself was in his driving. What should have been a horn-honking, tyre-screeching, risk-taking charge into Dublin was a casual Sunday afternoon tootle into town. All we needed to complete the picture was a tartan blanket on the back seat and a tin of boiled sweets.

Because I was spending most of my time looking at my watch and checking how many kilometres were left before we hit Dublin, I failed to focus on the sadness of the occasion. Peter was my last lift. This was it, the hitch-hiking was over. No longer was I to spread myself by a roadside and put myself at the mercy of a nation's drivers. I would miss it.

Well, bits of it, anyway.

'I could drop you at Sydney Parade Dart Station, my friends don't live far from there. It'll be quicker than suffering the city centre traffic anyway,' said Peter.

'And do you think I'll make it to Connolly Street for eleven?'

'Oh, I'm sure you'll be fine.'

Why do people do that? Say *I'm sure* when they're not sure at all. So often people will say 'Oh I'm sure you'll be fine' as an excuse for further dialogue on the subject: 'I've got to make this speech to a group of fundamentalist Shi-ite Muslims about the worthlessness of Allah, and I'm a bit worried about how it might go down.'

'Oh, I'm sure you'll be fine.'

It was just after 10.30 when we arrived at Sydney Parade Station. The barrier was down in the middle of the road.

'That means a train is coming; if you hurry you might get it,' said Peter.

'How long for the next one if I miss it?'

'They come every fifteen minutes.'

'Shit, I'd better not miss this one then. Bye.'

I dashed off, barely finding the time to shake Peter's hand. My last lift, treated with the dismissive familiarity of a spouse on a daily run to the station. Poor fella wasn't even invited to sign the fridge.

I did the best hurrying I could do given that hurrying with this load wasn't easy. As I rushed into the station, the train was drawing into the 'Trains To Dublin' platform, and I knew this was the train I *had* to get. Another fifteen minutes would be too late. There was no time to get a ticket, I would have to risk any fines which might be incurred. Just get that train! I ran past the ticket office, fridge rattling and wobbling behind me until there, directly ahead, horror of horrors, were mechanised ticket barriers. I had no chance of getting through, over, or under any of these, and the gate which had been placed there to accommodate the heavily laden, needed to be released by the man in the ticket office. I called out to him.

'Hello, could you please open the gate! Please! I must catch this train.'

He looked up, casually.

'Do you have a ticket?'

'I don't, but I'll buy one at the other end or whatever, just please open the gate!'

'It's just that you're not supposed to–'

'PLEASE! I'M THE MAN WITH THE FRIDGE AND I HAVE TO BE AT CONNOLLY STREET STATION TO BE ON *THE GERRY RYAN SHOW*!'

I'm not sure whether this made any sense to him or whether he was simply terrified by the urgency with which he was being addressed, but either way he pressed the button which released the gate. I bundled myself through and reached the train just as the automatic doors were closing. I tried to grab the inside of a closing door to force it back open again, a trick which I knew worked on London's Underground, but on this occasion the force of the closing door was too great and I had to withdraw my hand or risk losing it. The train pulled out of the station, and with it went my chances of making my Triumphal Entry on time. I got out my mobile phone and called *The Gerry Ryan Show*. The lines were engaged. No doubt they were busy making last-minute arrangements for a very exciting live link-up with their outside broadcast unit.

While they did so, the main protagonist in all this paced anxiously on a suburban station, somehow believing it would speed the oncoming train towards him. Either Peter had been wrong about the interval between trains or the pacing had worked, because seven minutes later another train rolled into the station.

The train stopped at a disappointing number of stations. Sandymount. Come on train, you could go faster than this. Lansdowne Road. We were just dawdling. At Pearse Street I noticed that passengers were beginning to stare at me. I couldn't fathom why. Okay, I was sweating, and I had a fridge with me on a trolley, but apart from that I was perfectly normal. Tara Street. Tara Street sounded like a star in a cheap skinflick. A woman got on with twin babies in a double-barrelled pushchair. They were too young to know that there was something odd about me, but they looked up at me in a way which suggested they instinctively knew there was. Bastards.

When we crossed the River Liffey I knew that we were nearly there. It was 10.53 am. At Connolly Station a guard helped me down the stairs with the fridge just like a mother might be helped down with a baby in a pushchair.

In homage to Hollywood suspense films, I headed for the rendezvous outside the station at 10.59. Any second now I would be hailed by cheering crowds, thrilled that I hadn't let them down after all.

I emerged from the main doors and on to the steps, and there before me was – wait a minute, this couldn't be right – an ordinary street on a Tuesday morning at 11.00? Where were the adoring fans? The hordes of well-wishers? The supporters of the cause with their domestic appliances by their sides? Nothing. No one. Just cars.

I realised that I must have the wrong spot. 'Outside the main doors at the front entrance' I had been told. This must be some kind of side entrance. This meant I had missed the eleven o'clock welcome live on *The Gerry Ryan Show*, silly idiot that I was, because I had not been bright enough to go to the right entrance.

I turned round and started to head back into the station. To my left, an old man in a kilt and carrying some bagpipes was approaching me.

'Is that a fridge?' he said.

It was going to be difficult to adjust to not hearing that question quite so often in the coming months.

'It is.'

At least the answer was simple.

'What's your name? Is it John?' the man asked, gently caressing his bagpipes.

'No, it's Tony.'

'Oh. Right, that's odd, because I was told to meet a John Farrell here at eleven o'clock.'

'Well I'm definitely not John Farrell.'

'But they did say something about a fridge.'

'Who did?'

'RTE.'

'RTE radio?'

'I don't know. My wife took the call.'

'Have you been booked to come here by RTE?'

'I have, yes.'

'Oh, I get it now. They've got you to play us through the streets on my triumphal entry. John Farrell is the reporter on the ground. I'm supposed to meet him too. The trouble is, we're both in the wrong place, we're supposed to be at the main entrance.'

'This is the main entrance.'

My heart fell.

'What?'

'This is the main entrance of Connolly Station.'

'Oh.'

Well, maybe for some reason the crowd had assembled somewhere else. At that moment a man came towards us, holding a mop in his hand, and gesticulating. He may have looked a worn out, intense, and slightly crazed individual, but you couldn't expect to attract the most balanced members of society to march through Dublin with kitchen implements. At least we had one marcher.

'Hello Tony, I'm John,' he said.

Make that no marchers. This was John Farrell, the crack reporter.

'Nice to meet you,' he continued. 'God, you look great – look at the colour on you, you look like you've been round the West Indies, not Ireland.'

Suddenly he didn't look crazed at all. It's amazing how something as little as a person holding a mop can change the way you view them.

'Come on, we'd better get going,' he said, eagerly.

'But hang on John, there's no one here. Are you sure we're in the right place?'

'We're in the right place all right. These things tend to kick off slowly.'

He'd done this before? He went on, 'When you start it then everyone sort of finds it and gets involved. Have you got a radio walkman with headphones?'

'I have.'

'Well, put it on, and listen. Gerry is just setting the whole thing up now, and if we cross over there to that callbox, I'll give him my first report. Keep listening because I may put you on to him at any point.'

As we crossed the disappointingly uncrowded street, I put on my headphones and couldn't believe what I was hearing. Dramatic music, in fact the soundtrack from *Ben Hur*, was building to a climax. Then Gerry Ryan's voice cut across it, in a sensational and melodramatic tone.

'He came across from the pond, the young man and his fridge travelling over land and sea searching for a meaning and purpose in their lives. We speak of Tony Hawks, the Fridge Man. Tony Hawks who came to live amongst us for all but a short while, a Messiah of sorts. We felt ourselves not worthy to touch the hem of his fridge, but then we realised that he was but an ordinary man, his fridge but a little fridge, the son of a bigger fridge – the Big Fridge – the huge, gigantic Fridge in the Sky.'

My, he was certainly going for it.

'He travelled the length and breadth of our nation – he became part of our lives. We received Tony Hawks and his fridge into our hearts. Today is the end of his fruitful odyssey.'

His tone now changed and the epic music faded as he tried for the first live link-up.

'Brenda Donohue is in the ILAC Centre in Dublin, wondering where Tony and his fridge are. How is your wondering, Brenda?'

'Good morning to you Gerry Ryan. We have a big crowd here just by the fountain at the ILAC Centre and we are awaiting the arrival of Tony Hawks. This is his final destination, this is his final port of call, and people have turned up from all over the country and I have to say that the atmosphere this morning is one of high expectation. You know that feeling of calm before the storm, there's tension in the air, there's longing, there's expectation – we can't wait to see him, we're curious about what he and his fridge look like. We have Mrs Burn who has come all the way from Drogheda, I am surrounded by the women of the Portobello School of Childcare who've all turned up with some domestic appliances, and not just that, they have a chant for Tony, so if he's listening, if he's making his way to the ILAC Centre here in Dublin, we have a chant for you Tony, on the count of three, tell Tony what you want to say to him. 1 . . . 2 . . . 3 . . . GO TONY GO TONY GO TONY GO! GO TONY GO TONY GO TONY GO!

This was all unbelievable. What was happening at the procession's point of destination was in stark contrast to the scene at its inception. Where I was, there was no real feeling of 'calm before a storm', more a worry that not even a light breeze was on its way.

Meanwhile, back on national radio, Gerry Ryan responded passionately to the girls' chant,

'Isn't that wonderful! If I was Tony Hawks, and I was standing beside my little fridge outside Connolly Street ready to make my triumphant entry into Dublin, then that would touch my heart.'

Well, I was. And it did.

John started waving to me from inside the callbox where he was waiting with the receiver to his ear. On air, in my headphones I heard the reason why, from Gerry himself.

'We now make our way to Connolly Station in Dublin where John Farrell our reporter on the ground is with Tony. John?'

From the callbox, John gave me the thumbs up. How was he going to deal with this situation? Compared to what was happening at the ILAC Centre, in fact compared to anything anywhere, our march was an abject failure. How would John handle this? I soon found out.

'Oh Gerry, I'm so excited. This man has been going all over Ireland for the last three weeks and two days and he has made a profound impression wherever he has gone. I came here today with my humble kitchen mop and my ice tray, so I am a man prepared. Although, having said that, nothing could have prepared me for meeting the Fridge Man. First of all I should tell you that he has a tan which makes him look like he has been camping in the outback of Australia for the last three weeks, it's amazing. His fridge has been autographed by hundreds of people who are wishing him well and saying how much they enjoy and love his fridge, and now his fridge has come home. We have a bagpiper here, Christy Riley is here to welcome him and I think in the background you can hear him starting to play again . . .'

John had clearly french-kissed the Blarney Stone. He had chosen to describe the scene, to borrow a word from the politicians, disingenuously. The rest of us call it bullshit. What a day! It began with horseshit, now it was bullshit – I was just pleased there were no elephants on the march. I looked into the callbox and saw John frantically signalling to Christy to start playing. '. . . Christy has been entertaining the crowd here with his bagpipes for the last hour or so – ah, there he goes! It's a very loud, full sound Gerry, and it's drawing lots of attention. We're about to start our procession, but I thought maybe first you'd like to have a word with Tony.'

It was my turn now to be waved at frantically. I moved forward and took the receiver as John handed it to me.

'Tony, how are you?' asked Gerry. 'Is the excitement mounting?'

'Gerry, it's at a fever pitch here. I can't tell you the excitement there is around the place.'

What the hell, I thought I might as well play ball. A bit of mythologising never hurt anyone. Well, apart from the millions of victims of cruel and repressive fundamental religions. It hurt them a bit.

'I don't think I've ever seen a people like it,' I suggested, 'I have captured the hearts of the Irish people, no question. I am overwhelmed by the response here.'

'I think it now behoves us to prepare for you to continue on your triumphant march,' announced Gerry, silkily leading the show into a commercial break. 'Caesar enters Rome, ladies and gentlemen.'

And so the march began. It wasn't the exact scene I had pictured in my mind's eye over breakfast in Wexford the previous morning. By now though, my initial disappointment had subsided and I was beginning to draw some perverse satisfaction from this pitiful response to my radio appeals and rallying cries. I had now decided that for a march which was truly pointless, it was entirely fitting that it should be met with such spirited apathy.

I took a moment to observe John, and saw that he wasn't remotely surprised by the lack of numbers on the ground. He had expected as much. I had been naive. Of course, it had been a form of naivety which had borne me so successfully to this point, but this was Dublin, and Dublin was reality. Dublin was to be the big slap round the face. This was a thriving city of commerce, and it was a Tuesday morning just after eleven o'clock. People had work to do, lives to lead, mouths to feed and, thank God, radios to listen to.

Radio listeners were sharing in one of the more spectacular and strangely moving days in their capital's history. There was however a substantial gap between the listeners' perception of what was going on and the events which were actually taking place. For those tuned into RTE2 on FM, whether they were in Donegal, Galway or even up in Tory Island, this event was an emotional climax to a touching story, as throngs of well wishers lined the route, tossing garlands and waving to their hero. For the marcher, just setting off from Connolly Station, it was difficult to view it quite like that. There were three of us. Myself, a roving reporter with a mop, and a pensionable bagpipe player who didn't have the first clue what was going on.

We made our way down Talbot Street and into a pedestrianised shopping zone. Dublin's busy shoppers, sadly out of radio contact, looked on with stunned bemusement. Were we making our way to a fancy dress function? Why were a man with a fridge, a fellow holding a mop, and a bagpipe player, marching proudly through a shopping precinct?

There wasn't a hint of self consciousness about the three of us. Why should there be? Presumably Christy dressed up in his kilt and went out with his bagpipes several times a week; I had spent an entire month in the company of a fridge; and waving a microphone about was John's chosen metier. As for the mop, well I think we'd all forgotten about that, and John was using it as a staff to assist his marching gait. For a few minutes we all chatted freely, oblivious to our surroundings and the alleged momentousness of the occasion.

As we crossed O'Connell Street and made our way up Henry Street, Christy told me a story of how an irate wife, who had grown tired of her husband's sloth, had hired him to come and play the bagpipes outside their bedroom window at the crack of dawn in order to get the idler out of bed. The man hadn't appreciated the joke and had pelted him with shoes, perfume bottles and whatever was to hand. Christy pronounced it the worst gig he had ever had. I hoped that after today it would still occupy the number-one slot.

For a while the fridge had seemed heavier than usual as I dragged it on its trolley behind me. Perhaps fatigue was setting in, because for almost the first time, it was beginning to feel like the burden I had expected it to be at the outset, but which it had never become. Then I looked behind me and saw the reason. A small boy on roller blades was rather cheekily hitching a lift, holding on to the handle of the fridge door and allowing himself to be pulled along. I smiled. Although he was getting heavy, I didn't tell him to let go.

This was fitting and proper. This was a gesture I was happy to make, a symbolic repayment to all of those who had given me rides in the last month and made my journey possible.

Just before the junction of Henry Street and Upper Liffey Street, I noticed that we had lost a third of our marchers. John was nowhere to be seen. This was slightly worrying since he was the only one who had any idea where we were supposed to be going. The numbers now involved in the Triumphal Entry had plummeted to two. As if two people marching triumphantly wasn't embarrassing enough, Christy and I might soon have to suffer the further indignity of asking directions. Biblical comparisons were no longer appropriate.

As I stood on a bench looking back down the street to see if there was any sign of John, I could hear in one ear Brenda Donohue's voice coming from the earpiece which was relaying me *The Gerry Ryan Show*.

'We have a huge crowd here in the ILAC Centre and we're all desperate to see Tony. We were hoping that he might have made it here by now, and we seem to have lost all contact with John, so we simply don't know where they are . . .'

A few hundred yards away I could just make out John running towards us, his mop looking like an oversize relay baton. When he caught up with us I asked where he had been and offered my available ear for the answer.

'Sorry about that, Tony, this guy called me on my mobile and it would have been awkward to get rid of him,' explained John.

'Couldn't you have told him that you were involved with a live nation-wide radio broadcast?' I enquired.

'Well, it wasn't that easy. You see he's in prison, and he said that this was the only time he was allowed to use the phone.'

I didn't bother to find out any more, thinking that it might be better not to know.

Interruptions from convicts behind us, we were now ready to complete the march to end all marches. With our numbers once again bolstered to three, we were feeling pretty good about ourselves. I was just considering introducing the 'What do we want? We don't know' chant when Christy launched into a spell of uplifting bagpipe music. This certainly made us the centre of attention.

John gave Gerry another update, which I could barely hear over Christy's now slightly jarring bagpiping. Brenda O'Donohue was interviewing people who had brought along domestic appliances to the ILAC Centre. Amongst the paraphernalia was a hairdryer, washing powder and some dirty laundry, a tin opener, a whisk, some curling tongs, and one woman had turned up insisting that her friend was a charlady she had brought along specially.

'That's marvellous, Brenda,' said Gerry. 'Stay tuned, fridge followers. I don't think since the Eucharistic Congress of the 1950s, have we seen such an outpouring of love for one man returned back home.'

He was upping the ante at each commercial break. This was going to take a lot of living up to.

'I think we're going to have to hurry now,' said John, on returning from the callbox where he had reported in to Gerry. 'If we don't get a move on, we won't reach the ILAC Centre until after twelve, and then the show will be over.'

The show will be over. I felt a pang of sadness. For me too, the show would be over. I wasn't sure whether I wanted it to be.

'Come on!' said John, with surprising urgency, 'I think we're going to have to run.'

Dublin's shoppers were treated to a new spectacle; that of the three adults running through the city centre with their burdens of eccentric and assorted accoutrements. Christy wasn't a natural runner. He was in his sixties now, and had probably not had any reason to run anywhere for twenty years or so.

As I ran, fridge rattling noisily behind me, I glanced at him, flushed and bathed in sweat, and felt pretty confident that he was experiencing something which would push the 'waking the lazy husband at dawn' gig down one place to number two.

We turned a corner and ahead of us I could see my unlikely and unglamorous journey's end – a shopping mall poetically called the ILAC Centre. With the end in sight, we moderated our sprint into a more dignified jog, and made our way into the centre, not knowing what lay in store. A huge cheer greeted us, emanating from a much larger crowd than I had expected. Okay, it wasn't as huge as Brenda had made out, but there must have been about a hundred people all gathered in the central concourse of the shopping centre. A woman with a microphone was waving me over. This must be Brenda, because her mouth movements were synchronised exactly with the words I was hearing in my earpiece.

'Gerry, Tony has made it! We've got the fridge! We've got John Farrell, we've got our piper – my, he looks a little tired, and we've got this huge crowd who I'm sure are going to show their appreciation for Tony and his fridge who after a month of travelling round the country have made it here to the ILAC Centre in Dublin. So, let's hear it for Tony!'

Another huge cheer went up as I bowed before them. John signalled to poor Christy to start playing, but he was woefully short of that most precious of faculties for a bagpipe player – breath. He collapsed exhausted on to a bench next to two old ladies and did his best, desperately trying to puff air into his instrument's windbag. He looked like a dying man. All he could manage was a sound which resembled a police siren struggling to run on a dying battery. In the studio, someone had the wisdom to feed in more of the rousing *Ben Hur* music to drown him out. Brenda ushered John over to the microphone.

'Before we talk to Tony, John Farrell, what was the journey like for you?'

'It was a real religious experience for me Brenda, because I had no idea how much people's lives were affected by humble domestic kitchen appliances. But the Fridge Man has let me see the light and I see it in the faces of all the crowd here. It's been a wonderful, wonderful day.'

'Brenda,' said Gerry back in the studio, 'get Tony over to the microphone, I want to ask him how he feels.'

Right on cue I joined Brenda at the microphone.

'Tony, you've done it, well done,' said Gerry. 'You must be very proud. How are you, and how is your fridge?'

'We are both absolutely thrilled. As you know this fridge was christened Saiorse, which means freedom in Gaelic, and everyone has recognised that it is a free fridge, free to do what it wants, free to go where it wants and free to be what it wants, and if a fridge can achieve that, then what are the limits on us?'

'A profound thought indeed, Tony. Tell me, would it be fair to say that this fridge is the closest thing in the world to you?'

'Yes,' I laughed, 'that's my own personal tragedy, thanks for highlighting it.'

'Now in a minute we have a little ceremony to perform but before we do that perhaps you'd like to say a few words to the crowd there – Tony Hawks – your final thoughts.'

It was time for another impromptu speech. I wanted to do this moment justice.

'Gerry, I can't tell you how moved I am by the response here – there are literally thousands of people, possibly. They go back for – if not for miles, then for yards, well a number of feet anyway. I just want to pay tribute to the people of Ireland and to the people who have given me lifts along the way. This fridge here is the first fridge to have hitch-hiked round this fair isle of yours. Presumably it won't be the last, I expect there to be a lot of copycat incidences, people taking different domestic appliances out on the road with them, and I'm proud to have opened up that avenue for them. There have been highs on this trip, like taking the fridge surfing in Strandhill, and there have been lows, like when the fridge kept falling off its trolley on the long walk through Galway town centre, but throughout it all there has always been someone on hand with a friendly word and more often than not, a pint of beer, and for that I just want to say a resounding thank you.'

A warm round of applause greeted my words. Gerry wound things up, 'Well, it only remains for us to complete this odyssey with a special ceremony. Brenda has with her *The Gerry Ryan Show* fridge magnet mayoral chain of office to bestow on Tony, complete with a selection of fridge magnets specially sewn on. Brenda, over to you.'

'Tony,' announced Brenda formally, 'Ireland now pronounces you its Fridge Man.'

The crowd cheered, the music from *Ben Hur* reached its crescendo, and I bowed before Brenda like a victorious Olympic athlete as she placed the mayoral ribbon around my neck. I looked out at the unlikely scene before me and waved to the smiling and laughing onlookers with genuine affection and gratitude.

To my surprise, a tear was rolling down one cheek.

24

For Sale: Fridge, One Careful Owner

It was a case of the Emperor's new clothes. Once the radio broadcast was over, so too was the fantasy which had sustained it. All of a sudden the Fridge Man felt rather ordinary. The feeling of triumph had disappeared into the ether as quickly as the airwaves. It had all been great fun, a bit of a laugh all right, but it had all been a bit silly and now the silliness was over. The crowd dispersed almost immediately. People had meetings to attend, jobs to go back to, or children to collect from school. No one could afford the time that had been granted to me on the rest of my travels. City life didn't permit such obeisance to whimsy.

The finale might have been fakery, but everything which had preceded it had not. For me this was real. The journey may not have changed the lives of the people of Ireland, but it had changed mine. I was a different, a better person. I had made discoveries, learned some important lessons. From this day forth I was going to stop for hitch-hikers, laugh along with happy drunks in pubs, and respect the right of the bad guitarist to play along with the rest. I had learned tolerance, I had learned that you could trust in your fellow man for help, and I had learned a new and pleasurable way of acquiring splinters.

Of course, in an ideal world *The Gerry Ryan Show* would have been an evening radio show and we would have had the night ahead of us to keep on partying. But it wasn't. It finished at twelve, midday.

'Are you up for a quick drink?' asked Brenda.

Was I up for a quick drink? I was up for twenty-four hours of non-stop partying.

'Yes, that would be nice.'

'Just give John and me ten minutes to sort a few things out and we'll be right with you.'

'Right.'

I stood there feeling lost. I felt lonely too. I had spent a month travelling on my own and I hadn't once felt lonely until now. I wanted my new friends to be with me. I wanted to see Andy and his family from Bunbeg. I wanted to see Geraldine, Niamh, Brendan and all the gang from Matt Molloys. I wanted to see Bingo with his surfboard, Tony from Ennistymon with his accordion, the Mother Superior, Brian and Joe the hardwood flooring boys, and my friends from Cork and Wexford. I wanted to hug them all. I wanted to see someone who had been touched in the same way as I had by this fanciful and fantastic experience. Someone who *understood*.

There was such a person here.

'Tony? How the hell are you?' said a woman's voice.

It was Antoinette, from the the *Live At Three* TV interview I had done in the first week.

'Antoinette! I'm just fine, how are you?'

And I gave her just the biggest hug. It was my hug for everybody, but poor Antoinette had to endure it. Rather shaken, she freed herself and introduced me to Kara, who had kindly organised the mobile phone for me.

'We heard you on the radio,' said Antoinette, 'and it sounded so amazing, we just had to leave work and come down here.'

'You should have come on the march. Why didn't you come on the march?'

'What, and make eejits of ourselves? Not likely – we leave that stuff to you.'

The difference between their jobs and mine, summed up rather neatly.

'I'm going for a drink now,' I said, 'with Brenda and John, will you join us?'

'We'd love to. Are you all right, you look a little confused.'

'I am a bit. It all feels so odd – it having finished. Such an anti-climax. I think I might go to pieces.'

'Oh, I'm sure you'll be fine.'

The journey may have been over, but one consistent theme endured. Someone being there to save the day. This time it was to be Antoinette and Kara. As the low-key celebration day drew to a close Antoinette turned to me.

'What are you going to do now?'

'In all honesty, I haven't got a clue.'

'Why don't you come with us?' said Kara. 'Mary from the office is leaving and we're going to her leaving lunch.'

'I'd love to, but I can't just crash it.'
'You can and you will.'

It had been an odd way of celebrating my achievement, crashing someone else's do, but it had served the purpose and taken my mind off the
fact that it was all over. After the meal had finished I took a cab to Rory's,
the bed and breakfast where I had stayed when I had first arrived, thus
giving my journey a nice symmetry.

There seemed to be traffic everywhere. Everything seemed to be happening quickly and lots of people seemed to be doing it. It was a shock
after the calm of rural Ireland. In those quiet backwaters I had discovered a direct correlation between the pace of life and the amount of time
it took a barman to serve you with a pint of stout. It was most endearing
because although it might take the barman an age to spot you, serve you,
fill the pint glass three-quarters full and then wait an age for the head to
settle; when you were passed that pint, it came with an introduction into
their conversations, and into their lives. That probably existed here in
Dublin too if you were in tune with things, but I wasn't ready to readjust,
I was so unsettled by the sheer volume of people. If Dublin was a shock,
how was I going to feel when I hit London?

In the cab I changed my mind about staying on. Formerly, I had
planned on remaining in Dublin for a few days, taking a look around and
generally wallowing in the glory. However, now it didn't seem right,
partly because the job I had come to do felt like it had been done, and
partly because there wasn't sufficient glory for satisfactory wallowing.
Wouldn't it be better to go home, recharge the old batteries, and come
back to look up old friends refreshed and reinvigorated? That was
decided then, I would sort out a flight in the morning and head off in the
late afternoon.

One question remained. What was I going to do with the fridge?
Again I had another rethink. My first idea had been to try and sell it. I
was amused by the idea of taking out an ad in the local paper:

FOR SALE: FRIDGE, ONE CAREFUL OWNER, LOW MILEAGE,
TRAVELS WELL, POSSIBLE SEA WATER DAMAGE, NEVER
PLUGGED IN, MUST BE SEEN.

My second idea had been to get Gerry Ryan to auction it off on air and
to donate the money to charity. This was the most noble course of action
and probably what ought to have been done, but the trouble was I was
too damn close to the thing now. When I looked down at it, I felt a gen-

uine affection for it. I knew that these weren't normal feelings to have towards a fridge, but I simply couldn't let it go. We'd been through too much together. This wasn't any ordinary fridge, this was Saiorse Molloy, completely covered from top to bottom in signatures from well wishers and friends. These were my memories. I would keep it in my office at home. After all, a bottle of mineral water would become holy water when it was placed in a fridge which had been blessed by a Mother Superior. And late at night I could drink the odd toast by mixing it with a drop of distinctly unholy spirit.

Rory was pleased to see me.

'Ah, you made it then. Can I sign the fridge?'

'If you can find room.'

He scanned its surface and could find no available space.

'I'll have to sign it underneath,' he said, and lifted it up and did just that.

'You'll be out tonight having a big celebration I suppose.'

'Not really.'

'Why not?'

'Well, it hasn't really come together, and I don't think I really want to do any celebrating tonight.'

Rory looked at me much as he had when I had first arrived all those weeks ago with a fridge in tow. Like I was mad.

I could have gone out and made a night of it, Antoinette and Kara had been kind enough to invite me to join up with a group of friends for a drink, but I simply wasn't up to it. Instead I went for a walk, ate a quiet meal alone and returned to watch TV in my room.

Things had fizzled out rather.

I found myself watching a political debate between Bertie Aherne and John Bruton, the two contenders for the top job in Irish politics. With only a few days of the election campaign to go, the two of them slugged it out with the same accomplished caution that I'd seen only a month ago in the British general election. There was very little to choose between them. Both were smarmy and both were brilliant at manipulating and evading questions. Were they like this all the time I wondered?

'How are you today, Bertie?'

'I'd like to answer that question in two parts if I may, but first let me deal with the question you asked last Thursday . . .'

It was by no means ideal, spending my last night in Ireland watching

TV in my hotel room, but nothing else had transpired and I simply didn't have the energy or will to force anything to happen. Maybe this was good for me. This was 'back down to earth' time. I had been living a fantasy and now it was time to re-enter the real world where smug politicians slugged it out on TV for the votes which would enable them to shape our futures. The real world, the future. Where fridges stayed in kitchens.

I tried to lift my spirits with a phonecall before I finally turned in for the night. I rang Kevin to tell him that he owed me a hundred pounds. He was out. I wasn't having much luck tonight. Then I rang Saoirse's family at Matt Molloys in Westport to let them know of their relative's success. I spoke with Niamh. She was thrilled.

'I can't wait to tell the others. We'll have our own little celebration. Thanks a million for calling,' she said.

I could turn in for the night now, knowing that somewhere someone was as excited as I was about having accomplished something quite this silly.

You can always count on family. I went to sleep with a warm feeling in my heart.

Rory's establishment must have gone up in the world because breakfast was cooked by a member of staff, and the improvement was considerable. So too was my general mood when I received a call on my mobile from Deirdre, one of the team on *The Gerry Ryan Show*.

'Tony, I think with all the excitement yesterday, we forgot to mention that we want you to come to lunch with us today. We thought you might like to meet Gerry and the team. We'd certainly like to meet you.'

'That would be wonderful, thanks.'

Maybe things weren't to end quite as unceremoniously as I had expected.

In the cab on the way to the restaurant, I started trying to guess what Gerry Ryan looked like. It was strange to have spoken to someone so much over the course of a month, but not to have any idea what their appearance might be. He and his team were probably equally intrigued as to the nature of my physical characteristics, but at least for them I would be easy to recognise. Unless anyone else entered the restaurant pulling a fridge behind them, there was unlikely to be any mix up.

The waiter informed me that the Gerry Ryan party of eight were at the rear of the restaurant. I made my way through and a little cheer went up from the relevant table as soon as the fridge was spotted. The man at the head of the table immediately got to his feet and came forward to greet me.

'Tony,' he said, 'it's great to meet you at last.'

It was weird because Gerry was exactly as I had pictured him – slightly receding reddish hair, trendy glasses and a light stubble.

'Gerry, it's great to meet you too,' I replied.

'I'm not Gerry, I'm Willy. That's Gerry over there.'

I looked across. Gerry stood up. How odd. He wasn't supposed to look like that. He was tall, well built with a healthy head of black hair, and the beginnings of a slight paunch.

'Tony', he said, coming forward to shake my hand. 'You look great. You have no right to look so well, not after what you've been through.'

I was introduced to the rest of the party, all of whom I had spoken to on the phone at one point or another. Willy, Paul, Jenny, Siobhan, Deirdre, Joan and Sharon. I was invited to open the champagne. I struggled with it, I always do, but eventually out popped the cork and the celebration began that I had so longed for yesterday.

At one point Gerry leant forward, filled my wine glass with the beginnings of yet another bottle of white wine, and said, 'Tony, there's one question I've been longing to ask which I couldn't ask you on air. Did you have sex at all on your travels?'

Giggles and teasing whoops and hollers greeted the question.

'Well, I finally started to get a little more attention than the fridge after I reached Cork, but you'll have to read the book to find out.'

'You're going to write a book about this?'

'Yes, I decided that last night.'

'Good idea,' said Gerry. 'I suppose that means I'll be in it. You'd better be nice, and don't mention this.'

He smiled and patted the beginnings of his slight paunch.

'I won't,' I replied with all the sincerity I could muster.

'Hollywood will probably make a film about it one day,' said Paul.

'Yeah, if they do, who do you think they'll get to play Tony?'

Deirdre's query prompted furious debate. Johnny Depp was a favourite choice, as was Mel Gibson, but most votes went to Bruce Willis. Yes, I could see that working. I had always seen myself as a kind of Bruce Willis who didn't rush around and blow things up quite so much.

After dessert I invited the party to join me at the fridge for photos.

Then I tore off the 'Mo Chuisneoir' sign which had adorned the door of the fridge since Donegal, allowing the signatures and messages of Gerry and the team to have pride of place on the front of the fridge where they belonged. After all, without their help it might have been a different story.

Gerry looked down at Saoirse.

'I can think of easier ways of making a hundred pounds,' he said.

'I know, but can you think of a better one?' I replied.

He thought for a moment.

'No I suppose not. Not really.'

We returned to the table for dessert wine. These people knew how to have lunch. It was nearly five o'clock, and what's more the restaurant was still full. My taxi arrived and I got up to go. Gerry Ryan stood and raised his glass, and the rest of the table followed suit.

'To the Fridge Man!' he said, loud enough for everyone in the restaurant to hear.

'To the Fridge Man!' came the response.

As I walked out of that restaurant pulling my fridge behind me for the final time, everyone on Gerry's table began applauding politely. Astonishingly, some people on a few of the other tables started to join in. Others looked up to see what was going on, and when they saw me and a fridge, they too joined in, possibly thinking it was somehow expected of them. Soon everyone in the restaurant was applauding, with cheers, whistles and laughter thrown in for good measure.

I felt great. The anti-climax of yesterday didn't matter anymore. I understood now. Yesterday had been phoney, this was real. Yesterday I had been saying 'Look at me'. It hadn't been right and it hadn't really worked, and I should have known that, having learned that lesson when Elsie had showed me off in the golf clubhouse in Ballina. *Now* it was working, and it was working because I was walking humbly out of a restaurant with no airs and graces, affectations or histrionics. The restaurant's diners picked up on this and were offering their spontaneous and unaffected appreciation of someone for whom they had a peculiar nagging respect. This moment was a special one and I cherished it.

I looked round and saw that the Gerry Ryan table were still all on their feet, and others in the room were rising to theirs. Just incredible. When the Hollywood script is written this ending might be considered too schmaltzy. Tough. They wouldn't be interested in this anyway – this *happened*.

So it was that a Triumphal Exit and not a Triumphal Entry was to prove the fitting climax to this strangely moving adventure. I was glad that I was to leave Ireland exactly as I had found it over the previous four weeks: warm, accommodating and enjoying a drink.

By the time I reached the taxi, my eyes had welled up with tears.

'Are you all right there?' said the cabbie as he opened the door for me.

'Yes, I'm just happy.'

'Oh right. Where to?'

'Dublin airport.'

I was leaving Ireland. The affair was over, but the friendship had just begun.

Epilogue

Roisin hasn't called.